pocket pc handbook

pocket pc handbook

dan hanttula

Hungry Minds™

Hungry Minds, Inc.

New York, NY ■ Cleveland, OH ■ Indianapolis, IN
Chicago, IL ■ Foster City, CA ■ San Francisco, CA

Pocket PC Handbook

Published by
Hungry Minds, Inc.
909 Third Avenue
New York, NY 10022
www.hungryminds.com

ISBN: 0-7645-3568-4

Printed in the United States of America

10 9 8 7 6 5 4 3 2 1

1O/RT/QS/QR/FC

Distributed in the United States by Hungry Minds, Inc.

Distributed by CDG Books Canada Inc. for Canada; by Transworld Publishers Limited in the United Kingdom; by IDG Norge Books for Norway; by IDG Sweden Books for Sweden; by IDG Books Australia Publishing Corporation Pty. Ltd. for Australia and New Zealand; by TransQuest Publishers Pte Ltd. for Singapore, Malaysia, Thailand, Indonesia, and Hong Kong; by Gotop Information Inc. for Taiwan; by ICG Muse, Inc. for Japan; by Intersoft for South Africa; by Eyrolles for France; by International Thomson Publishing for Germany, Austria, and Switzerland; by Distribuidora Cuspide for Argentina; by LR International for Brazil; by Galileo Libros for Chile; by Ediciones ZETA S.C.R. Ltda. for Peru; by WS Computer Publishing Corporation, Inc., for the Philippines; by Contemporanea de Ediciones for Venezuela; by Express Computer Distributors for the Caribbean and West Indies; by Micronesia Media Distributor, Inc. for Micronesia; by Chips Computadoras S.A. de C.V. for Mexico; by Editorial Norma de Panama S.A. for Panama; by American Bookshops for Finland.

For general information on Hungry Minds' products and services please contact our Customer Care department within the U.S. at 800-762-2974, outside the U.S. at 317-572-3993 or fax 317-572-4002.

For sales inquiries and reseller information, including discounts, premium and bulk quantity sales, and foreign-language translations, please contact our Customer Care department at 800-434-3422, fax 317-572-4002 or write to Hungry Minds, Inc., Attn: Customer Care Department, 10475 Crosspoint Boulevard, Indianapolis, IN 46256.

For information on licensing foreign or domestic rights, please contact our Sub-Rights Customer Care department at 650-653-7098.

For information on licensing foreign or domestic rights, please phone +1-650-653-7098.

For sales inquiries and special prices for bulk quantities, please contact our Order Services department at 800-434-3422 or write to the address above.

For information on using Hungry Minds' products and services in the classroom or for ordering examination copies, please contact our Educational Sales department at 800-434-2086 or fax 317-572-4005.

For press review copies, author interviews, or other publicity information, please contact our Public Relations department at 650-653-7000 or fax 650-653-7500.

For authorization to photocopy items for corporate, personal, or educational use, please contact Copyright Clearance Center, 222 Rosewood Drive, Danvers, MA 01923, or fax 978-750-4470.

Library of Congress Cataloging-in-Publication Data

Hanttula, Dan.
  Pocket PC handbook / Dan Hanttula.
    p. cm.
  ISBN 0-7645-3568-4
  1. Pocket computers.   I. Title.
QA76.5 .H3555   2001
004'.16--dc21   00-054071

 is a trademark under exclusive license to Hungry Minds, Inc.

About the Author

Dan Hanttula is a handheld industry expert, covering the market for over a decade and speaking at PDA conferences and vertical market trade associations throughout the United States. Dan Hanttula was the Windows CE platform editor for Pen Computing Magazine for four and a half years and he has become a regular on the Windows CE "AlternaTip" segment of ZDTV's *Screen Savers* television show offering advice on handheld devices to viewers. In addition, he has published hundreds of articles for *Pen Computing Magazine*, ZDTV, CNET, Microsoft, and other print media and online news sources. Last year, he launched www.semperaptus.com, the news and review source for Internet-connected PDAs, cell phones, and other web-ready appliances and is a contributing author for www.PocketPC.com.

In addition to his addiction to handheld computing devices, Dan is an avid James Bond enthusiast and collector of Coca-Cola memorabilia. The treasures in his collection include a 1957 Coke machine and the prop cellular phone used in *Tomorrow Never Dies*. But seeing the HP Jornada 420 Palm-size PC in the Bond movie, *The World Is Not Enough*, is one of Dan's proudest moments because it combined two of his most feverish passions: Windows Powered handheld devices and James Bond.

Credits

Acquisitions Editor
John Gravener

Project Editors
Marty Minner
Colleen Dowling

Technical Editor
Piroz Mohseni

Copy Editor
Richard H. Adin
KC Hogue

Proof Editor
Cindy Lai

Project Coordinators
Joe Shines
Danette Nurse

Graphics and Production Specialists
Robert Bihlmayer
Rolly DelRosario
Jude Levinson
Michael Lewis
Victor Peréz-Varela
Ramses Ramirez

Quality Control Technician
Dina F Quan

Book Designer
Kurt Krames

Illustrator
Gabriele McCann

Proofreading and Indexing
York Production Services

Cover Image
© Hewlett-Packard Company

To Nancy Ellen Hahn, my co-author of
the greatest love story never written.

Will you marry me?

Foreword

Hewlett-Packard Company has long been recognized as one of the world-wide leaders in the handheld computer market. HP entered the personal computing arena more than 25 years ago with the first handheld scientific calculator and continues to develop new products that shape the landscape of handheld computing.

The HP Jornada 540 Series Color Pocket PC powered by Windows has generated a lot of interest from consumers and press alike ever since its unveiling in April 2000, and continues to be a great selling product and receive winning reviews from popular trade publications. The HP Jornada was the first Pocket PC on the market, and HP's first handheld PC offering that is flexible enough to be used as a professional and entertainment tool — all in one pocket-sized device! The Pocket PC platform enables you to check e-mail, review Word and Excel documents, surf the Web, listen to digital music, and read electronic books.

Dan Hanttula, the author of this book, does an excellent job of explaining the many ways that you can use your Pocket PC more efficiently, creatively, and productively. So whether you are looking to buy a Pocket PC, or you already own one and want to get the most out of it, this book will provide you with all the information you need.

Enjoy your Pocket PC!

Boris Elisman
Group Marketing Manager
Personal Appliances and Services Organization
Hewlett-Packard Company

Preface

Just a few years ago, desktop computers broke the "hundreds of megahertz" speed barrier and were able to boot up in minutes to perform complex word processing, spreadsheet, and communications functions. Today, you can carry a computer with the same amount of CPU, word processing, spreadsheet, and communications functionality in the palm of your hand. This cigarette-pack sized powerhouse is called the Pocket PC.

Up and running in just fractions of a second, the Pocket PC puts Word documents, Excel spreadsheets, appointments, contacts, and a great deal more under your control when you're miles away from civilization. And, best of all, it weighs mere ounces (including the power supply) compared to the many pounds of a laptop computer.

Hewlett-Packard Company was the first to market with a newly designed Pocket PC: the HP Jornada 540 series. With a sleek, stylish design that is unmistakably HP and a third-generation "Windows Powered" operating system supplied by Microsoft, it was an undeniable success. It was so popular, in fact, that the first few shipments of the device quickly sold out and HP had to work hard to keep up with demand.

Because of the enormous popularity of the platform, Hungry Minds has partnered with HP to develop a Pocket PC handbook, rather than another book on the popular Palm Pilot products. Although leading the market in mind share and sales, the Palm Pilot does not have the functionality or expandability that exist in the Pocket PC and, therefore, makes for a number of shallow and repetitive books. Instead, covering the Pocket PC platform allows for this multifaceted, advanced-use handbook that contains original ideas and can productively coexist with volumes of other Pocket PC guidebooks, including *Pocket PCs for Dummies*, another Hungry Minds publication.

Who Should Read This Book

The *Pocket PC Handbook* is designed for owners of any Pocket PC who are excited by the opportunity to expand their knowledge of the product and wish to utilize the Pocket PC and the built-in applications to the fullest extent. While this book uses the HP Jornada Pocket PC as a model for our examples, the information contained within this manual can be applied to any of the Windows Powered Pocket PC devices.

This handbook is especially indispensable for Pocket PC users who consider themselves:

- New and potential users who are interested in learning the capabilities of the Pocket PC while discovering how to get the most out of their Pocket PC experience.

- Advanced users who are familiar with the general features of the Pocket PC, but want to learn advanced tips and tricks that will impress fellow Pocket PC owners, and help them work more efficiently and effectively.

- Super users who believe they know everything about the Pocket PC. (I'll stake my reputation on the fact that even the most advanced user will learn something new in this book.)

How This Book is Organized

This book has been carefully organized to follow the natural flow of how you would normally familiarize yourself with a Pocket PC. For this reason, the majority of all readers should be able to start at the point at which they feel comfortable and then read straight through to the end of the book.

- **Part I: Pocket PC Basics** — introduces you to the Pocket PC's features and functions. This part of the book explores the hardware, the operating system, and the three methods of inputting information into your Pocket PC. There's also a chapter on caring for and maintaining your Pocket PC.

- **Part II: Applications that Really Apply Themselves** — familiarizes you with the built-in applications and teaches you how to use each program to its utmost potential with real world examples. In special chapters on the Pocket Outlook suite and ActiveSync, you will learn how Pocket PC applications can work together and how desktop synchronization software can vastly improve your Pocket PC experience.

- **Part III: Getting More From Your Pocket PC** — marks the beginning of the cutting-edge portion of this handbook. Choosing software and hardware accessories to meet your specific needs are discussed in this section, as well as an in-depth look into Internet connectivity. Chapter 17, "Advanced Personalization For Your Faithful Companion" should be of particular interest to users that are interested in personalizing and fine-tuning their Pocket PC.

- **Part IV: Pocket PC Challenges** — takes you into the real world to confront the problems you may face while using your Pocket PC. Memory, power constraints, and ways in which you can work together with the prevalent line of Palm PDA products are covered in this section.

- **Part V: The Technology and Tomorrow** — designed for the techies and engineers, this part of the book includes the Pocket PC product specifications, complete information on other devices that work with the Pocket PC, and a glimpse into the future of the Pocket PC and the entire Windows Powered device platform.

Helpful Icons

This book has four icons that indicate additional information in various forms:

Warning

The Warning icon indicates that caution is needed for a procedure that requires special preparation or certain risks.

Cross-Reference

The Cross-Reference icon guides you to more information on the current topic in another section of the book.

Note

The Note icon signifies additional observations or clarification of the topic at hand.

Tip

The Tip icon designates words of advice that are valuable time savers.

Where to Go from Here

This book has been carefully organized so that beginning and advanced users can begin at a level where they are comfortable.

- ***Beginners:*** *If you are considering purchasing or have just purchased a Pocket PC*, begin at Chapter 1 to acquaint yourself with the product and its feature set.

- ***Advanced users:*** *If you have been using your Pocket PC for more than a month and are comfortable with the basic features*, skip to Chapter 6 to discover the advanced features and functionality of the Pocket PC.

- **Super users:** *If you are already using the Pocket PC applications at their utmost potential,* Chapter 16 introduces you to ways of expanding the Pocket PC. Using third-party software and hardware, you can expand the device beyond what it is normally capable of accomplishing.

- **Users in trouble:** *If you are experiencing problems with your device,* jump to Chapter 21 and Appendix A. These sections will help you get your Pocket PC back in order so you can enjoy the rest of the book.

Contact Information

I encourage you to contact me with your comments and suggestions. And although I regret not being able to offer technical support for Pocket PC issues, I would thoroughly enjoy hearing about your experiences with the Pocket PC. Above all, I'm interested in how useful you found this book to be in streamlining the operation of your Pocket PC and how it strengthened your reliance on the most personal and expandable handheld computing device available.

E-mail: danh@semperaptus.com
Internet: www.semperaptus.com

Acknowledgments

Personally, I have to thank Nancy Hahn, my best friend and the woman that always said, "you can do it" throughout the arduous and taxing process. To my parents, who have raised me with an understanding that knowledge, above all else, is the greatest power a man can wield. My father has worked all his life to become an expert in his field and never asked for anything more than the ability to work harder, while my mother has been instrumental in developing the minds of our future in her capacity as a teacher and tutor, before my birth and now, in the prime of her life. Thank you for being such wonderful examples of the lessons you teach.

Professionally, I have endless praises for the staff at Hungry Minds, including my acquisitions editor, John Gravener; my development editor, Martin Minner; my technical editor, Piroz Mohseni; and my project editor, Colleen Dowling. Thank you to Chee Chew and Ed Suwanjindar at Microsoft, as well as Crystal Duncan and Brandi Cook at Wagner Edstrom. I would also like to express my gratitude to Kevin Havre, HP technical marketing manager; Debbie Rivers, HP product manager; and the entire Hewlett Packard organization for making this effort possible.

Finally, special thanks to Cherie Britt of Britt PR, who furnished me with endless insight into the Hewlett-Packard Pocket PC and without whom completion of this book would not have been possible.

Contents at a Glance

Contents

Chapter 17: Advanced Personalization for Your Faithful Companion 241

Chapter 18: Killer Apps for the Pocket PC 271

Applications That Really Apply Themselves

Hardware Features and Functionality

IN THIS CHAPTER • A quick introduction to your Pocket PC

• Pocket PC equipment

• Pocket PC quick setup

Congratulations on your purchase of a Pocket PC. This device is the most faithful personal companion you can own. It obediently stores all of your personal information and is also charged with entertaining, educating, and assisting you in decision making. With all this power, it's a wonder it still fits in your pocket. But the portable design is exactly what makes it so successful. After all, what good would a personal secretary, entertainment coordinator, or counselor be if they were not available at a moment's notice?

At first glance, the Pocket PC is all business. With its elegant exterior and sleek controls, it's suitable for the boardroom, but is just as appropriate in the family room or on the streets. Several hardware companies develop Pocket PCs for different purposes. The HP Jornada series targets business professionals who prefer beautiful yet conservative styling and trusted hardware. Compaq Computer Corporation's striking chrome iPAQ line of Pocket PCs speaks to the rebellious attitude of the flamboyant who want a machine that says, "Look at me." And Casio has developed a number of products with the intention of winning over the techno-elite crowd who demand fashion-conscious color options or exclusive features, such as a rugged casing or interchangeable battery packs.

Regardless of which brand you own, the Pocket PC weighs less than 10 ounces, is slightly larger than a deck of playing cards, and houses a 320×240 pixel, touch-sensitive screen. Although each Pocket PC contains a different processor chip, all of them run at speeds in the hundreds of MHz — much faster than virtually any other personal digital assistants (PDAs) on the market — and contain 16 MB (or more) of memory. With the "instant on" capability, the Pocket PC truly is available in a moment's notice. Simply push the Power button and the device comes to life in milliseconds, awaiting your command.

Pocket PCs belong to a larger category of products referred to as "Windows Powered" devices because they run a Microsoft Windows operating system designed exclusively for mobile computing. Windows Powered hardware includes a set of larger handheld computers called the Handheld PC, which are easily distinguished from the Pocket PC by its keyboard and the horizontal orientation of the screen, and a cellular Smart Phone, which has many of the same features as your Pocket PC. In addition, there are a few unconventional Windows Powered devices, such as an in-car computing system dubbed the Auto PC (which is essentially a communications-centric computer with a Global Positioning System (GPS) and mobile phone capabilities, and is designed to fit where your car radio does today) and Internet-connected television-top boxes such as WebTV.

The advantage of owning a Pocket PC that belongs to the family of Windows Powered devices is that you can communicate with many of these devices, increasing their functionality and usefulness. Examples of the advanced communications features in Windows Powered devices are: trading electronic business cards with friends and associates that own a Pocket PC, Handheld PC, or Windows Powered cellular phone, or beaming an address from your Pocket PC's address book into the Auto PC to receive spoken step-by-step directions on how to get to your destination. Additionally, because Microsoft developed the operating system, Windows Powered devices have excellent communications capabilities with Windows desktop computers and the entire Microsoft Office suite of applications.

But, in this guidebook, your journey is not to explore the entire line of Windows Powered devices, but rather to master a single device. There are hundreds of ways to put your Pocket PC to work, and you will learn about all of them in the next 25 chapters. Begin your travels by acquainting yourself with the Pocket PC.

A 60-Second Introduction to Your Pocket PC

Take a moment to examine the Pocket PC with the power off. Aside from the touch screen previously mentioned, you must become familiar with a number of hardware features in order to successfully master your Pocket PC. Figure 1.1 identifies the location of each of the special items on the HP Jornada, including the Power, Voice Recorder, and application buttons; Notification L.E.D.; Scrolling controls; and Speaker.

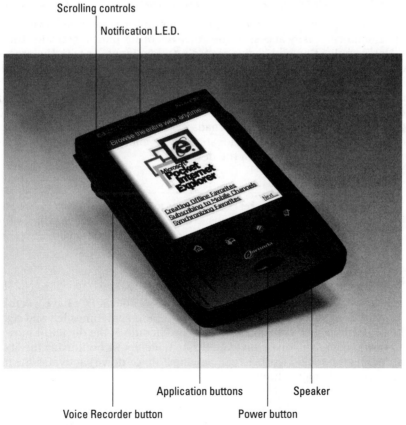

Figure 1.1 Pocket PC hardware features

Hardware buttons

Every Pocket PC has hardware buttons that provide instant access to many of the most frequently used features of the device. Naturally, the Power button is the most popular hardware button and always stands apart from the other buttons on the device in order to distinguish itself and prevent unintentional deactivation of the device. The application buttons are grouped together as a panel that launches Pocket PC programs in an instant, even when the device is powered down. This prevents the multiple steps of pressing the Power button and searching through the menus to run the application.

Cross-Reference

The section titled "10 Things Every User Should Change in the Control Panel," in Chapter 17 explains how to customize the hardware buttons to start the applications that you choose.

Voice Recorder button, microphone, and speaker

Popular enough to receive special placement on the side of the device where your thumb can easily access it, the Voice Recorder button activates the Pocket PC Notes application and begins recording audio input. As with the programs activated by the application buttons, the Voice Recorder can be activated even when the device is off, which makes recording a fleeting thought extremely fast and effortless. Audio is recorded via the microphone, which can be seen in a nearly imperceptible hole above the scrolling controls. The microphone icon etched into the hinge of the HP Jornada case helps detect the microphone port and Figure 1.2 reveals the exact location of the microphone. Audio playback occurs through the speaker on the device.

Note

If you are shopping for a Pocket PC, make sure to select a device with the speaker mounted on the front. This feature ensures clear playback of recordings and will not impede the system alarms when the device is set down or enclosed in a carrying case.

Scrolling controls

Occasionally referred to as the Action button, all Pocket PCs have a scrolling lever that enables you to move up and down (and sometimes left and right). The HP Jornada has a rocker switch on the left side of the device. It moves up and down to enable you to navigate through menus without using the stylus. Depressing the rocker (rather than moving it up or down) activates the item that is currently highlighted.

Scrolling controls

Microphone

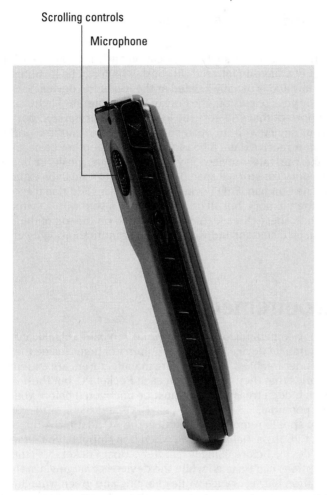

Figure 1.2 Side view of the HP Jornada, providing a view of the voice recorder microphone and scrolling controls

Tip

In addition to navigating menus, the scrolling control can be used to close items. For example, when you are viewing a pop-up window or any item with an Ok button, simply depress the rocker switch in order to save the settings and close the window.

Additional hardware features

Concealed among all of the previously discussed features of the Pocket PC are a few additional functions that differ slightly in location and function on each Pocket PC model. All Pocket PCs have an infrared (IR) port, which can be identified as a black reflective window and is usually located at the top of the device. Similar to the remote control for your television, the Pocket PC uses infrared light to send information. It is important that you note the location of your infrared port, as you will need to align your device with the corresponding device's infrared port when you wish to transmit or receive data. A headphone jack is another basic feature of the Pocket PC, used for privately reviewing voice recordings, music, or books on tape. Finally, the memory (or storage space) on all Pocket PCs can be expanded via a memory slot. The Compaq iPAQ Pocket PC requires an additional accessory in order to install extra memory, but all other Pocket PCs ship with a memory card slot. For easy reference, these three features are located on the top of the HP Jornada unit, but will be discussed individually and far more thoroughly in future chapters.

Pocket PC Accoutrements

Everyone loves getting something for free and, while you paid a significant amount of money for your handheld device, there are a number of items inside the box that you should consider freebies. The hardware manufacturers are extremely generous in the accessories that they include with each Pocket PC, but these accessories are sometimes hidden treasures that must be uncovered before you can use them to their fullest potential.

The first item you should remove and install is the AC adapter. Although the battery in the Pocket PC is partially charged when it is shipped, you should completely charge your device before using it remotely. Most Pocket PCs (the Casio being the only exception) can be used while the device is charging. On the HP Jornada, the notification LED is orange while charging and green when fully charged. The AC adapter can be connected directly to the Pocket PC, or attached to the docking cradle.

Cross-Reference

The HP Jornada comes with a special travel charger that works with many different accessories. For complete information, check out the "Special Jornada Hardware Enhancements" section of Chapter 23.

Every Pocket PC comes with a docking cradle or a serial cable. These products are used to connect your Pocket PC to the desktop. Hewlett Packard has an innovative docking cradle with what they call the "one cable on the desk solution." This means that the docking cradle has only one cable that extends from the base of the station until it continues under the desk, where it splits into a power cord and a PC connector. With the power off, connect your cable or cradle to the desktop PC and then install ActiveSync using the CD-ROM.

While you have the ActiveSync CD-ROM in your drive, and while your Pocket PC is charging, take a moment to browse through the contents of the CD-ROM. The disc includes a number of free Pocket PC applications and supplementary programs for the desktop that a majority of Pocket PC users never discover. Here is a brief summary of the contents in the ActiveSync CD-ROM and their location:

- **Microsoft Outlook 2000** (\Extras\Outlook\)**:** A full retail version of Microsoft Outlook, the personal information manager (PIM) for your desktop computer. Schedule + v7.0a, Outlook 98, or this application must be installed on your system if you wish to synchronize your Pocket PC.

- **Microsoft Internet Explorer v5.0** (\Extras\IE5\)**:** A full version of Microsoft Internet Explorer for your desktop computer. Version 5.0 or later must be installed on your system in order to create and synchronize Mobile Favorites. Mobile Favorites are Web pages that can be automatically downloaded to your device.

- **Windows Media Manager** (\Extras\Media\)**:** A desktop program to assist you in copying digital music (in MP3 or WMA format) to your Pocket PC. Installation of this file is completely optional.

- **AvantGo Advertisement** (\Extras\AvantGo\)**:** An HTML page discussing the features and benefits of using AvantGo.

- **E-books for Pocket Reader** (\Extras\MSReader\books\)**:** 29 free books that can be copied to your Pocket PC, including *The Importance of Being Earnest* by Oscar Wilde, and *Little Women* by Louisa May Alcott.

- **Pocket Money Setup** (\Extras\MSMoney\)**:** A program that must be run in order to connect your desktop version of Microsoft Money 2000 with the Pocket Money application. A version of Pocket Money for the Handheld PC is also included on this CD-ROM.

- **Transcriber** (\Extras\TScribe)**:** A free handwriting-recognition program for the Pocket PC.

- **Pocket Streets v3.02** (\Extras\Pstreets\)**:** A street map program that enables you to quickly locate restaurants, hotels, and other points of interest, or enter an address to quickly jump to the location on the map. A subdirectory includes 14 maps of major metropolitan areas.

Warning

The maps included on the ActiveSync CD-ROM cannot be used if you download the new version of Pocket Streets (2001) from the www.pocketpc.com Web site.

In addition to the ActiveSync CD-ROM, most Pocket PCs ship with an additional disc from the hardware manufacturer. This disc contains third-party software for which the hardware manufacturer has already paid software developer licensing fees so that you can freely use the products. A complete list of these applications can be found on the CD-ROM label, the CD-ROM case, or on the box that came with your Pocket PC.

Cross-Reference

For complete information on the applications that come with the HP Jornada Pocket PC, skip ahead to the "HP Exclusive Software Applications" section of Chapter 18.

And finally, most manufacturers include an inexpensive slipcover with each Pocket PC. Although most users prefer to purchase a more stylish and functional protective case, I strongly recommend that you use the protective slipcover until you find a suitable replacement. This is because slipping the device in your pocket with keys or spare change, inadvertently dropping it, or even the act of simply setting it on an uneven surface can cause harm to the incredibly fragile screen. One side of every slipcover has a section reinforced with plastic, which should always be the side that the Pocket PC screen faces when enclosed in the case. The Hewlett Packard line of Pocket PCs ship with a metal cover that is both stylish and incredibly protective. This cover should always be used — it can be accented with an additional exterior case, or you can purchase striking case covers in alternate colors.

Quick Setup of Your Pocket PC

The first time you power up the Pocket PC, the device runs you through a number of setup procedures. The first procedure enables you to set the screen alignment by using your stylus to tap in the center of the target. The target moves around the screen a number of times until the touch screen is properly calibrated. It is very important that you hold the stylus in a comfortable and normal manner, as the device will expect you to tap the screen in the same way in the future.

After the screen alignment, you are introduced to the tap-and-hold feature by performing a cut-and-paste on a sample appointment. Complete this correctly, and you can advance to the final stage of setup, which is the regional settings. Because the Pocket PC is a worldly device, you need to tell the system where you normally reside. This information is used to program your world clock, manage your agenda, and track the date and time of files in your Pocket PC. Select the city or region that is closest to your home or work and ensure that the time zone matches your locale.

Tip

If you plan to synchronize with your desktop computer right away, you do not need to adjust the Pocket PC clock. ActiveSync (the desktop software that synchronizes your Pocket PC with the computer) automatically sets the time using your PC clock. But you need to make sure that your regional settings are correct on both devices.

Summary

Now that you have completed this chapter, you have successfully set up your device and should be comfortable with the nomenclature of the hardware features on the Pocket PC. Feel free to return to this chapter as a reference if you are having difficulties remembering the functionality of a specific button or want to reacquaint yourself with the hardware features.

The next logical step is to power up your device and explore the Pocket PC interface. That is exactly what you will be doing in Chapter 2.

The Pocket PC Interface

IN THIS CHAPTER
- Basic elements of the Pocket PC
- Work faster with a stylus
- The Start menu
- How is this different from my desktop?

love the term "interface" because it loosely means "to work with" or "to interact with," all words that are very engaging. But when used in reference to the
Pocket PC, *interface* describes all of the visual elements that appear on the
screen and enables you to navigate and control the Pocket PC. Still, true to the
original description, the Windows Powered interface is so engaging that you will
quickly become skilled at using the interface to work faster and smarter than
ever before. But in order to get to that point, you must become familiar with
some naming conventions.

Basic Elements of the Pocket PC

Figure 2.1 shows a sample window of information on the Pocket PC. At the top of
the screen is the Navigation bar. In this example, the navigation bar contains four
elements:

■ The *Start menu icon*, which should be familiar to users of the Windows
   desktop operating system. This is where you access all of the applications
   on the device. This icon is discussed in detail later in this chapter.

■ The *program title* is a dynamic field that always displays the name of the
   active program. This can provide vital clues to what program you're in if
   you turn on your device and cannot recognize what application is currently
   running.

■ The *system time* simply displays the current time like a clock.

■ The *Ok button* is used to save information and close the window. Although
   it is shown in the example screen shot (see Figure 2.1), the Ok button does
   not appear everywhere on the Pocket PC interface. It is only used on pop-
   up windows that contain information you can create or edit. A new or existing Pocket Word document is an example of a window of information you
   can create or edit.

Note

While you can close pop-up windows using the Ok button, you never have to exit
programs on the Pocket PC. Applications simply run in the background until you
use them again.

While the content area in Figure 2.1 is irrelevant to our discussion of naming
conventions, there are two very important interface features within the content:

■ *Tabs* are a vital part of the Pocket PC interface because they provide quick
   access to other pages of information. Similar to an index tab in a binder,
   Pocket PC tabs enable you to quickly switch back and forth between pages.

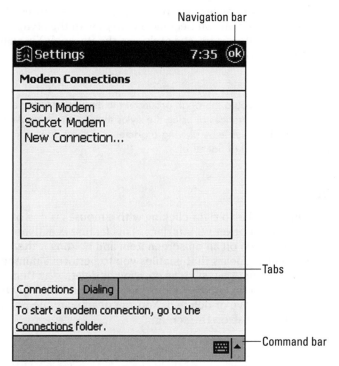

Figure 2.1 A sample Pocket PC pop-up window

- *Links*, on the other hand, enable you to jump to related information that is available in another location. Indicated by underlined text, a selected link will transport you to the new information (in this example, the Connections folder) and may not provide a way back to the information you were previously examining.

At the bottom of Figure 2.1 is the *Command bar*, an invaluable tool that adapts itself to the active application. In our example, a solitary function (the Input panel button described in Chapter 3) is visible, but the Command bar also contains entire menus, buttons, and icons that display information and provide access to the advanced features of each program.

Work Faster with a Stylus

One of the biggest challenges that a new Pocket PC user faces is working with a stylus. While a pen is a very close real-world relative to the stylus, most users are reluctant to simply place a pen on a screen because of the preconceived notions about non-interactive television sets and computer monitors. However, it's necessary to use the stylus to access many of the advanced features of the Pocket PC. With a little practice you can become as adept with the stylus as you are with a pen. For avid computer users, the stylus on the Pocket PC is analogous to the mouse on your desktop.

Tip

Although this handbook gives you a thorough grounding in the Pocket PC operating system, you will only learn the nuances of using the stylus through practice. And the best way to practice with the stylus is by playing a game . . . so put down this book for 10 minutes and play a round of Solitaire!

Tap and hold

The tap-and-hold feature (similar to right-clicking with a mouse) is one of the most powerful features in the Pocket PC interface. This feature is activated by simply placing your stylus down on an on-screen item and holding it there for a few seconds. A pop-up menu appears that enables you to perform a number of actions, including common functions, such as copying or deleting an item. Figure 2.2 shows the pop-up menu for an e-mail, which enables the user to reply to or forward the e-mail, as well as save or delete it. You can deactivate the pop-up window by tapping anywhere else on the screen.

Note

Pop-up menus activated by using the tap-and-hold feature only make changes to a single item. Use the menus on the Command bar to make global changes.

Unfortunately, the only way to tell if an item has a pop-up menu is to try it. In most cases, any individual item will reveal a pop-up window when you tap and hold it. Tasks, calendar entries, files, and contacts all reveal pop-up menus using this technique. Even buttons on the Command bar have pop-up windows to explain what they do. Select Start ⇨Programs ⇨In box. In the Command bar, tap and hold both of the icons to the right of the Services menu (visible in Figure 2.2). You will see two pop-up windows that say Connect and Send/Receive Mail. Although you might never have been able to figure out what these buttons do by examining them, the tap-and-hold function clearly explains their functions in just seconds. One more little-known tap-and-hold secret: if you tap and hold the system clock in the navigation bar, a pop-up window displays the current date.

The one exception to the rule are the icons in the Program menu. In order to keep you from deleting the application shortcuts, no menu is available when you use the tap-and-hold feature on these items.

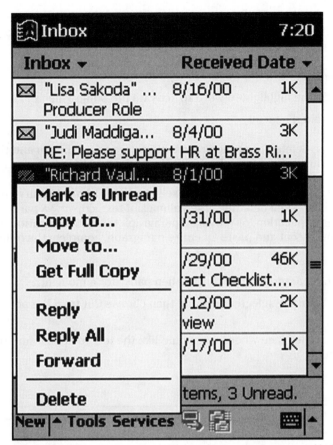

Figure 2.2 The pop-up menu is opened by using the tap-and-hold feature on an e-mail item.

The single-, double- and triple-tap tricks

When working with text in any application (such as an e-mail or Word document, for example), keep the Pocket PC's stylus tapping tricks in mind. A single tap anywhere moves the cursor to that point in the body of the text. To begin typing in the middle of a sentence, tap once at the place where you would like to insert the text and then begin typing.

A double-tap with the stylus highlights an entire word. This is extremely useful if you want to correct a word in the middle of a sentence or if you want to use Transcriber to spell check the word.

If you tap where a space appears between words, the gap between the words and the word that appears before the space is selected. You can use the following technique to remove a word from a paragraph quickly:

1. Tap the space beyond the word you wish to remove.

2. Tap and hold the highlighted word to activate the pop-up menu.

3. Select Cut from the menu.

The word will be deleted from the document you were working on and the paragraph will be instantly reformatted with the correct spacing between the words.

Performing a triple-tap in any document selects an entire paragraph of text. This feature is handy when deleting large volumes of text, copying a paragraph for use in another application, or moving a paragraph to another location in the document. To quickly cut and paste an entire paragraph, complete the following steps:

1. Triple-tap the paragraph quickly and then pause for a moment.

2. Tap and hold on the selected text and then choose Cut from the pop-up menu.

3. Tap and hold the place where you would like the text to appear and then select Paste.

Tip

The single-, double- and triple-tap tricks work perfectly even when you do not have an input method activated. However, if you turn on the keyboard, Character Recognizer, or Transcriber before you begin to tap, you can quickly delete the selected text by typing new content.

The Start Menu

As with all Windows operating systems, the Pocket PC's functionality centers on the Start menu. This is the tool for running and switching applications, locating documents, and getting help. Best of all, it is always accessible, no matter where you are. Figure 2.3 shows the Pocket PC with the Start menu active. As you can see, there are six elements on the Start menu: the Shortcut bar, Start menu application icons, Programs, Settings, Find, and Help.

Shortcut bar

Start menu application icons

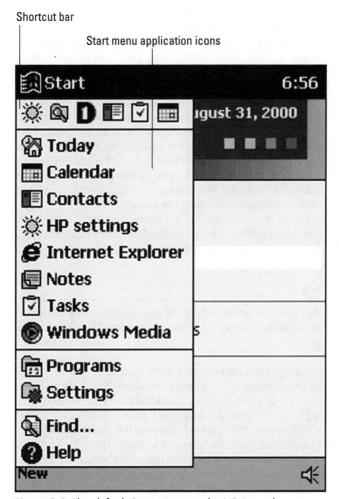

Figure 2.3 The default Start menu on the HP Jornada

The Shortcut bar is adjacent to the Start menu button because it is the most frequently used feature. It is designed to display the graphical icons of the last six applications that you have run on your Pocket PC. Selecting an icon will run that program. If you only use six Pocket PC applications (and shame on you, if that is true), they will always be available from this Shortcut bar. Some users overlook this bar and go straight to the Programs menu, even though the application they wanted was available with a single tap. Once you become accustomed to looking for the program's icon (instead of the name), you will find that the Shortcut bar is an extremely efficient application switcher.

Directly beneath the Shortcut bar is a set of Start menu application icons. Your Pocket PC hardware manufacturer has selected these applications as the most important programs in your device and given them this prime real estate on the Start menu. Naturally, you might disagree, and that is OK. Shortcuts to any application can be placed in this area, and the point is that these should be your principal applications that you would like to have quick access to at all times. You can place as many shortcuts as you like on the Start menu, but I recommend seven or less, because the Start menu detaches from the left side of the screen when more icons are added. This makes the entire Start menu harder to use because you must reposition your stylus after you select the Start button.

The Programs menu item opens an icon-driven list of all of the applications installed on your device. If you are looking for an application that you have just installed from your desktop, or you want to find one of the built-in software packages, this is where you should head. The Programs menu also contains folders (such as the Games folder) that contain icons and help organize the Programs menu if there are too many icons cluttering the screen.

The Settings menu item is the Pocket PC equivalent of the desktop computer's Control Panel. Here you can make changes to the Pocket PC operating system and configure the device's various communications, hardware controls, and security features.

 Cross-Reference

Chapter 17 provides comprehensive instructions on customizing the Start menu and Programs menu and includes a section on "Ten Things Every User Should Change in the Control Panel."

The Find feature in the Start menu offers a more powerful search tool than is available on any desktop computer. Designed to explore both files and databases, the Find function scours every information repository on your device for the information you are trying to find. Figure 2.4 displays a search for the term "Nancy," which returned results from my calendar (displaying her flight schedule and her day off) and a Word document that contains her name in the title. The find feature also listed my contact card, because I have her name in the Spouse field, and an e-mail in my in-box from her. The arrows to the right of the Find and Type fields enable you to recall your last six searches and limit the search to specific file types and sizes.

Although the Find feature will scour all of your databases, it only searches for files in the My Documents folder and subfolders within My Documents on your device and memory card. This means that the Find feature will not locate files installed by third-party applications (that are located in \My Device\Program Files\), or any system files that reside in the Windows directory.

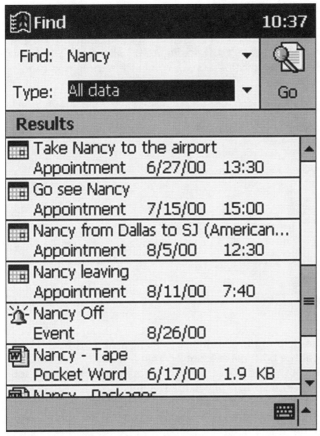

Figure 2.4 The Find feature in action

Last, but definitely not least on the Start menu, is the Help command. A pure stroke of genius, the Help command is designed to display context-sensitive help based on the active application. This means that if you are currently in Pocket Word and you select Start ➪ Help, a document appears that is specifically designed for assisting you with Pocket Word.

Tip

If you are having trouble getting context-sensitive help, check to make sure that the correct application name appears in the Navigation menu at the top of the screen before you select Help from the Start menu. If the name is different from the program you are trying to receive help on, run the application from the Start menu again. If the correct Help menu still does not appear, select Start ➪ Help to load the Help application and then select View ➪ All Installed Help from the toolbar. This displays a list of all of the Help files installed on your Pocket PC.

In many applications, the Help command provides assistance based on the action you are trying to perform. For example, launch Pocket Word on your Pocket PC, create a new document, and select Edit ⇨ Format and then launch the Help command by choosing Start ⇨ Help. Figure 2.5 shows the resulting Help file. As you can see, the documentation assists you in formatting text in a Pocket Word document.

Figure 2.5 The Help window

Navigation in the Help window is similar to using a Web browser. The Command bar arrows shown at the bottom of Figure 2.5 enable you to move backward and forward. Hyperlinks in the text connect you to related information. An index of all help items available for the program you are reading about is available by selecting View ⇨ Contents. This is an invaluable feature when you would like to learn more about a product, but do not know where to start. Many applications include an introduction to the program in their Help file. Pocket PC games (such as Solitaire) even include complete rules on how to play.

Tip

If you press the Ok button at the top right corner of the screen, your Help window closes and you lose the ability to retrace your steps using the forward and backward arrows if you launch Help again. To keep your place in the Help window, return to the application by tapping on the Start menu and selecting the application from the Shortcut bar. When you want to return to the Help window, select Start ⇨ Settings ⇨ System tab ⇨ Memory ⇨ Running Programs tab. Highlight the Help item and press the Activate button.

How is This Different from My Desktop?

Although the Pocket PC is a Microsoft Windows Powered device, it is extremely different from the Microsoft Windows operating system that runs on your desktop or laptop computer. The Windows Powered operating system has been developed from scratch, specifically for use on handheld computers, to accommodate many of the unique features discussed in this handbook, such as instant-on capability, longer battery life, and using the stylus for data entry.

Moreover, the Pocket PC is designed as a PC companion that complements your desktop computer. The operating system and all of the built-in applications are simplified versions and do not perform some of the higher-level functions and calculations that the desktop counterparts can. This is because of the Pocket PC's limited memory. The operating system and applications on the Pocket PC are allocated approximately 16 megabytes of storage space. Anyone who has installed an operating system or Microsoft Office knows that the desktop versions of these software packages are hundreds of megabytes. Besides, bigger files translate to longer wait times and slower response. And no one likes to wait!

Note

Applications designed for your desktop computer cannot be installed on your Pocket PC because the file formats differ. In order to work, programs must be specifically written to work on the Pocket PC.

One place where Microsoft did not cut corners is in communications features. Although it is not necessary for you to know all of these terms, the Pocket PC supports TCP/IP, SLIP, PPP, SMTP, and POP3. Basically, this means that the Pocket PC uses Internet-standard communication protocols. So although the Pocket PC may be deficient in some areas, the Internet communications features are first-rate.

Cross-Reference

Chapter 16 provides complete information on how to connect your device to the Internet using popular online services and Internet service providers (ISPs).

Summary

This chapter should have augmented your proficiency with the stylus, made you at ease with the Start menu, and given you a better understanding of the differences between the Pocket PC and your desktop PC.

However, the principal difference between the Pocket PC and the desktop is how you enter data. Chapter 3 explores the different input methods and helps you choose the right one for you.

Input Methods

Although Pocket PCs are most commonly used for looking up and reviewing data, the device would be considered ineffective if you could not enter information. In fact, the ability to write a fleeting thought or record an associate's new phone number on the run is one of the best benefits of constantly carrying a PC companion. But without a visible keyboard for entering information, many people are lost.

Thankfully, after many years of research and development, Microsoft has created a number of input methods to suit every person's unique writing style. The three input applications that ship with the Pocket PC are the keyboard, Character Recognizer, and Transcriber. Each application uses different techniques to convert screen taps to text; pressing the Input panel button on the Command bar activates them all. As you can see in Figure 3.1, pressing the Up arrow alongside the Input panel button enables you to select your input method. The bullet next to the words "Character Recognizer" indicates that it is the default input method on this device. Note also that the icon inside the Input panel button changes to reflect the current input method.

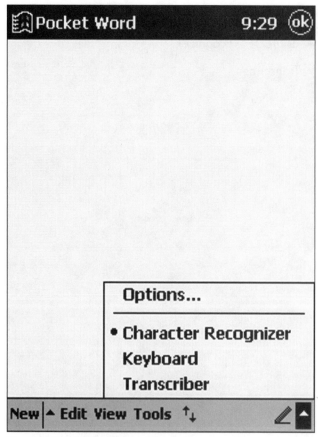

Figure 3.1 Selecting an input method

Finding an Input Method

The Input panel changes its appearance to display the default input method. Shown sequentially in the preceding figure are the icons for the keyboard, Character Recognizer, and Transcriber.

Although most users are unaware of this, two special keyboard layouts can be accessed from the soft keyboard. The first layout, reachable by pressing the 123 key in the upper left-hand corner, reveals a keyboard containing special numeric keypad and symbol sets. The second layout, accessible via the accented äü key in the bottom row of the keyboard, uncovers a keyboard that enables you to enter foreign language letters and symbols.

Note

Once you have selected your preferred method of data entry, the Pocket PC remembers your choice and defaults to it whenever you push the Input panel button.

Choosing an input method depends on many factors. Having a clear understanding of the advantages and disadvantages of each of them will make it far easier to decide which one to use.

The Keyboard

The most straightforward input method is the soft keyboard. Modeled after the computer equivalent, this input method places a miniature keyboard at the bottom of the Pocket PC screen that can be used without any practice. Figure 3.2 shows the keyboard being used in the Pocket Word application. Notice the Word Completion feature, which tries to deduce the word you are typing and places its best guess just above the keyboard. Pressing on the word will type it into your sentence and place a space directly following it.

Tip

If you want to lock down the Shift or international character key, give it a quick double-tap.

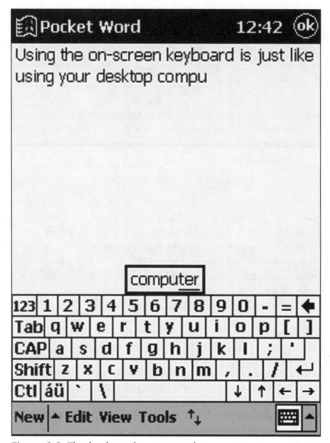

Figure 3.2 The keyboard input panel

Word completion is just one of the advantages of having an on-screen key-board. Microsoft has integrated a number of elegant shortcuts that increase your data entry speed when using the keyboard. The keyboard has a special set of gestures that enable you to capitalize a letter, move forward or backward, and enter a carriage return. A helpful set of illustrated instructions for each of the gestures is listed in the input settings for the keyboard. You open the keyboard Input Settings applet in either of two ways:

■ Select Start ⇨ Settings ⇨ Input.

■ Press the arrow to the right of the Input panel button and select Options.

Tip

You can quickly capitalize a single letter using the keyboard by pressing your stylus on the letter and then dragging up and releasing.

Customizing the Keyboard Input Settings

Figure 3.3 displays the Input Settings screen with the keyboard selected. It is important to note that the gestures listed on this screen work consistently on the soft keyboard. However, if you increase the size of the keys, you can select the "Use gestures . . ." checkbox to remove the four keys and make a more efficient use of space. Also, note the hyperlink at the bottom of the window to align the touch screen. If your typing is accurate, but the Pocket PC seems to be misinterpreting the characters, use this hyperlink to increase the precision of the screen's alignment.

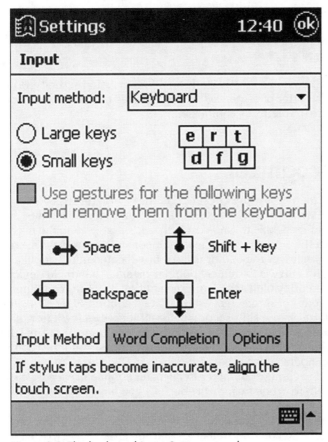

Figure 3.3 The keyboard Input Settings panel

Note

If your screen looks vastly different from Figure 3.3, press the Down arrow on the Input method field at the top of the screen and select keyboard from the drop down list.

The second tab of the keyboard Input Settings applet enables you to customize the Word Completion feature. You can deactivate it if you find it distracting; otherwise, you can change the quantity of letters that it waits for you to enter before suggesting a word and increase the number of words that it suggests. The first feature is essential to enhancing the program's accuracy. Test it out by increasing the amount on the "Suggest after entering X letters" line to four or five. It won't make a suggestion for smaller words, but you'll find it far more accurate in the words it does suggest. The second feature is desirable if you use words that are very similar and Word Completion has a hard time matching the letters to the word you want to spell.

Tip

Use the Word Completion feature as an on-the-fly spell checker. If you do not know how to spell a word, type the first few letters. The word pops up above the keyboard when you get close.

The Options tab contains mostly irrelevant configuration settings. However, the "Capitalize first letter of sentence" setting ensures that every time you begin a new sentence the first letter is capitalized.

Character Recognizer

The second input method for the Pocket PC is the Character Recognizer. It involves a style of writing one character at a time, in a specific manner, so that the application can recognize it. Once each character is written, the user must lift the stylus from the screen. Almost instantaneously, the character is recognized and placed wherever the cursor is currently located in the application. This method of data entry is extremely popular on small handheld devices because of the incredibly high speed and recognition accuracy,combined with the very small amount of screen real estate that it requires. Figure 3.4 shows the Character Recognizer in the split-second before it identifies the letter "e". Notice that there are three distinct writing areas in the recognition pane. The left side is designed for capital letters, the middle area for lower case, and the right side is designed for numbers and symbols.

With speed and accuracy, Character Recognizer sounds like a data entry dream. However, there is one major drawback — you have to learn to write the way that the program wants to see characters. Fortunately, most of them are simply lowercase versions of the letter you wish to write. One frustrating exception is that Character Recognizer demands that the letter "I" be written from bottom to top, and the letter "L" printed from top to bottom. However, time and practice will eliminate these minor nuisances and provide you with the most accurate recognition system available in a handheld computer.

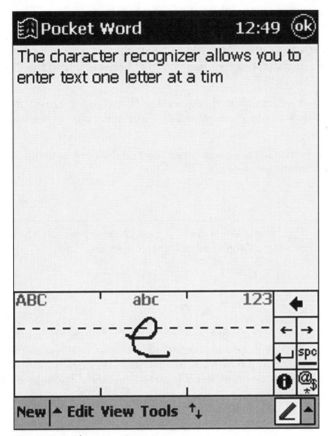

Figure 3.4 Character Recognizer

Note

Appendix E contains a quick reference table with all of the gestures that Character Recognizer can identify. Remove the pages from the book and store them with your Pocket PC for a quick and easy reference when you need to check how to write a specific symbol.

Customizing Character Recognizer

As with the keyboard, the options for Character Recognizer are available once you have set it as your default input method. Simply select Start ⇨ Settings ⇨ Input or press the arrow to the right of the Input panel button and select an option from the Options tab:

■ **Uppercase mode** — greatly increases the recognition accuracy for users who generally write in block print style.

- **Lowercase mode** — the system default. This mode has a few options of its own:

  - A single-stroke method of writing is available to boost your data entry speeds even faster, but requires you to adhere closely to the Character Recognizer's alphabet.

  - Left-handed writers should activate the "Right to left crossbar" feature, so that you can cross your Ts, Fs and the + sign in the opposite direction.

  - Users who write in languages other than English can activate the accented characters feature.

Tip

Ex-Palm Pilot users: If you would like to use a single-stroke character set, which is very similar to the Palm Pilot's Graffiti, select Uppercase mode.

Transcriber

The final data-input method is my personal favorite. Transcriber is handwriting recognition at its finest. Using the same recognition engine that was implemented and refined on the Apple Newton, Transcriber has been developed after years of real-world experience on earlier Windows Powered devices as a third-party application.

Note

On most Pocket PCs, including the HP Jornada, Transcriber needs to be installed from the ActiveSync CD-ROM in order to appear on the list of active input options. To install it, open the \Extras\Tscribe folder on the ActiveSync CD-ROM and double-click the setup.exe file while your Pocket PC is connected to the computer. Once the application is installed on the device, you will have to soft-reset your system. Appendix A has complete information on how to perform a soft reset.

Using Transcriber is easy. Set it as your default input method by pressing the Up arrow next to the Input panel button and selecting Transcriber. Next, press the Input panel button to activate it and then start writing. Figure 3.5 shows Transcriber in operation with text about to be recognized. In this example the Transcriber toolbar and pop-up symbol pad are turned on. However, it is important to notice that when Transcriber is activated, a rectangle with a white background appears behind the Transcriber icon in the bottom-right corner. Were the toolbar and symbol pad not activated, this white rectangle would be the only indication that Transcriber was active and ready to recognize text.

Figure 3.5 Transcriber handwriting recognition

Tip

If you want to take a break from writing without letting Transcriber convert your current notation to text, leave your stylus down on the screen, on the last letter you have written. When you are ready to resume the sentence, lift up the stylus and begin writing the next letter.

In addition to the remarkable recognition engine, Transcriber comes with some impressive extras. The toolbar and pop-up symbol pad make the recognition application easier to use, but the real gem is the built-in spell checker. Transcriber automatically checks the spelling of words as it recognizes them, but it also has a pop-up spelling advisor that you can call upon by simply highlighting any word and drawing a "V" from left to right with the two lines nearly overlapping each other. Figure 3.6 has an example of the pop-up for an obvious spelling error and also displays the feature's ability to add words to its dictionary. Bear in mind that the pop-up spelling advisor can also be used on words that are spelled correctly, just in case Transcriber changed a word you wrote into something that you didn't mean. Also, if you draw the correction symbol on the screen when nothing is selected, Transcriber activates the pop-up symbol pad.

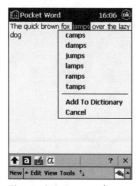

Figure 3.6 Transcriber's pop-up spelling advisor

Tip

If you have just jotted a line but it didn't appear as recognized text after the handwriting disappeared, tap in the window where you want the text to go. You should see a flashing cursor appear in the window. Write the phrase again and it will materialize where you placed the cursor.

Customizing Transcriber

If you have read straight through thus far, you undoubtedly know that you can reach the customization applet for Transcriber by selecting Start ⇨ Settings ⇨ Input or by pressing the arrow to the right of the Input panel button and selecting Options. The Options button uncovers a number of simple features, including activating and deactivating the feedback sounds when recognizing text, displaying an intro screen (which I recommend turning off, because having it on greatly increases the load time), and activating the icon bar, which we mentioned earlier. In addition, you can alter the color and size of the "ink" that appears when you write on the screen.

The Recognizer tab has two sliding scales that enable you to adjust the amount of time between when you stop writing and when it begins to recognize the text (which is helpful if you often find Transcriber begins recognizing before you have finished writing), and a speed versus quality setting. In addition, one checkbox enables you to control whether the program automatically adds a space after each word that it recognizes; another checkbox activates Transcriber's Separate Letter mode. While I strongly suggest that everyone activate the first checkbox feature, users should only initiate Separate Letters mode if they constantly write each letter separately, that is, disconnected from all other letters. While this feature does increase the recognition speed of the Transcriber application, it effectively disengages the program's ability to recognize cursive handwriting.

Transcriber tips

Although you will learn tricks to improve your accuracy later in this handbook, here are a few tips you can use right away as you get started with this handwriting recognition program.

Cross-Reference

Chapter 17 begins with an advanced section on how to improve your text entry accuracy using Transcriber. If you would like to get a head start on better handwriting recognition, skip to that chapter before continuing to other sections of the book.

Changing writing orientation

If you tend to use long words or work in an industry with long, technical terms, you may want to consider rotating the direction in which Transcriber recognizes text. Figure 3.7 shows an example of Transcriber performing handwriting recognition sideways. Although Pocket Word and the entire Pocket PC graphical interface still appears in the portrait format, the device can be rotated 90 degrees and text can be written in landscape mode.

Figure 3.7 Writing sideways on the Pocket PC

To change the direction in which Transcriber recognizes text, activate the Transcriber icon bar by selecting Start ⇨ Settings ⇨ Input ⇨ Options button and selecting the Show icon bar checkbox. Open a document and activate Transcriber. When Transcriber loads and the icon bar appears, tap on the directional arrow on the left side.

Transcriber enables you to write in six different directions. To identify which direction Transcriber is expecting you to write in, examine the directional arrow you just tapped. The arrow should always point upward (toward the top of your head) before you begin writing. Figure 3.7 shows Transcriber set so that the device is rotated 90 degrees counter-clockwise. This is the most convenient position for right-handed users who prefer to write in landscape mode.

Cross-Reference

HP Jornada users can permanently rotate the screen on their device for all applications. For step-by-step instructions on how to perform this trick, refer to Chapter 17.

In addition to being able to rotate Transcriber left, right, and upside down, you can use two diagonal settings. Figure 3.8 shows the right-diagonal setting with text being entered into Transcriber. Although this method of entering data reduces the amount of writing area and limits the length of the words you can write at the beginning (top of the screen) and ending (bottom of the screen), it is more ergonomically correct. Because you are not bending your wrist downward to keep the screen perfectly vertical in portrait mode, and you do not have to struggle to try to hold the entire length of the device in landscape mode, this middle-of-the-road option enables you to hold the device at a comfortable angle and write in the available space. Carpal tunnel sufferers, such as myself, find this feature a welcome alternative to the rigid options of portrait or landscape orientation.

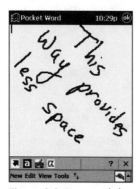

Figure 3.8 Diagonal data entry

Note

Because Transcriber uses the entire screen for recognition, text selection is performed in a slightly different manner. To select text, tap and hold the beginning of the information you wish to select. When you hear Transcriber beep, begin moving the stylus to the right (or downward, if you wish to select multiple lines of text). When you have highlighted your entire selection, lift the stylus from the screen. A faster, alternative way to select a single line of text is to draw a line over the text from left to right.

Recognition mode

Another feature on the Transcriber icon bar is the Recognition mode icon. By default, it appears as a lowercase letter "a". When tapped, this icon toggles to an uppercase "A", and then the staggered numbers "1" and "2". The purposes of this icon are to tell Transcriber when you are entering a word in all capital letters and to enhance the recognition of numbers.

When entering abbreviations such as USB (Universal Serial Bus), Transcriber frequently capitalizes the first letter and then converts the remaining characters to lowercase letters. To solve this problem, tap the Recognition mode icon once and the icon changes to a capital "A", indicating that Uppercase mode is active. Enter the text and Transcriber will print every letter in capital letters. When you have finished, tap the Recognition mode icon once to return to the regular mode. Another way to quickly change the case of a word or phrase is to highlight the text and then drag the stylus straight up (as you would when writing the letter l, but from bottom to top). This will capitalize the selected text if it is lowercase or convert a capitalized text to lowercase.

Likewise, when you are entering a large quantity of numbers and symbols, tap the Recognition mode icon twice and it will activate Numerical mode. Transcriber will assume that all characters entered are numbers or symbols, which greatly enhances recognition speed when entering math equations. To return to the default mode, tap the Recognition mode icon once.

Tip

When you are entering a large amount of data or creating complex formulas in Pocket Excel, switch to Transcriber and activate the Numerical mode by tapping the Recognition mode icon twice. It is far easier on your eyes than trying to type formulas on the soft keyboard.

Transcriber gestures

As with the keyboard, a number of Transcriber gestures perform standard cursor control functions. Figure 3.9 shows each of the cursor control functions. As you would expect, the Enter gesture performs a carriage return, the Space gesture inserts a space, and the Tab gesture moves the cursor one tabbed space to the right. The Backspace gesture moves the cursor one space to the left, deleting the letter (if applicable) that was to the left of the cursor. If text is selected, performing the Backspace gesture deletes the highlighted text. Note that the Backspace gesture is drawn from right to left.

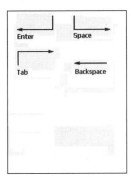

Figure 3.9 Cursor control gestures

Note

All of the cursor control gestures perform their respective actions at the cursor's current location.

A second set of gestures enables you to quickly perform complex editing functions. Figure 3.10 lists each of the gestures for Copy, Cut, Paste, and Undo. The Copy and Cut functions require you to select text; these functions perform in the same way as the Cut and Copy functions on your desktop computer. Paste inserts the cut or copied information where the cursor is positioned. If text is highlighted when Paste is selected, the new text overwrites the highlighted content. The Undo command automatically cancels the last action performed. Because the Pocket PC has multiple levels of Undo, you can perform the Undo gesture a number of times.

Tip

Transcriber's undo gesture works on the Pocket PC even in programs where the Undo feature does not appear in the menu. For example, if you cut-and-paste a file, you can activate Transcriber and perform the Undo gesture to return the file to its original location.

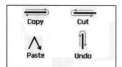

Figure 3.10 Text editing gestures

One final tip for using Transcriber requires a leap of faith. If you trust Transcriber to be able to recognize your handwriting even if you cannot see the words you are writing, you can write on top of your previous words. Write a very long sentence from the top of the screen to the bottom of the screen. Without pausing, start another sentence at the top of the screen, writing over everything you have already written. You may repeat this as many times as you like. When you finally stop writing, Transcriber will quickly translate everything you have written down in perfect order. I have performed this trick many times, and no matter how quickly or how much I write on the screen, Transcriber is always able to keep up with me.

Summary

Now that you have finished the first three chapters of the handbook, you should be comfortable with using all aspects of the Pocket PC. From here, you can skip to anywhere in the book and do extremely well.

If you continue on to Chapter 4, you will learn the valuable skills of protecting your device from damage, deterioration, and theft using free and inexpensive solutions available locally and on the Internet.

Care and Maintenance
of Your Pocket PC

IN THIS CHAPTER • Protecting your device from physical harm

• Theft-proofing your Pocket PC

• Securing your personal data

• Cleaning and covering your Pocket PC's touch screen

When you use the Pocket PC to its fullest capabilities, it contains your most personal and vital information. In addition, because it is always within reach to jot down phone numbers, notes and tasks, your Pocket PC will be the most up-to-date repository for your information. The frightening fact is that by damaging the device, having it stolen, or simply mishandling the unit, you can instantly lose all of the data that you have worked so hard to record. A few simple precautions can help to prevent any circumstances from prematurely severing the bond between you and your Pocket PC.

Protecting Your Device from Physical Harm

Without a doubt, the most common event that results in data loss is damage to the Pocket PC. And while I have heard abnormal stories of devices being run over by automobiles or dropped through a hole in a gangway while boarding a plane, the majority of the messages I receive are from people who simply mishandle the device during use or drop it a few feet to the ground. Although protecting your device from an automobile or plane incident might be unachievable there are a few easy steps each user should take to ensure that a short plunge does not spell the end of days for his or her Pocket PC.

Cross-Reference

Using a memory card in your device makes it simple to recover data from a damaged Pocket PC, because the memory card can simply be removed from the broken system and inserted into a new one. Study the "Using a memory card" section of Chapter 19 in order to find out how to automatically store all of your Word, Excel, Notes, and Inbox attachments on a memory card.

The HP Jornada ships with a metal cover that attaches to the device and stores the stylus when not in use. Keep this metal cover attached at all times. It is a passive protection device that keeps other objects from scratching the screen and damaging the front of the device. In addition, practice opening the cover partway, rather than all the way, to prevent it from locking in place during use. Should you ever drop the device while working on it, you'll increase the chance that the cover will close and protect the front of the Pocket PC.

Tip

To personalize your HP Jornada and help distinguish it from other Pocket PCs, take the metal cover to an engraving shop and ask them to engrave your name on the cover. This is an inexpensive way to have a customized and easily identifiable device.

If you dislike the metal cover or own a Pocket PC that does not have a protective cover, consider using a carrying case. E & B Company (www.ebcases.com) offers a line of reasonably priced "slipper" cases for the Pocket PC that enable you to operate your Pocket PC while it is inserted in the case. This helps guarantee that the device is protected at all times and offers slight protection against Pocket PC plunges. For more robust device drop defense, consider an "organizer-style carrying case. These cases generally consist of a Pocket PC zippered compartment and a separate wallet/checkbook compartment. By its very nature, this multiple-section design offers a padding that protects the device from small to medium falls. I personally use a wallet case from Targus Inc. (www.targus.com) and have experienced numerous drops from approximately 4 feet with no visible or functional damage whatsoever. If you want the best of both worlds, check out RhinoSkin Inc. (www.rhinoskin.com) for a line of super-slim wallet cases and water-resistant sport cases.

Theft-Proofing Your Pocket PC

Once the Pocket PC has been protected from destruction, it must also be protected from abduction. Handheld computers are easy to steal and even easier to lose because of their small size. They can be simply pocketed by a crook or misplaced and forgotten on a restaurant seat or in a taxicab. Fortunately, there are ways to protect yourself from experiencing these mishaps.

To begin, locate the "Solutions and Resource Guide" that came with your Pocket PC and look for the insert from ReturnMe.com. Figure 4.1 shows the top of the insert, which includes a loss-prevention ID tag. The service is free to all Pocket PC owners; all you have to do is sign up on their Web site or fill out the back of the card. If your Pocket PC is ever lost, someone who finds it simply calls the 800 number and Returnme.com sends Fed-Ex to their door to pick it up, and it will be returned to you the next day. You are only charged a fee if your device is returned to you via their service. If you cannot find your "Solutions and Resource Guide", visit www.returnme.com, where you can order a pack of 11 Returnme.com ID tags for $9.95.

The Pocket PC also has a built-in system for conveying your contact information should your device be found and activated by a curious passerby. Select Start ⇨ Settings ⇨ Owner Information from the startup screen. Figure 4.2 shows the Owner Information screen with the several different contact information fields, so you only need to provide the personal information you feel comfortable disclosing. Be sure to activate the "Show information when device is turned on" checkbox (it will be hidden if you have the keyboard active) so that your contact information appears every time the Pocket PC is activated.

Figure 4.1 ReturnMe.com's loss prevention ID tag

Tip

After you have entered your owner information, select the Notes tab and type **REWARD IF FOUND** in all capital letters. Activate the "Show information when device is turned on" checkbox so that it appears with your contact information. This provides an incentive for good Samaritans to go through the extra effort of returning your device to you.

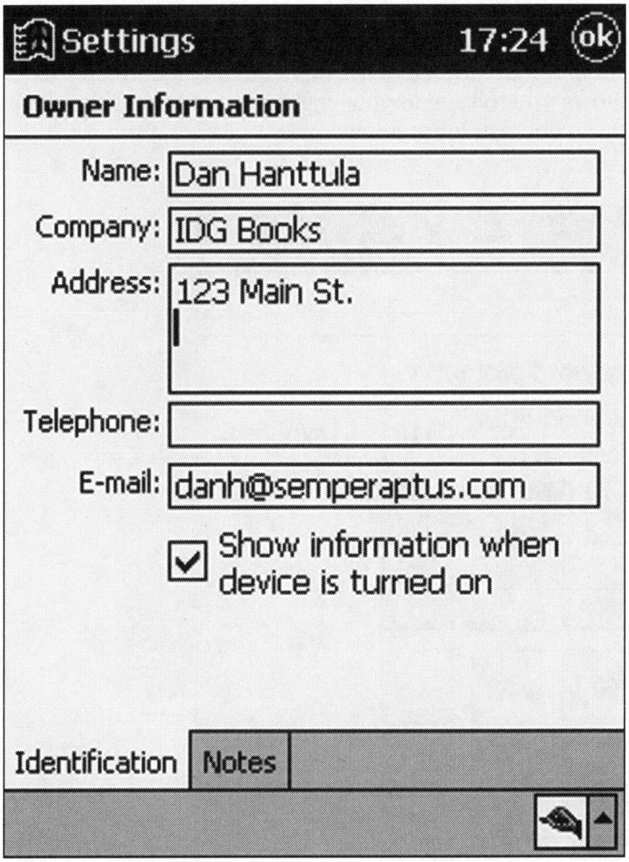

Figure 4.2 The Pocket PC Owner Information data entry screen

Securing Your Personal Data

With everything done to ensure the safe return of the Pocket PC from honest people, now it is time to prevent dishonest people from accessing or erasing your data. This is accomplished by the use of the Pocket PC security. Select Start ⇨ Settings ⇨ HP Security to open the control panel Security applet. Figure 4.3 shows the fully activated security system. The first checkbox, labeled "Enable password protection," sets the device to request a password at device activation. The second checkbox enables you to set a selectable delay before the Pocket PC asks for your password again. With my Pocket PC configured to the settings shown in the following screen shot example (Figure 4.3), I can turn on my device and enter the password, and the Pocket PC will not ask me to enter the password again for another ten minutes, even if I turn the power off. This is a convenient setting if you frequently find yourself going back to your device after a minute or two and if you do not leave the device unattended after use. The numeric keypad allows you to type in your password and the CLR button erases the password entry so you can input a new one.

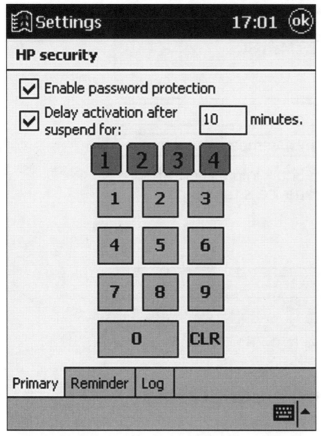

Figure 4.3 The fully activated control panel Security applet

Tip

Once you have customized all of the security settings to your preferences, make sure to close the dialog box by selecting the Ok icon in the upper-right corner. If you switch to another application without closing the security settings dialog box, anyone can access your security settings without entering a password.

Other features in the Security applet include the capability to set a failsafe question and answer backup password, and system access logging. The failsafe backup system, available in the Reminder tab of the Security applet, enables you to designate a personal question such as "What is my mother's maiden name?" If you forget your main password, the HP Jornada asks you the failsafe question and gives you access to the device if you answer it correctly.

Warning

If you forget your main password, you will not be able to erase it without deleting all the information on your device. Answering the failsafe question correctly enables you access to your data so you can back it up onto a memory card or your desktop. Once you have safely backed up your data, you should perform a *hard reset* (See Appendix A for instructions) on your device.

The Log tab of the Security applet enables you to record every successful and failed login attempt at system startup, and in trying to access the Security applet itself. This is incredibly useful information if you suspect someone of tampering with your device in a corporate or family environment. You can catch your co-workers (or your kids) red-handed by checking the date and time of the access attempts and checking their alibis. If that is not extreme enough, you can even export the log file to your desktop for use in a court of law. Just don't drag me in as an expert witness!

Note

Because the Log feature of the Security applet records every power on of the HP Jornada, the file can become rather large after extended periods of time. To clear the cache, select Start ⇨Settings ⇨HP Security ⇨Log tab and press the Clear Log button. The security log will be erased without any confirmation.

Cleaning and Covering Your Pocket PC's Touch Screen

Now that you've learned how to protect your device from sudden and extreme damage, it's time to learn about a silent aggressor that is far more sinister. It attacks your Pocket PC while you sleep, eat, and even while you are working. This bold scoundrel is dirt. When dirt gets on the case of your device there is not too much to worry about. A sweep of the hand or maybe even scraping the dirt away with a fingernail easily does the trick. But when that same dirt molecule attaches itself to the Pocket PC screen, you have a minor emergency.

Brushing away at lodged dirt particles or trying to forcefully remove them frequently causes the most dreaded result in handheld computing: a scratched screen. What's more, many long-time Pocket PC users have experienced dragging the stylus over a piece of dirt that they did not see on the screen, and then heard the dreaded chalkboard scratching noise while watching the dirt particle and the stylus create a permanent trail across the screen. You can prevent this problem by cleaning the screen frequently with a common household window cleaner, sprayed on a soft, lint-free cloth. If you are looking for a more chic way to clean your screen in style, you can purchase Brain Wash, a two-step cleaning kit that is essentially a pair of disposable cloths; one is laced with cleaning solution and the other is dry, to quickly soak up the solution. It is available complete with a *karma cloth*, a soft leather cloth for quickly removing dirt, from Concept Kitchen (www.conceptkitchen.com).

Tip

For a quick and cheap cleaning solution; purchase a small eyeglass lens cloth from your local drug store. Fold it up tight and store it in your carrying case. You never know when it will come in handy!

But dirt is not the only enemy to the screen. Eventually, simply using a stylus will wear down the smooth, glossy coating of the Pocket PC touch screen. You can protect your screen from dirt and everyday wear-and-tear with a screen protector. Screen protectors are thin, flexible plastic sheets that rest on top of the touch screen. Often, in addition to functioning as a protection device, the screen protector also helps to reduce glare on the screen. HP sells custom screen protectors as an accessory on the Jornada Web site (www.hp.com/jornada).

Summary

Just as superheroes face evil villains on a daily basis, you — as a super Pocket PC user — must face the dangers that try to assault your Pocket PC. Armed with the knowledge that this chapter has provided, you should succeed at every turn. If you implement all of the suggestions, you can even stay ahead of the enemy by owning a device that is well protected and well maintained.

The next chapter is the final segment of our "Pocket PC Basics" section. It will help convey an overall understanding about how each of the Pocket PC applications can be used in day-to-day work.

Pocket PC Applications

IN THIS CHAPTER
- Finding countless hours of pleasure in your Pocket PC
- Using a Windows Powered device in school
- Traveling with your Pocket PC
- Employing your Pocket PC at work

Anyone can purchase a Windows Powered device for a couple hundred dollars. In fact, some might consider the purchase an impulse buy, just to have something cool or to keep up with the Joneses. However, using a Pocket PC effectively requires an awareness of the device's capabilities and an understanding of how to apply those capabilities in everyday situations.

In this final chapter in the "Pocket PC Basics" segment, you can peruse a list of real-world scenarios matched up with their related Pocket PC application and the chapter that describes the procedure.

Finding Countless Hours of Pleasure in Your Pocket PC

- Carry electronic pictures of your family and friends (Image Expert CE, Chapter 18)

- Keep track of your personal contacts (Contacts, Chapter 9)

- Learn about alternate e-book formats with free and inexpensive electronic texts (Advanced e-book Tutorial, Chapter 20)

- Listen to audio books through your Pocket PC (Microsoft Reader, Chapter 12)

- Monitor your portfolio, bank accounts, and expenses (Pocket Money, Chapter 11)

- Play games on your Pocket PC (Gaming software in "Entertainment", Chapter 18)

Using a Windows Powered Device in School

- Convert your thesis into an e-book and beam it to your classmates (Microsoft Reader, Chapter 12)

- Duplicate entire documents to your Pocket PC faster than a copy machine (Capshare, Chapter 16)

- Track your homework assignments, complete with due dates and notes (Tasks, Chapter 6)

- Carry all of your English reading materials and a dictionary in the Pocket PC (Microsoft Reader, Chapter 12)

- Take notes in class without wasting paper and faster than your classmates can type (Pocket Word, Chapter 11)

Reasons to Bring Your Pocket PC When You Travel

- Access your AOL or MSN account anywhere from your Pocket PC ("Online Services and the Internet," Chapter 16)

- Check the time anywhere in the world in seconds (Pocket PC Clock, Chapter 6)

- Connect to the Internet wirelessly (The Novatel Wireless Sled in "Going Wireless", Chapter 16)

- Enter a flight in another time zone correctly (Calendar, Chapter 6)

- Extend the battery life on your HP Jornada during travel with a special accessory (HP Jornada extended battery in "Increase Your Power", Chapter 19)

- Receive turn-by-turn directions to any street address in the United States (GPS solutions in "Find Your Way", Chapter 19)

- Learn the lay of the land in a strange town (Pocket Streets, Chapter 13)

- Leave your travel clock at home now that you own a Pocket PC (Pocket PC Clock, Chapter 6)

Employing Your Pocket PC at Work

- Check your daily schedule, e-mail and tasks from one location (Today screen, Chapter 9)

- Create a professional e-book of your company policies, industry terminology or employee phone directory (Step-by-step instructions in "Making an e-book", Chapter 20)

- Find out where the technology will go in the future ("The Future of the Pocket PC", Chapter 25)

- Keep your personal Outlook data off the corporate network (Pocket Outlook, Chapter 9)

- Make high-speed connections with your desktop computer (ActiveSync, Chapter 15)

- Receive and open native Word, Excel, and HTML file attachments on the go (In box, Chapter 10)

- Set up a meeting and keep track of the attendees using the Calendar feature (Calendar, Chapter 6)

- Separate your work contacts from your personal contacts (Contacts, Chapter 9)

- Store network passwords, voicemail access codes, and health insurance information (eWallet, Chapter 18)

- Take notes in a meeting without stopping for a moment (Pocket Word, Chapter 11)

- Track your business trip expenditures (Pocket Money, Chapter 11)

Summary

If you aren't excited yet about everything that a Pocket PC can do, I don't know what to tell you. You have now completed the entire Pocket PC Basics section of this handbook and should have a firm grasp of how to use the Pocket PC to explore the rest of the book, as well as a great overall knowledge of the inner and outer workings of the Pocket PC.

Now it's time to have some fun. The next part of the book, "Applications that Really Apply Themselves," focuses on using each of the Pocket PC software applications to their fullest extent. The previous list of real-world uses was just a teaser, so jump to the next section and get with the programs!

Applications That Really Apply Themselves

The Pocket PC Clock and Calendar: Superior Time Management

IN THIS CHAPTER ● Set up home and visiting cities

● Wake up with daily alarms

● Calendar: get the view you want with the information you need

● Add U.S. and international holidays to your Pocket PC

● Enter a flight in another time zone correctly

● Arrange a meeting from the palm of your hand

● Reschedule appointments in seconds

One of the most indispensable features of the Pocket PC is how it helps you manage your time. The device functions as a multiregion timekeeper, a wake up call, and an appointment book, and even schedules meetings in less than 60 seconds. With all this functionality in the palm of your hand, you might not be able to make excuses for missing a meeting or your spouse's birthday but, on the other hand, you will never lose track of an appointment or oversleep past an important meeting in a different time zone.

Setting Up Home and Visiting Cities

The Clock is the foundation of all time management on the Pocket PC. It works in tandem with each personal information application to control when task reminders, appointment alarms, and birthday notifications appear. In addition, the Clock stamps the date and time on files that you create and uses regional settings to communicate with other devices when you set up appointments with other users. You can see how critical it is for you to set up your Clock correctly.

Cross-Reference

For instructions on how to keep the Pocket PC Clock accurate by using the Naval Atomic Clock system, check out Chapter 15, "ActiveSync: Desktop Connections for Maximum Speed and Security."

To open the Clock's control panel applet, select Start ⇨ Settings ⇨ System tab ⇨ Clock. Figure 6.1 shows the applet with the home time zone activated. Note that although the visiting time zone is not selected and is grayed out, it still displays the correct time for that location. The Pocket PC will default to Redmond, Washington (the location of Microsoft headquarters) as the home city, but you can change it to the city that you reside in. If your city is not listed, simply select one from the list that is in your time zone.

You can ensure that you have made the correct selection by examining the second drop-down menu, which shows the Greenwich mean time (GMT) equivalent. In our Figure 6.1 example, you can see that San Francisco, California is correctly reported as being located in the Pacific time zone for the United States. If you are certain you have selected the correct city but the GMT time zone is incorrect, you may adjust it by selecting the correct time zone from the second drop-down dialog box. Each time you change the location and GMT options, the current time adjusts itself to reflect these settings. Therefore, you should verify that the displayed time is accurate whenever you make changes.

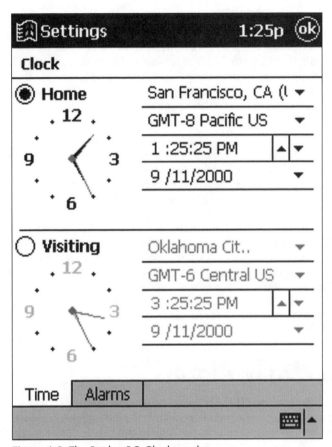

Figure 6.1 The Pocket PC Clock applet

Tip

If you would like to quickly check the current time in another region without permanently changing your location, select the time zone from the drop-down list on either the home or away clock. The current time in that region will be displayed on the clock to the left as soon as you make the selection. To return to your previous settings, press the Ok button. When the dialog box appears asking if you would like to save the changes, select No.

As with a traveler's pocket watch, the visiting time zone stores a second location so that you can quickly switch between home and away locations. This dual-zone feature enables you to easily change the Clock settings when traveling and to accurately enter flight information for air travel that has layovers in other time zones. If you do not travel often, consider setting the visiting time zone to a region where you frequently make long distance phone calls. That way, you can quickly check if you are calling the party at a reasonable hour, or if you are calling a business during their hours of operation. While the current time for the visiting zone is always displayed on the Clock applet, you can change the time system-wide by selecting the radio button to the left of Visiting and then selecting Ok.

Warning

When you select the Visiting option, all of the appointment times in your calendar are changed to reflect the time that they occur in the visiting zone because the Pocket PC assumes that is your local time. To display appointments in the home zone time, simply open the Clock applet and select the "Home city.

Another Clock feature that is often overlooked is the ability to set the Pocket PC to display military time. Select Start ➪ Settings ➪ System tab ➪ Regional Settings ➪ Time tab to display the Clock's regional options. Using the Time Style drop-down menu, select the HH:mm:ss option to display six o'clock p.m. as 18:00. The HH:mm:ss option displays single digit hours with a leading zero (for example, 6:00 a.m. would be shown as 06:00). To return to standard time, simply select either of the options with a lower-case h.

Wake Up with Daily Alarms

Once you have set the Pocket PC Clock, you can use the alarms to wake yourself up in the morning, or remind yourself of repetitive tasks that you perform on a regular basis. You can access the alarm settings in the Clock applet by selecting Start ➪ Settings ➪ System tab ➪ Clock ➪ Alarm tab. Figure 6.2 shows the Alarm applet with a set of real-world alarm uses. The second line of each Alarm setting enables you to choose which days of the week that the reminder appears. Consequently, you can set a daily alarm to remind you to let the dog outside every night and then set a second alarm to remind you to take out the trash the day before the garbage company makes their rounds.

Setting an alarm using the applet is a simple five-step process:

1. Open the Clock applet (Start ➪ Settings ➪ System tab ➪ Clock ➪ Alarm tab).

2. Each of the four sections of the applet is a separate alarm. Enter text to replace the placeholder. This is the text that will appear when the alarm goes off. You may enter up to 63 characters, but only approximately 40 will be displayed.

3. Tap the respective initials of the days of the week that you would like the reminder to notify you. A gray letter indicates that the alarm will sound on that day.

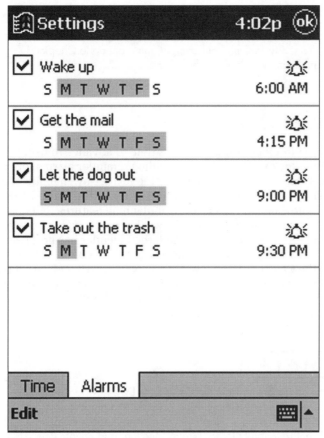

Figure 6.2 The Pocket PC Alarm applet

4. Tap the Alarm Bell icon to personalize the alert with a personalized sound, the message display, and the flashing Pocket PC notification light.

5. Finally, tap the time (which defaults to 6:00 a.m.) to display an analog clock with hour and minute hands that you can drag to the chosen alarm time, and a text box, if you would prefer to type the alarm time in yourself.

Once you begin the process of setting the Alarm applet, your Pocket PC will automatically activate it by selecting the checkbox next to the alarm. Select Ok to close the applet window and save your changes. You can deactivate the alarm, but save all of the settings by simply deselecting the checkbox next to the alarm.

Tip

For details on how to create custom audio alarms, such as a recording of your dog barking when you need to take him out at night, jump ahead to Chapter 17, "Advanced Personalization for Your Faithful Companion."

Setting the Calendar

Now that you have your clock configured, it is time to advance to using your calendar. Although the Clock works well for providing reminder alarms for repetitive tasks, the Calendar takes scheduling one step further by enabling you to set time slots for tasks and enter all-day appointments for birthdays and anniversaries. In addition, the Calendar has advanced planning features that enable you to schedule recurring appointments as daily, weekly, monthly, or yearly events based on the day of the week or the date. And, the Calendar has group-scheduling capabilities that enable you to organize meetings in seconds. (For example, icons available in the Calendar Day view, shown in Figure 6.3, indicate inportant information in a small amount of space.) But first, you need to decide how you want to look at your calendar because you have several options and each is designed to appeal to a different personality.

Figure 6.3 The icons above are used in the Calendar's Day view to denote key information for each appointment without using an extensive amount of space. From left to right, they are: Reminder Alarm Set, Recurring Appointment, Additional Notes, Event Location Entered, Group Meeting, and Private Item.

Tip

To cycle through all of the different Calendar views, press the Calendar hardware button while the Calendar application is running. It automatically swaps displays in this order: Day, Agenda, Week, Month, and Year.

Day view

The Day view, as shown in Figure 6.4, is similar to a standard pocket-organizer Calendar view and is the default display mode for the Calendar. As you can see, the day is divided up into one-hour slots; the screen cannot display the entire day without scrolling up and down. In addition to the Appointment icons, appointments have color-coded bars to their left that define their status. Dark blue is the default for new appointments and denotes that you are busy. Light blue represents tentative appointments, and white connotes events where you are unoccupied. Appointments scheduled outside of office hours are defined by purple appointments.

Figure 6.4 The Calendar Day view

Users who want a more detailed Calendar view or who frequently schedule appointments that begin or end on the half-hour mark may want to expand their Calendar view. Select Tools ➪ Options to open the Options window, and activate the "Show half-hour time slots" feature. This expands your Calendar view to display the day in 30-minute increments, but also limits the screen to displaying six hours of appointments at once.

Tip

Although you can enter a detailed appointment by selecting the New button, you can do this much more quickly in Day view: Highlight the time frame for the meeting on the calendar and begin entering the name of the appointment.

In Day view, using the hardware scrolling controls moves the calendar forward and backward by a single day. To navigate quickly between days of the current week, use the Navigation bar on the top of the screen. To traverse longer time periods, select the date in the Navigation bar to activate a Calendar Month Navigator, as shown in Figure 6.5. Selecting a date from the calendar transports the Day view to that date and closes the Navigator. A little known fact is that selecting the month or year on this calendar enables you to quickly jump between larger time periods. In Figure 6.5, the year has been selected — this enables you to scroll in annual increments or enter a numerical value to jump straight to that year. Close the Calendar Month Navigator by tapping anywhere else on the screen and then selecting the arrow and box icon. You will be returned to the current day.

Figure 6.5 The Calendar Month Navigator

Agenda view

As with Day view, Agenda view displays one day of the week at a time. However, this mode is the no-nonsense version of a daily calendar. Figure 6.6 demonstrates the same day that we previously examined in the Day view. Notice how all of the

Appointment icons have disappeared, except for the Additional Notes icon. Also, it is important to observe how easily all of the appointments fit in this display. While the Agenda view gives no visual indication of the amount of time between meetings (which was indicated by an empty space between appointments in Day view), it does an excellent job of displaying an entire day at a glance.

Figure 6.6 The Calendar Agenda view

The Navigation bar and controls for the Agenda view are exactly the same as the Day view. One subtle nuance of the Agenda view is that it grays out appointments that have already occurred for the day, as shown by the first appointment in Figure 6.6. This gives a nice visual indicator of what you have already accomplished and gives prominence to the next appointment when you are looking over an extensive list. One expense of using the Agenda view is that you lose the capability to simply highlight a timeslot to create a new appointment. The New menu must be used to enter an event.

Note

The Pocket PC calendar extends from January 1900 to December 2999. So even though the device probably will not last several lifetimes, you can still schedule appointments that far in advance!

Week view

Popular with business people, the Calendar's Week view conveys a graphical overview of the week ahead. Resembling Day view, appointments are color-coded to indicate status and the display delivers an accurate picture of the amount of leisure time where empty spaces appear. Figure 6.7 reveals the Week view starting with the same day used in the previous illustrations. As you can see from this example, the wider, colored blocks are overlapped by thin lines which extend the entire day. These thin lines indicate all-day appointments.

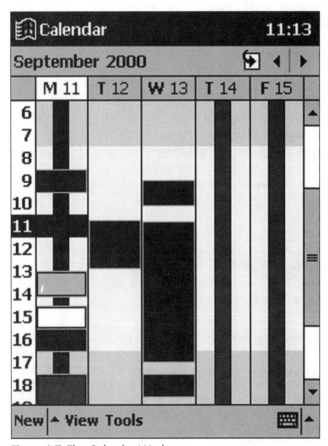

Figure 6.7 The Calendar Week view

Navigating in this view is similar to the previous displays. Activating the hardware scrolling controls or using the arrows in the Navigation bar will pilot you forward and backward in one-week increments. Note that the application, by default, only displays five-day (Monday–Friday) work weeks. To change this setting, select Tools ➪ Options and increase the Week view to the six-day or seven-day week options. Tapping the month in the Navigation bar activates the Calendar Navigation mentioned earlier; tapping the year displays a list of years that enables you to quickly navigate to last year or the upcoming three years with one tap of the stylus. An "Other. . ." feature permits you to manually type a numerical value for years outside of the pick-list. Icons available in Calendar Month view are shown in Figure 6.8.

▰◢☐▮

Figure 6.8 These icons are used in the Calendar Month view to communicate appointments throughout the day. From left to right, they are: Morning Appointment, Afternoon Appointment, and All-Day Appointment.

Tip

Although the Week view display has been streamlined by the elimination of text, you can quickly determine the details of a specific appointment by single-tapping the time block. The event name, location, date, and time will be displayed in the Navigation bar at the top of the screen for five seconds.

Month view

Month view is the typical wall-calendar view with an interactive touch; the calendar uses special icons to communicate committed time slots for each day. Figure 6.9 shows a sample month with the afternoons primarily booked. Month view navigation works like the Week view, with one exception: tapping the month triggers a list of all twelve months of the year. However, one might not expect that, as with the Week view, the hardware scrolling controls and the arrows in the Navigation bar will pilot you forward and backward in one-week increments. Selecting any day with the stylus takes you to the Day view for that date.

Tip

Due to a bug in the Windows CE calendar, all-day calendar items that are entered on your desktop computer and downloaded to the Pocket PC are not displayed in the Month view. To prevent this, enter all-day events in the Pocket PC and synchronize the Pocket PC to copy them onto the desktop.

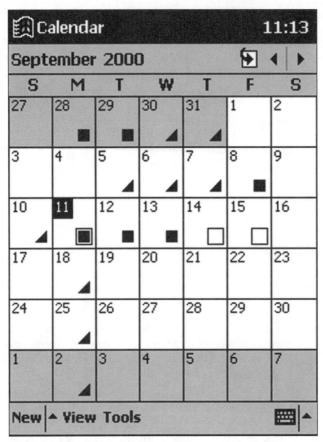

Figure 6.9 The Calendar Month view

Year view

The final view available in the Pocket PC calendar is the Year view. This annual overview is generally only used for navigating to a specific day for additional information. Figure 6.10 shows that the current date is highlighted in a black square and — on color devices — Sundays are indicated with red. The figure also shows an enlarged date (August 10), which appears when you tap and hold a specific day on the calendar. This feature is useful for ensuring that you select the correct date in the middle of all the tiny numbers. The controls on this view include the Year Pick list, the Return to Today icon, and arrows that move in annual increments. The hardware scrolling controls advance the calendar in three-month segments.

Figure 6.10 The Calendar Year view

Add U.S. and International Holidays to Your Pocket PC

To make the Pocket PC practical for international distribution, the Calendar application does not contain national holidays for any country. However, you can add holidays to the Calendar quickly and easily by first setting them up on your desktop computer. To add national holidays to the desktop version of Outlook, open the application and select Tools ➪ Options ➪ Calendar Options button ➪ Add Holidays button. A pop-up window appears, containing more than 70 countries. Activate the checkbox of any nation and press Ok to instantly populate your calendar with the holidays for that region. The next time you synchronize, the holidays will be copied to your Pocket PC as normal, all-day appointments.

Note

To add personal holidays, such as birthdays, anniversaries, and company vacations to your calendar, create an appointment by using the New button on your Pocket PC and then change the Type field from normal to all day.

To remove a single holiday from your Pocket PC, view the holiday using Day or Agenda view and then tap and hold the holiday name at the top of the screen. Select Delete Appointment and answer "yes" to the delete confirmation to permanently remove it from your device. To remove an entire set of holidays from your Pocket PC, open Outlook on your desktop and select Tools ➪ Options ➪ Calendar Options button ➪ Add Holidays button. Deactivate the checkbox of the nation's holidays that you wish to remove and then synchronize your Pocket PC.

Enter a Flight in Another Time Zone Correctly

Now that you have mastered the Pocket PC Clock and Calendar applications, you are going to use them together in a real-world situation. Imagine that you have a cross-country flight with one layover. Although the flight departs from your time zone, it will almost certainly stopover in another time zone and then land in a third. Although some might consider it a mental challenge to try entering all of the correct arrival and landing times by calculating their local-time equivalent, it is far easier to use your boarding pass and let your Pocket PC do all the work. Here is how to do it:

1. Run Calendar and navigate to the day of your flight.

2. Select New and enter the starting point and ending point for the first leg of your flight in the subject area. Enter your flight number in the Location field. Enter the flight's take-off time in the Meeting Start Time area and then press Ok to save the appointment.

3. Select Start ➪ Settings ➪ System tab ➪ Clock.

4. Activate the Visiting City function and then select the location of your layover as the visiting city. Press Ok to save these changes and change the system clock to visiting time.

5. Return to the Calendar and open the flight appointment. Change the end time to the actual time that the plane lands. Press Ok to save the changes.

6. For the next leg of the flight, go to Step 2 and repeat all the remaining steps, but change the visiting city to the final destination when you return to the system clock. Once you save the appointment, simply go to Start ➪ Settings ➪ System tab ➪ Clock and activate the Home City function to return the Pocket PC to your local time zone. The flights will be correctly entered into the Calendar and should accurately display your arrival time. During each leg of the flight, set your Pocket PC to the location where you are about to land. That way you can catch a glimpse of how quickly you need to make your connection!

Tip

For the return flight, simply reverse the process, starting with the clock set to the travel destination time zone, then to the layover time zone, and finally ending in your local time zone.

Arrange a Meeting in the Palm of Your Hand

My favorite feature of the Pocket PC Calendar is the ability to automatically schedule meetings with coworkers, friends, and family. The application uses the Pocket PC Clock and In-box to deliver e-mail invitations that Microsoft Outlook 2000 users and fellow Pocket PC owners can employ to automatically place the appointment in their Calendar and instantly send you a confirmation response.

Cross-Reference

If you want to invite someone who does not use Outlook or their Pocket PC for e-mail, read the "Using Infrared to Transfer Information" section of Chapter 9 to find out how you can beam a meeting invitation to them!

To use your Pocket PC to invite other people to a meeting or event, complete the following steps:

1. Create a normal appointment using your Pocket PC (be sure to enter a descriptive name and clear location so people understand the invitation and where to go).

2. In the appointment, tap the Attendees item and a complete list of all of your contacts who have e-mail addresses appears. Select everyone that you wish to invite and then press Ok to save your list.

3. Finally, select the Notes tab to enter a description. This will appear as the body of the e-mail that your invitees receive.

4. When you have filled out the appointment to your satisfaction, press Ok to save the appointment and generate an e-mail.

Figure 6.11 is a sample e-mail invitation generated by the Calendar application. As you can see, invitees have the ability to decline the invitation or respond with tentative or confirmed attendance. Choosing any option generates an automated e-mail response to you with the respondent's answer; the latter two options automatically place the appointment in his or her calendar.

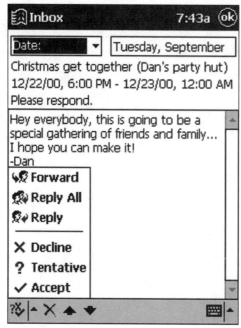

Figure 6.11 An E-mail invitation received on a Pocket PC

In addition, any changes you make to the event (such as a change of location or start time) can automatically be sent to all invitees. The Pocket PC will detect changes and ask you if you would like to inform the attendees of the modifications. It's like having an event coordinator that takes care of the invitation list for you!

Note

Don't worry if you are inviting people from other time zones; the Pocket PC sends the appointment with the date and time formatted by time zone. For example, if members are attending a meeting via telephone, the 1:00 p.m. West Coast conference call correctly appears as a 4:00 p.m. call in the Pocket PC of an East Coast attendee.

Reschedule Appointments in Seconds

If your schedule is like mine, arrangements are constantly being changed. A lunch meeting at noon today could quickly change to a dinner meeting at six o'clock tomorrow night. The Calendar application has the ability to keep up with your ever-evolving schedule and includes a special feature to quickly move appointments to their new time slot.

Warning

If you use the method described in the following section to cut and paste a recurring appointment, the recurrence pattern will be deleted and the appointment will be set to Occurs: Once. To prevent this from happening, open a recurring appointment by tapping it. When the Calendar application asks you if you would like to open just this one occurrence, select No so that you can edit every instance of the recurring appointment. Tap once in the top half of the screen to edit the Calendar item and change the time of the appointment. To change the date of the recurring appointment, tap on Occurs and select Edit Pattern.

When an appointment changes date or time, open Calendar and find the scheduled item that you had previously entered. Tap and hold the item until the pop-up menu appears and then select Cut. Figure 6.12 shows the pop-up menu with the Cut option selected. If the appointment is changed to a different time on the same day, scroll to the new time slot. Otherwise, use the Navigation bar at the top of the screen to navigate to the day on which the appointment occurs. Tap and hold the line corresponding to the new appointment time and when the pop-up menu appears, select Paste to insert the appointment.

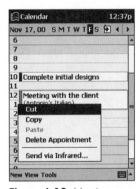

Figure 6.12 Moving an appointment

Adding another instance of an existing appointment is accomplished in a similar manner. It is advantageous to make copies of existing appointments so that you do not have to reenter all of the duration, location, category, type, reminder status, and sensitivity information from scratch. To make a copy, tap and hold the original appointment, as shown in Figure 6.12. This time, select Copy from the pop-up menu. Now navigate through the calendar to the date and time of the second appointment. Tap and hold the start time and select Paste from the pop-up menu. An exact duplicate (minus any reoccurrence settings) has now been added to a new day.

Note

If you set up a group appointment and change any of the details of the appointment, the Calendar application will ask you if you would like to send out the updated information. If you select yes, an E-mail will be dispatched to all meeting attendees which automatically updates their Outlook calendars with the modifications.

Summary

In this chapter you have learned how to work with the Pocket PC Clock and Calendar applications using real-world examples and supplemented with a few advanced-user tricks. The next chapter focuses on how to get the most from the Tasks application of the Pocket PC, an invaluable asset for keeping track of your daily action items and long-term goals.

Tasks: A List-Maker's Paradise

IN THIS CHAPTER • Utilizing the Tasks application

• Learning to create time-delayed and repetitive tasks

• Setting your task reminders

• Learning superior task-sorting tricks

W e each spend part of our day running errands or taking care of action items from business meetings. Thankfully, the developers of the Pocket PC recognize this as an important factor in organizing our lives, and have included the popular and invaluable Tasks application to make quick work of our responsibilities. Although the application is far more powerful than a handwritten list, the developers of this application have also taken great pains to keep it uncomplicated and easy to use.

Using the Tasks Application

Initially exhibiting only two controls, the Tasks application toolbar consists of Show and Sort By drop-down menus. The Show drop-down menu, on the left-hand side, is divided into two parts and offers a number of ways to manage which tasks are displayed. The first section of the drop-down menu enables you to display tasks by category; you may activate a single category, display tasks of all categories, or just display tasks that have been created or modified recently. The second section features active or completed tasks, which can be toggled back and forth or deactivated to show all tasks. Completed tasks are easily identified by their activated checkbox (indicating that the action item has been fulfilled). Active tasks have a hollow checkbox indicating that the item must still be finished.

Note

Active tasks are action items that either have no start or end dates, or those that are designated as "active" because today's date falls between the start and end date, making it a task that you should be working on.

The Sort By drop-down menu offers five methods for arranging the tasks: status, subject, start date, due date, and the system default, priority. Which organization style you use depends on how detailed you are in entering your tasks. The easygoing user should choose to sort by subject, which is just in alphabetical order based on the task name. Detail-oriented people who enter due dates for all of their tasks should prioritize by due date. People who are disorganized or become frequently distracted, should sort by status, so the completed tasks fall to the bottom of the list. Personally, I prefer to sort by priority (see Figure 7.1) and only display active tasks because once I've completed an action item, I never redo it.

[! | ↓]

Figure 7.1 The respective icons shown here denote high- and low-priority indicators in the Tasks application.

The Priority option enables you to rank each task by its urgency. There are three priority levels: high, normal, and low. By default, all new tasks are set to normal priority. I use this feature extensively as it makes an excellent visual indicator of tasks that require my immediate attention and those that I may ignore without suffering consequences.

Tip

If you tap and hold the stylus in the space between a task's check box and text description, a pop-up menu appears, enabling you to set the priority of the task.

If you have been using the Tasks application for even a short time, you have undoubtedly become comfortable with the simple "list" interface. If you feel familiar enough with the application, you can make one quick change that will save you countless hours over the course of using the Tasks application. While running the application, select Tools ⇨ Entry Bar to add the Tasks entry bar directly above the task list (as shown in Figure 7.2). This optional entry bar gives you quick access to the Tasks application to create new tasks quickly and easily. And, you can save one extra stylus tap by selecting the priority before entering the text; when you click the high or low priority buttons, the Pocket PC automatically places the cursor in the "Tap here to add a new task" area and activates your input panel.

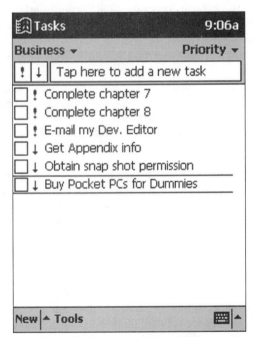

Figure 7.2 The Tasks application with entry bar activated

Tip

Here's a special trick to quickly entering many tasks with the same category (for example, the business category): Create one task and set its category to business, and then open the Show drop-down and select Business. Thereafter, every new task will automatically be in the business category. To discontinue this feature, open the Show drop-down and select All Categories.

Setting Time-Delayed and Repetitive Tasks

Although most tasks are simple action items that are currently underway and can be erased once completed, some tasks are considerably more complex. Take, for example, the responsibility of taking out the trash. It must be done every Tuesday night in preparation for an early Wednesday morning pickup and it repeats every week. Obviously you do not want to stare at the "Take out the trash" action item in your task list all week long, so you need to create a *time-delayed task* that only appears at appropriate times.

Open the Tasks application, select New, and begin by entering a name for the task. Tap on the Starts field and select the upcoming Tuesday from the pop-up calendar. Notice that when you select it, the Tasks application automatically populates the due date as the same day, which is appropriate in this case because the trash must be taken out on Tuesday. Next, tap the Occurs field on the task to activate the drop-down dialog box and select the Every Tuesday option from the list.

Tip

In addition to enabling you to modify an existing recurrence setting, the Edit Pattern option in the Occurs drop-down dialog box enables you to create complex patterns for tasks that occur regularly. For example, this is how you set up biweekly items or tasks that occur on the first or last weekday of the month.

Press Ok to save the task and check to see if it appears on your task list. If it does, select the upper-left drop-down dialog box in the Tasks application (just below the Start menu icon) and ensure that the Active Tasks option is checked. This will hide all tasks that begin later than the current date. Tasks without a specified start date will still appear on the list when Active Tasks is activated. Using this method you can create tasks for depositing your paycheck on the first and fifteenth of the month, or create long-term reminders for medical check-ups and automobile services. These tasks will not appear on your list until it is time for you to attend to them.

By default, the Tasks application does not display task start and due dates, making it extremely difficult to quickly identify which items from the task list are due today. To activate this feature, select Tools ➪ Options ➪ Show start and due date. This changes each task on the list to a two-line display, showing half as many tasks on the screen at one time, but revealing vital time-sensitive information for each item.

Setting Task Reminders

Just like a list on paper, the Tasks application is worthless if you do not remember to check it. But, true to the "personal assistant" style of Pocket PC applications, the program has a built-in reminder application that will automatically notify you of important task items each day. At 8:00 am, the Pocket PC displays a list of tasks that have the Remind me feature activated and, by default, meets either of the following rules:

- If a start date is specified, the reminder sounds on that morning, indicating that the task has become active.

- If a due date has been specified but no start date has been entered, the alarm appears on morning of the due date.

Figure 7.3 reveals the Reminder dialog box that appears on mornings when task alarms have been set. In the dialog box, you can see that both the name as well as date-relevant information is displayed on-screen for each task. The Dismiss and Dismiss All buttons enable you to remove the reminders from your screen; the Snooze button enables you to delay the reminders to pop up at a later time. Each item can be selected individually and then set to appear after a delay of anywhere from five minutes to one week. This enables you to constantly remind yourself of important tasks, while putting off tasks that are of lower priority.

Figure 7.3 The Reminder dialog box

To activate the task reminder, you must first create a new task or open an existing one. Tap the Reminder field to activate the drop-down menu and select Remind me. The Pocket PC automatically sets a reminder date based on the start or due dates using the formula listed previously. If you wish to modify the day on which the reminder occurs, tap the date that appears directly beneath the Remind me text and then select the appropriate day from the pop-up calendar.

Tip

If you wish to automatically set the reminder feature on all of the tasks that you create on your Pocket PC, select Tools ⇨ Options ⇨ Set reminders for new items. Now when you set a start or due date for an item, the application automatically activates the Remind me feature for that task. The alarm date will be set based upon the rules listed previously.

There are a few troubling issues around the reminder feature that keeps the Tasks application from being the perfect assistant. For example, if you create a new task with a starting date of the current day or earlier, you will not receive a reminder alarm regardless of when the task is due, unless you manually modify the reminder date using the steps described previously. Also, reminders cannot be set for tasks that do not have a start date or end date specified, indicated by a grayed-out Reminder field.

Superior Task-Sorting Tricks

Knowingly created as the tongue twister title for this handbook, this section is much easier to master than to repeat ten times quickly. Being able to quickly accomplish your tasks means that you need to be able to organize them in a manner that makes sense. Although priority is an excellent start, a family of four can easily create a number of high-priority tasks that will completely fill the screen. If all the tasks need to be completed in one day, it can be tough to arrange the list into a usable format.

Even though the Tasks application enables you to assign categories to each action item, the categories are not visible from the task list and, more importantly, you can not sort the list by categories. This means if you have a shopping list in the Tasks application, the items will not appear adjacent to each other. To solve this problem, I have created a system called the "all-caps category."

This system involves creating a group prefix of all capital letters and a colon to be used for all tasks having to do with a specific group. For example, three items on a shopping list would be entered as STORE: Bread, STORE: Milk, STORE: Potatoes. This way, when the Tasks application sorts the tasks by alphabetical order, the entire shopping list will be grouped together, making shopping (and using the Tasks application) far easier. Figure 7.4 illustrates the allcaps category system for a busy day. Capital letters are used for the category names because they are easier for the eye to disregard. Less creative individuals may choose to simply group tasks by using a number. For example "1:" would be the prefix for groceries and "2:" would indicate work tasks.

Figure 7.4 The Tasks application with "all caps category" tasks

Tip

Because the Tasks application displays numbers before letters when sorting, I use an all caps category of "911:" for tasks that absolutely must be completed first.

Regardless of how you sort, display, and name your tasks, you should set start and end dates whenever they are available. The Pocket PC keeps track of the information and displays a complete record of your active, high priority, and overdue tasks on your Today screen. In addition, overdue tasks display in red on color devices, indicating that those tasks need your immediate attention.

Cross-Reference

For complete information on the Today screen and how to configure it to display detailed task information, read Chapters 9 and 18.

Summary

This chapter disclosed the secrets behind successfully entering and managing a list of action items and errands regardless of the number of tasks or their complexity. In the next chapter you will learn how to manage contacts, the key to communications within the Pocket PC.

Contacts

IN THIS CHAPTER
- The Contacts application
- Learning to enter contacts faster and easier
- Easier navigation of the address book

Without question, the majority of Pocket PC users consider the Calendar and Contact programs the most critical. They are the most frequently used applications because they store the vital information that users may require access to anytime and anywhere. The Contacts application is where addresses and phone numbers are stored; this application is similar to an electronic version of a Rolodex. Accordingly, the developers of the Contacts application took their job very seriously. With 45 unique fields for storing information about a single contact, along with the capability to enter handwritten notes and voice recordings, the Contacts application proves itself as a personal information manager with no equal.

Note

The Contacts application on the Pocket PC contains a Children field, intended for entering the names of a contact's offspring. Outlook 2000 does not contain this field, so although you may view this information on your Pocket PC, it will not show up on your desktop when you synchronize.

Using the Contacts Application

Figure 8.1 shows the notes field of the contacts application. The speaker icon in the upper-left corner indicates that a voice note was recorded for this contact. Note that pressing the voice recorder button while viewing or editing a contact automatically switches to the notes field for that contact and inserts the voice recording there. Drawings and voice recordings are viewable on the desktop version of Outlook as graphics and .wav files.

Cross-Reference

For information on how to receive contacts from Palm Pilot users via infrared, check Chapter 22, "The 'All my Friends Use a Palm Pilot' Constraint."

The Contact application commences in a simple list view, showing the contact name and the primary method of communication. The primary method of communication is selected by the application from the contact's phone numbers and e-mail addresses in the following order: work telephone, home telephone, mobile telephone, pager, work fax, and e-mail. (Note that home faxes, as well as secondary phone numbers and secondary e-mail addresses, are not considered to be primary communication methods.)

Figure 8.1 A contact's notes field

Tip

Many users prefer to sort their contact list by first name, rather than last. Unfortunately, this cannot be accomplished on the Pocket PC. Instead, users that synchronize their contacts with Microsoft Outlook can modify the sort order by opening each contact and changing the File As field to the user's first and last name. Future contacts can be automatically set by selecting Tools ➪ Options ➪ Contact Options and setting the default File As order to First Last. However, because this setting is only available on the desktop, contacts entered (or edited) in the future on the Pocket PC will still have to be manually changed from the desktop.

If you prefer a different phone number to be displayed, simply select the blue letter (usually a "w" or an "h") on the far right of the contact and the application displays any of the primary contact fields listed previously for you to choose from. The program will remember your selection for each contact so that you can it set up to display the most frequently used number for each contact. The drop-down menu that is activated by selecting the blue letter also makes a nice method for quickly looking up phone numbers because the font is much larger than it is when you actually open the contact.

Entering Contacts Faster and Easier

The Contacts application has a few secret features that enable you to enter contacts much more rapidly once you begin using them. Moreover, these shortcuts are so simple that you will be embarrassed that you had not found them earlier.

Region and country settings

In the Contacts application, select Tools ⇨ Options and take notice of the options in the second half of the window. Figure 8.2 shows the Options window with the Area code and Country and Region settings already filled out. Entering an area code into the respective window on the County and Region settings advises the Contacts application to automatically populate every Telephone Number field with the area code from this screen. Changing the default is as simple as overwriting text, but this simple trick will save you an immeasurable number of taps with the stylus just because you will never have to enter your local telephone area code number again.

Figure 8.2 The Contacts Options window

Tip

After you have entered a telephone number for any contact, Pocket Outlook automatically copies the area code from the first number whenever you tap another Telephone Number field.

Like the default area code, you can enter a default country or region for addresses. Select the region from the Country/Region drop-down menu in which most of your contacts reside. The Contacts application automatically adds the country or region you selected to every address you enter. Do not worry, setting a default country in the Contacts application will not change or affect the Pocket PC's regional settings that control time, currency, and date formatting; the information in this drop-down is only used when creating new addresses.

Preformatted name and address entries

In addition to the regional and country settings, the Contacts application has preformatted fields for entering complex addresses and names. You can access these fields by tapping a down arrow icon in each field. Figure 8.3 is an example of the pop-up window that appears for the Names field. To access this window, create a new contact and tap the down arrow at the upper-right corner of the screen. In addition to the first, middle, and last names, the pop-up window offers title and suffix fields.

Figure 8.3 The preformatted Names window

Note

You do not have to use the preformatted fields. For example, if you were to enter Dr. Henry Jones Jr. in the regular Name field, the Contacts application would automatically parse the prefix, suffix, and first and last names into the proper fields. The pop-up windows are provided for your assistance; using them is optional.

Name prefixes are not displayed on the contacts list. When you enter a suffix, such as Jr. or Esq., it will not be displayed in the normal list of contacts unless you have set the Contacts application to sort by first name (see tip in previous section, "Using the Contacts Application"). The same is true for middle names and middle initials. The address pop-up window contains separate Street, City, State, Zip, and Country fields. It is available in the Work, Home, and Other address fields. If you have already designated your regional settings, as described in the preceding section of this chapter, the Country field will be filled in. The Street field in the Contacts application supports three lines of text, in order to accommodate apartment numbers, departments, and mail stops.

Making the Address Book Easier to Navigate

After you become addicted to storing all of your phone numbers in the Contacts application, you may quickly find yourself with hundreds (or even thousands!) of contacts. And, if you use your Pocket PC to store business and personal contacts, there is no end to the number of records that you could accumulate. In these cases, navigating the massive pool of electronic information becomes an effort instead of a convenience. But there are many ways to surf through the information quickly and easily.

Cross-Reference

For complete information on using categories to filter your list of contacts, read "The Ins and Outs of Using Categories" section in Chapter 9.

Power scroll

The Contacts application has a special feature designed for extremely fast movement through hundreds of contacts. In normal mode, pressing the hardware scrolling controls up or down moves one record in the respective direction, and holding it for a moment allows you to continuously move that direction one record at a time. When you want to scroll past many records at a time, hold the scrolling control in the upward or downward position for four seconds to activate power scroll.

Figure 8.4 demonstrates power scroll's power to display letters of the alphabet one by one, which enables you to jump directly to the first letter of the contact you wish to locate. Power scroll scrolls sequentially through the letters in alphabetical order and, if you miss the letter you desired, you can simply reverse the direction you are depressing the scrolling control. Power scroll will beep just before it closes itself and jumps to the first contact name for the letter you have selected.

Tip

If you enjoy using the scrolling controls, you can also use it to open and close contact records. Simply use the up/down function to locate the name you wish to view and then depress the control. It will open the record you are viewing without using the stylus! Depress it a second time to close the contact.

Figure 8.4 The power scroll feature in Contacts

ABC tabs

If your first organizational tool was a DayTimer, you probably long for the file folder tabs that allow you to quickly jump to your contacts in the OPQ section. Although your days of paper organizers are (thankfully) long gone, you can bring back the days of old on your Pocket PC. Select Tools ⇨ Options and turn on the Show ABC tabs feature. Figure 8.5 shows the Contacts application with the feature enabled and, as you can see, the ABC tabs run horizontally. Because of this it is important to remember that activating this feature infringes on the display area, eliminating one contact record from the viewable area.

Figure 8.5 The Contacts application with ABC tabs

Just like its real-world counterpart, tapping any section of the bar takes you to the first record that begins with the letter you selected. However, as you have probably come to expect by now, simple imitation is not enough for the programmers who developed the Pocket PC software. For example, if you tap the LMN tab, you obviously jump directly to the first contact beginning with the letter L. A second tap, however, takes you to the first contact in the M section. And, the third tap will jump to the N portion. This wonderful extra touch gives the user the same functionality of an entire row of individual letters, but still provides the important benefit of a rather large target for the stylus to tap.

Quick find

While the previous methods for locating a contact are far flashier, the easiest and fastest way to locate a contact is to type the first few letters of the contact's first or last name into the search box at the top of the Contact window. It is faster than scrolling down the entire list and provides the accuracy of eliminating all of the contacts that do not contain the characters you are entering.

Note

If you employed the "sort by first name" tip discussed at the beginning of this chapter, you can only perform searches by first name.

For example, if I type "Hanttula", the Contacts application narrows the on-screen list to my family members for whom I have records. If I enter a comma and a space, I can then narrow my search by entering the first few letters of the person's first name. Selecting the button to the right of the search box clears the search window and returns my contact list to the entire list of records.

Tip

To address an e-mail to your entire family quickly, enter your last name in the Contacts search box. When the names appear, highlight all of them by dragging your stylus from the top to the bottom of the list. Now lift the stylus off the screen, then tap and hold any of the highlighted names. Select "Send E-mail to Contact . . ." and a preaddressed e-mail will appear in seconds.

Summary

If you have been reading this book straight through, you have the information you need to be proficient at using almost all of the Pocket Outlook applications. This chapter added the specialization in using the Contacts application, where previous chapters in this part of the handbook covered Tasks, Calendar and the Clock application.

The next chapter will tie all of these Pocket Outlook programs together and show you how to use some common features in the suite to make your Pocket PC experience a little more comfortable and a great deal more fun!

Pocket Outlook

IN THIS CHAPTER • The Today screen: your most valuable resource

• Managing multiple reminders

• Using quick entry arrows

• Keep Outlook data private

• Make Pocket Outlook easier on your eyes

• The ins and outs of using categories

• Using Infrared to transfer information

Following in the footsteps of Outlook on the desktop, the Pocket PC's Calendar, Tasks, and Contacts all work together in a suite called Pocket Outlook. Previous chapters of this book discussed the features of each and provided a glimpse of how some of the programs can work together. The Today screen, discussed in this chapter, is a powerful application that unites all of these applications to make managing your life a snap. In addition, the Pocket Outlook suite contains a number of features in common that provide security, user-friendliness, and better communication.

Making the Most of the Today Screen

Every morning, I start my day with a bowl of Frosted Flakes and a close look at the Today screen. And, although I could probably get by skipping breakfast every so often, the Today screen is a morning ritual that cannot be overlooked. Figure 9.1 shows a glimpse of my Today screen for a typical Monday morning. You can see that the Today screen displays information from several Pocket Outlook applications. The Clock's date and time occupy the top-right corner of the screen, the Calendar appointments are presented in the center of the screen, and summaries for the In-box and Tasks applications follow suit. At the bottom of the screen, in the Navigation bar, are the New button, Battery Status icon, and a control to mute the speaker. This application is the only one on the Pocket PC that provides such a concise summary of an entire day's work, all in one location. Best of all, it is completely customizable.

Figure 9.1 The Pocket Outlook Today screen

Tip

Several secret hotspots are located on the Today screen; tap the word "today" to go to the control panel applet to customize the Today screen or tap on date to go to the Clock settings. Naturally, tapping the Calendar, Tasks, or In-box plug-ins takes you directly to the corresponding application. The Battery Status icon (shown in Figure 9.1 at the bottom of the screen), which only appears under extremely low-power or battery-charging situations, provides a shortcut to the control panel's Power applet. And the New button works slightly differently than when it appears in applications. Pressing the New button here displays a list of items you can create (appointments, contacts, E-mail, spreadsheet, note, task, or Word document) without loading the application.

To access the Today screen settings, follow the instructions in the preceding tip, or select Start ➪ Settings ➪ Today. With the Today control panel applet open, you have the ability to configure each Today screen plug-in and to program the Today screen to appear after a preset period of inactivity. Because I consult the Today screen throughout the day, I have it set to appear when the device has been idle for one hour. The plug-in selection however, is a very personal and individual choice. I recommend everyone use the Up and Down buttons to arrange the information in the sequence they prefer and to deactivate features they do not use.

Tip

If you have already set up a password and owner display at startup, remove the owner information from the Today screen. You obviously know that this is your schedule, and the redundant information is using valuable Today screen space!

Once you have the Today screen plug-ins displaying the information where you want it, take a few moments to customize the data in each window. For example, in the Today control panel applet, highlight Tasks and press the Options button. Activate all of the checkboxes and the Today screen reports the number of high priority, overdue, and currently due tasks. I also recommend modifying the Calendar plug-in so that it displays all upcoming appointments for the day, as well as all day events. This feature, however, inhabits a significant amount of screen real estate if you have a busy calendar; whether or not you activate it depends on your personal preference. However, the Today screen automatically displays a vertical scroll bar when the information extends below the screen — so the information is still accessible, but you will have to scroll down in order to see it.

Cross-Reference

To alter the settings and add information to the Today screen, skip ahead to the "Customize your Today Screen" section of Chapter 18.

Managing Multiple Reminders

If multiple reminders go off at one time, or more than one alarm goes off while you have left your Pocket PC unattended, the Pocket PC displays a special screen that enables you to easily scroll through all of the reminders. Figure 9.2 is an example of the Multiple Reminder window with reminders for an appointment, an alarm, and two tasks.

Figure 9.2 The Multiple Reminder window

Although there are no icons to help differentiate tasks, appointments, and alarms, a clever user can identify each item by its description. Alarms are the easiest to spot because the date and time are bold and the text description (if you entered one) appears in plain text. The Wake up item in Figure 9.2 is an alarm. Appointment reminders — such as Breakfast with Mom in our example — offer the most information, providing the start and end times, as well as the location of the appointment below the bolded meeting name. Task reminders display the task name in bold and then show a start or due date. Pay bills today and Buy birthday present for Mike are the two task reminders in Figure 9.2.

If you turn on your device and the Multiple Reminder window appears, you probably won't be able to accomplish all the tasks and appointments that have piled up. The following quick procedure will enable you to whittle your list down to a more manageable size:

1. Quickly scroll through the list and stop at each action item that you have already completed and every meeting you have already attended. Tap each of these and press the dismiss button. You will never be warned about these again.

2. Once you reach the bottom, start scrolling upwards looking for items that are long-term or that cannot possibly be completed now. Tap each of these items and select a reasonable time delay from the drop-down list in the bottom-right corner of the Reminders screen (the delay options are as follows: 5 minutes, 10 minutes, 15 minutes, 30 minutes, 1 hour, 2 hours, 8 hours, 1 day, and 1 week). Be sure to select a different delay for each option you can postpone, so they do not all pop-up at once again, and try to make it a time when you will actually have free time to attend to the item.

Now you should have a fairly small list of items remaining. Keep the list on your screen, and scroll to the highest priority items first. Proceed to complete each item, marking it off as you do so and then continue on to the next most important task. Using this method, your Pocket PC has gone from a simple organizer to a prioritizing management utility. When you finish the last task on the list, be sure to pat yourself on the back and grab a cup of coffee, because the items you delayed in step two will appear on screen soon.

Tip

The Pocket PC scrolling controls can be used to quickly move between the Dismiss, Dismiss all, and Snooze buttons. The selected option appears only slightly bolder than the other buttons (such as the Dismiss button in Figure 9.2). Pressing one of these buttons performs that action on the highlighted reminder. Pressing the same button again repeats the same action on the next appointment. This is a fast way to dismiss appointments one by one, so that you can read each one but dismiss them quickly using only one hand.

Using Quick Entry Arrows

Hidden within the Pocket Outlook suite is a feature that can shave hours off of your data entry time: the quick entry arrow. When creating new appointments and tasks, a few of the fields contain down arrows that, when tapped, presents a drop-down list of the most frequently used entries. Figure 9.3 illustrates a new Calendar item with the Subject quick entry arrow activated. Although the arrow appears white on a black button because it is activated in Figure 9.3, the arrow normally appears as a small black arrow without any border.

Note

When creating a new item in the Contacts application, some fields contain drop-down arrows. These arrows are not quick entry arrows; they activate a pop-up window that enables you to correctly format a contact's name or address.

Figure 9.3 The quick entry drop-down list

As you can see in the screen shot, the items that appear in the list are a few of the most common appointments that you enter into your Pocket PC. Meet with, Lunch, Dinner, Visit, Call, Birthday, or Complete are automatically typed into the Subject line of your appointment with one tap of the stylus. In addition, the feature automatically adds a space following the inserted text, so you can enter more details about the appointment using the stylus. If you make a selection from the drop-down and then tap on the quick entry arrow again, choosing another option from the drop-down list erases all text in the field.

The next field in a new appointment contains one of the most useful applications of the quick entry arrow. When you tap the arrow in the Location field, the drop-down list displays the last eight locations you have entered in previous appointments. This is a great way to enter repetitive locations such as conference room names or your favorite restaurants. Although the list cannot be edited, the chances are pretty good that your favorite spots will rise to the top of the list, especially if you only use the Locations field for events that you are planning. Otherwise, if you enter locations for all of the events that you attend, the eight locations in the drop-down box may end up always being a random list of locations.

As with the Calendar, the Tasks application uses the quick entry arrow in the first field, which is Subject. The options on this drop-down list are Buy, Call, Complete, Create, Plan, Update, and Work on. Again, this list cannot be edited, but provides a fast way to enter the first word or two on many of the most common tasks. In addition, always using a drop-down list item ensures that similar items (telephone calls beginning with Call and purchases starting with Buys, for example) will be grouped together when the Task list is sorted by subject.

 Cross-Reference

For complete information on sorting to better organize your Task list, review the "Superior Sorting Tricks" section of Chapter 7.

Make Pocket Outlook Easier on Your Eyes

Although the Pocket PC is a success because of its small size and bright screen, the text that is displayed on the screen is not always big enough for farsighted and elderly people. The three most frequently used applications (Calendar, Contacts, and Tasks) all have the capability to display their information in a larger-sized (and bold) font. From either of these applications, select Tools ➪ Options and activate the "Use large font" feature. When you press the Ok button, you will instantly recognize the change. You may also notice that using a larger font reduces the number of records you can see on the screen at one time. This is especially evident in the Contacts application. If you find the larger font more to your liking, you will need to activate it in each of the three applications individually.

Keeping Outlook Data Private

If you often worry about big brother peering down at everything you do on your computer, fear not. Although many corporate networks enable users to peer into your schedule in the desktop version of Outlook, the Pocket PC has a special security feature that keeps your information private. The Tasks and Calendar applications in Pocket Outlook have a privacy feature that's accessible when you create a new record. Figure 9.4 reveals the location of this feature in the Calendar, which, when synchronized with your desktop, marks that period of time as "busy" on your desktop calendar, but does not reveal the details of the appointment to network users. The private feature in the Tasks application works exactly the same way to keep your action items from becoming public knowledge.

Figure 9.4 The Private feature in Calendar

Note

The details of private appointments can also be hidden when you print a paper copy of your schedule from your desktop. Select File ⇨ Print in Outlook and activate the "Hide details of private appointments" feature.

Discovering the Ins and Outs of Using Categories

You may have noticed that I have not mentioned Pocket Outlook categories until now. Categories are words or phrases that can group a set of contacts, tasks, or appointments. This feature is built into the Pocket PC and although the applications enable you to single out a set of categorized items, you cannot sort by category. This reason alone renders Categories almost useless in my opinion.

However, the one saving grace is that the Pocket PC Find feature searches the category field. This is very helpful, because if you have a category dubbed "The Cyberdyne Project," performing a search for that text would reveal every categorized contact, task, and appointment, even if the words never appear anywhere else in the individual records. When using each of the applications that support categories, you can activate the category filter by pressing the hardware button assigned to the application. For example, if I run the Contacts application and then press the hardware button assigned to Contacts, the program sequentially filters the list in the alphabetical order of the category names.

If using Categories appeals to you, the quickest way to categorize an existing list of contacts or tasks is to assign them from your desktop. Synchronize your Pocket PC to ensure you have the most current version of all records, then run Outlook on your desktop, and open the contacts or tasks section. Highlight all of the records you want to assign to a single group and then right-click one of them with your mouse. Select the "categories . . ." option and check the appropriate box next to the category. As soon as you save the changes by pressing Ok, the newly categorized records will be copied to your Pocket PC.

Tip

One compelling reason to use Categories is if you synchronize multiple Pocket PCs with a single computer. For example, you can create "husband" and "wife" categories that only download to the Pocket PC's of the respective man and woman. A third "us" category could be created for both users when they wanted to schedule mutual events or download common contacts, such as family members.

Using Infrared to Transfer Information

One of the most exciting features of the Pocket PC is being able to communicate with other Pocket PC users. You can exchange business cards, transfer documents, and even play games using the infrared port on your Pocket PC. And it doesn't matter what brand or model device you own — any Windows Powered device can transfer information with a Pocket PC.

 Cross-Reference

For information on how to transfer information with Palm Pilot users, check out Chapter 22, "All my friends use a Palm Pilot. . ."

In the Pocket Outlook suite, send an appointment, contact, task,or note by tapping and holding the record for a few seconds. Figure 9.5 depicts the pop-up menu that appears in the Notes application when an individual record is selected. Notice that this feature is hidden in the tap-and-hold menu. Uncovering the feature in this location is the only way you will know that you have the capability to send that particular item via infrared. As it happens, e-mail is the only object in the Pocket Outlook suite that cannot be sent to another user via infrared.

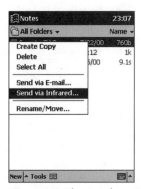

Figure 9.5 The Send via Infrared option

Receiving information from another user is far easier. While the sender is initiating a transfer using the preceding instructions, select Start ⇨ Programs ⇨ Infrared Receive and place your device in a position where the sender can align his device to yours. Figure 9.6 shows the Pocket PC patiently waiting a full 30 seconds to receive an incoming transmission. When the data transfer begins, you will see the name of the device which is connecting to you, a description of the content being transferred, a Progress bar, and a Cancel button to disconnect from the transfer. Once all the data is successfully received, the Pocket PC automatically stores the information in the proper location. This means that business cards go into the Contacts application, action items appear in the Tasks program, and so on. Once you have beamed someone a few times, you will get the hang of it. There is nothing as cool as wireless data transmission!

Figure 9.6 A Pocket PC awaiting infrared data

Tip

With some halogen and florescent lighting, you may experience transmission problems when sending or receiving data. In fact, this is the most common cause of data transmission errors. If this occurs, hold a piece of paper over the space between the two devices (to protect the infrared beam from disruptive light sources) and reinitiate the transmission.

Security and Infrared data transfer

Unlike other personal digital assistants (PDAs), the Pocket PC does not enable other users to begin sending unsolicited data to your device. Infrared receive must be activated (Start ➪ Programs ➪ Infrared receive) each time you receive data from another user, and it automatically turns off after the data has been transferred. In addition, the Pocket PC identifies the sending device before any data is transferred. If you do not recognize the device, simply press the Cancel button and the file will not be copied to your device, even if the transfer process has begun. Most importantly, infrared transfer is not possible beyond a few feet, so you do not need to worry about an unknown hacker beaming something malicious into your Pocket PC from across the room.

Note

If you begin an infrared transfer session with a device that is sending you more than one file, you must cancel the session before the first file is transferred. Otherwise, data will have been transferred to your device. If data has been received, check the screen to see what type of data was received, and then open the appropriate Contact, Calendar, Task, or Note application, or open File Explorer to delete the received files.

Transferring several files at once using infrared

Although File Explorer enables you to send any file via infrared, it only transfers one file at a time. However, if you use the Contacts, Notes, Tasks, Pocket Excel, or Pocket Word application to perform an infrared transfer, you will be able to send an unlimited number of files to another Pocket PC. To send multiple files to another device, complete the following steps:

1. Open the application that corresponds to the type of files you want to send (for example, to send contacts, open the Contacts application).

2. Tap-and-drag to select the files you want to send. If the items you wish to send are not adjacent to each other, activate the soft keyboard, tap the Control key, and then tap each file you wish to send individually.

3. Tap and hold one of the selected items and choose Send via Infrared . . . from the pop-up menu.

4. On the receiving device, activate Infrared receive (Start ⇨ Programs ⇨ Infrared receive) and align the infrared ports on the two devices.

The files transferred using this method will be accepted and are automatically stored in a location that is based on their file format. Contacts, appointments, and tasks are stored in the respective Pocket Outlook databases for each application. Voice recordings, notes, and all other files are saved in the My Documents folder of your device. Transferred files are stamped with the time that they are received, so sorting by date in File Explorer will place the transferred items at the bottom of the file list.

Figure 9.7 shows a Pocket PC sending multiple files. Note the new Progress bar that keeps you informed of the status of the data transfer, the text that displays the current file being transferred, and the number of files sent. If you press the Cancel button on either device during the transfer process, the window closes immediately. The other Pocket PC reports that the transfer process was cancelled and displays how many files were successfully transferred before the process was interrupted.

Figure 9.7 Transferring multiple files

Note

If someone tries to beam you a file that has the same name as a file already on your device, the Infrared receive feature automatically adds a number to the end of the filename. This means that you do not have to worry about incoming data overwriting your file. The only exception to this rule is in the Contacts application, where duplicate items can exist without any problems.

Summary

This chapter should supplement the lessons on the individual applications with big picture knowledge of how to use the entire Pocket Outlook suite in a consistent and competent manner. The next chapter focuses on the In-box, an essential tool for e-mail junkies like myself and one that provides more power than one would expect from a pocket-sized computing device.

CHAPTER 10

The Inbox: Your One-Stop Information Repository

IN THIS CHAPTER • Standard e-mail management

• Managing file attachments

• Making your Inbox even smarter

Although the program is a member of the Pocket Outlook suite because of its integration with the rest of the personal information manager (PIM) applications in the Pocket PC, the Pocket PC Inbox sets itself apart because it contains the functionality of a full-featured e-mail client. The application supports all of the popular Internet e-mail standards for sending and receiving mail, and employs the Pocket PC's connection capabilities to connect to Internet service providers (ISPs), corporate networks, and, of course, the desktop. Additionally, the installed Pocket versions of Word, Excel, and Internet Explorer enable the Inbox to receive file attachments from the corresponding desktop application. This means that native .doc, .xls, and .html files can be opened on your Pocket PC without any file conversions or extra software. With all this functionality, the Pocket PC sets the standard for communications capabilities in a personal digital assistant (PDA).

Using the Inbox

Designed to mimic the appearance of Outlook on the desktop, Pocket Inbox provides the familiar e-mail list and folder structure that is popular with most e-mail clients. Figure 10.1 demonstrates the Inbox with the folder list activated. Each e-mail service (shown as ActiveSync, Best.com, and Corporate account, in this example) has a separate file folder structure to separate messages from different services. Subfolders can be created to organize and clear up your Inbox.

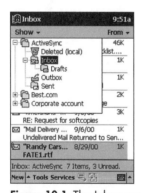

Figure 10.1 The Inbox service folders

Note

Although you have the ability to move and copy messages to subfolders, you cannot move a message from one e-mail service folder to another. When the folder list is closed, you can visually check which e-mail service is active, by examining the Inbox command bar. In Figure 10.1, the command bar at the bottom of the screen shows that the application is in the Inbox of the ActiveSync service and that seven items (three of which are unread) are currently in this folder.

Quickly collecting e-mail from any service you connect to (not ActiveSync) requires the use of the only two icons important enough to receive real estate on the Inbox navigation bar (see the following figure). The first button begins the connection process to your ISP, while the second performs the Send and Receive feature of the e-mail application.

Because Inbox supports several services, including Post Office Protocol 3 (POP3) Internet e-mail, Internet Message Access Protocol 4 (IMAP4) corporate e-mail, and ActiveSync, a number of different features are available for each service. Users with POP3 service — the most commonly used mail service for Internet service providers — can send messages using the MIME format, which is an encoding format that many desktop mail applications recognize. The Pocket PC IMAP4 support (for corporate users with IMAP4 server access) includes an intelligent connection to the server that reviews the size and content of the information that you receive against rules you have set for accepting the content, and enables you to synchronize your entire folder list from the server. Interestingly, HTML e-mail can only be read if it is downloaded from Outlook on the desktop via ActiveSync. All of the services automatically format Web address URLs as clickable hyperlinks and receive automated appointment requests impeccably.

Cross-Reference

For information on how to send appointment requests via e-mail, read the "Arrange a Meeting From the Palm of Your Hand" section of Chapter 6.

Addressing messages

When you create a new e-mail message, you can address the message by tapping the Contacts button in the bottom of the message, indicated in Figure 10.2. A pop-up window will display all of the e-mail addresses in the Contacts application. Activate the checkbox for all of the users that you would like to send the e-mail to and then press Ok. Inbox will return to the e-mail and enter all of the e-mail addresses in the To: field.

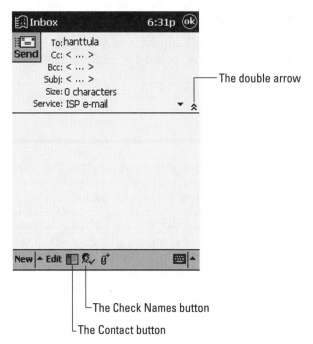

Figure 10.2 The e-mail composition window

Automatic addressing

Alternately, you can address an e-mail by entering part of the recipient's name in the To: field and then pressing the Check Names button, which is shown in Figure 10.2. The application will search for any contacts that contain the string that you have entered in the Name and E-mail Address fields, and then display the list so that you can pick from the matches that were in the Contacts database. For example, if I were to type in Hanttula and then press the Check Names button, a pop-up window with all of the members of my family would appear. If the application finds only a single match for the criteria you enter, the e-mail is automatically addressed to that person and the screen does not display the pop-up address list.

Tip

Although the Pocket PC does not support groups in the contacts list, you can quickly address a mass e-mail for your entire family by entering your last name in the e-mail To: field and then tapping the Check Names button. This will provide a list of all of your family members with the same last name. Check all of the boxes to address the e-mail.

Addressing an e-mail using an LDAP server

If your company has employed a Lightweight Directory Addressing Protocol (LDAP) server, you can enter a recipient's name in the Address field of an e-mail and have it checked against an address book on the server. To activate this feature, select Tools ➪ Options ➪ Address tab and activate the checkbox for the corporate or e-mail Web server that supports LDAP. If the LDAP server does not appear on the list, press the Add . . . button and enter the directory log in information. Inbox automatically checks the LDAP server when you press the Check Names button, but only if you are online and connected to the e-mail server.

Other e-mail composing features

Figure 10.2 also reveals the expanded header bar, which is only activated when you tap the double arrow in the header area. The additional fields that appear allow you to carbon copy or blind carbon copy other users, displays the size (in characters) of the e-mail, and allows you to select which service the e-mail will be sent through.

Saving and sending messages

To save a message that you are composing without sending it, press the Ok button. The application will store your e-mail in the Inbox folder of the service that you were going to send it in. Saved messages can be edited, copied, moved, or deleted while they remain in the Inbox. When you are ready to dispatch the message, open it and press Send.

When you press Send, the message moves to the application's Outbox. At this point, you can still edit, copy, move, or delete the message by changing to the Outbox. Once you connect to the service (ActiveSync, ISP, or corporate e-mail service) the message is sent when you press Send in the Inbox command bar. If you press Send on an e-mail while you are connected to your ISP (indicated by the Connect icon in the Inbox command bar appearing depressed), the message is immediately dispatched to the e-mail server and does not linger in the Outbox.

Tip

To save a copy of all the messages that you send, select Tools ➪ Options ➪ Message tab and check the "Keep copy of sent mail in Sent folder" option.

Standard E-mail Management

The left side of the Inbox uses three icons (see the following figure) to help you quickly identify the e-mails that you receive. They appear in the following order: text e-mail, e-mail with attachment, and meeting request.

If you are a fastidious Inbox organizer who only leaves e-mails that require action in your Inbox, you should consider updating ActiveSync to download all of your e-mail (by default, ActiveSync only downloads the last 3 days of e-mail and the first 100 lines of text). To modify the synchronization settings, open ActiveSync on the desktop and select Tools ➪ Options, highlight Inbox, and then click Settings. Deselect the options to save space, copy at most *xxx* lines and copy messages from the last *xx* days. As a result, any e-mails that you keep in your Inbox are also available in your Pocket PC, regardless of how old or how long the message.

Tip

If your Inbox contains more than just messages that require action, consider using the Unread message indicator to denote messages that require responses. Unread messages display the sender and subject in bold to distinguish them from messages that have already been read. You can return e-mail to its unread state by tapping and holding any e-mail item in the Inbox and then selecting Mark as Unread. The bold text calls your attention to these e-mails and reminds you that you have work to do.

When you are in the Inbox application, viewing the list of messages, use the scrolling controls to move up or down the list and to press the action button to open a message. While viewing a message, you can use the scrolling controls to page down through the message and then you can press the action button to close the e-mail.

Managing file attachments

E-mail without attachments is like a hamburger without ketchup — a bland existence and a waste of time. The Pocket PC enriches your life by allowing you to receive file attachments in the most popular formats used by offices. However, because attachments in e-mails can quickly become the rule and not the exception, you must be diligent about managing the attachments you receive.

Tip

You can quickly download documents attached to e-mail by double-clicking the transfer attachment icon in the e-mail while your device is synchronized or connected to an Internet service provider.

If file attachments are your lifeblood, like they are mine, you should set up ActiveSync to automatically download e-mail attachments to your Pocket PC. Open ActiveSync on the desktop and select Tools ➪ Options, highlight Inbox, click Settings, and then activate the Include file attachments feature. Every e-mail attachment will be automatically downloaded to your Pocket PC. Obviously this feature should be cautiously activated for users who frequently receive files that are many megabytes in size. Users that infrequently or almost never receive attachments should definitely activate this feature, because the few files that you receive will be there when you need them.

Tip

If you are using ActiveSync and want an extremely fast way to keep e-mail with a large file attachment out of your Pocket PC, simply drag it into another folder before you synchronize.

If you receive large files and cannot manage without them on your Pocket PC, you should consider buying a memory card. Although discussed in depth in later chapters, a memory card is an accessory that provides a separate space to store files and does not interfere with the Pocket PC's onboard memory. If you purchase a memory card, you can instruct Inbox to automatically store attachments on the card by selecting Tools ➪ Options Storage tab and activating the Store attachments on storage card feature. While you are on this screen, be sure to observe that the Storage tab displays the amount of free memory on the Pocket PC and on the memory card, and the current size of all of the attachments in your Inbox. This gives you an excellent glimpse of how much free memory you have and how much you need; use this snapshot to make sure that you are storing information in the right location.

Cross-Reference

For more information on conserving memory, walk through the steps in Chapter 19, "Memory and Power Constraints." You will save memory and have more room to download file attachments.

If you need a short-term solution for managing file attachments, you can delete an attachment without deleting the e-mail. Open the message, tap and hold the file attachment icon, and select Delete from the pop-up menu. The file will be removed from your device, but can be downloaded again later.

Finding messages

Although few users know it, you can search for the subject, sender's name, or text in the body of the e-mail using the Pocket PC's Find feature. In fact, you do not even have to launch the Inbox application to search for messages. To perform a search, complete the following steps:

1. Select Start ➪ Find.

2. Enter the text that you wish to search for in the Find field.

3. Tap the Type drop-down menu and select Inbox to narrow the search to e-mails only.

4. Press Go.

The Find application scours through all of the e-mail folders and returns a list of messages that contain the text that you searched for. Tap any one of the results to launch Inbox and open the message. If you wish to return to the search results, tap Start ➪ Find.

Deleting messages

When you delete messages, Inbox has three different ways to manage the deletion process. To control the way the deleted messages are handled, select Tools ⇨ Options ⇨ Message tab. The Empty deleted items field on this screen has three options: Immediately, On connect/disconnect, and Manually.

Immediately, as it sounds, erases the messages the moment you select Delete from the pop-up menu. E-mails that reside on your e-mail server will be removed from the server if you are connected, or will be removed upon your next connection to the server. The On connect/disconnect option performs a file deletion when you connect or disconnect to the e-mail server. This is the best option for users who are confident about permanently deleting files and are serious about conserving space.

The Manually option enables you to retain the messages in the Deleted (local) folder of each e-mail service until you decide to delete them. The deleted messages can be permanently erased individually by navigating to the Deleted (local) folder, tapping and holding an item, and then selecting delete. To erase all of the messages at once, select Tools ⇨ Empty Deleted Items.

Tip

To quickly delete all of the messages that have been received by the e-mail service, select Services ⇨ Clear All. (This feature will not work on the ActiveSync service folder.)

Making Your Inbox Even Smarter

Although most users only receive e-mail by using ActiveSync, you can easily take communications to the next level by downloading your e-mail using other methods beyond synchronizing with your desktop. A regular modem allows you to connect to a phone line anywhere in the world, a wireless modem connects you on-the-go, and a digital phone connection kit can attach your Pocket PC to a cellular telephone.

Cross-Reference

For a complete step-by-step guide to setting up the Inbox to send and receive e-mail over the Internet and for more information on the different ways to connect your device to the Internet, refer to Chapter 16.

A daily newspaper in your Inbox

Because the Inbox is built into your Pocket PC, it is the most portable information resource you can own. Instead of just using it for correspondence, enhance it by creating a set of news and information resources that arrive in your Pocket PC like a daily newspaper. Subscribe to text-based (not Hypertext Markup Language, or HTML) newsletters, and e-mail yourself corporate manuals or personal documents in Word format. Do not bother trying to funnel Web-based or interactive information into your device; Chapter 15 will teach you how to use Internet Explorer for that.

Folders and IMAP4

If your e-mail service is IMAP4, you can create a set of subfolders in the Pocket PC Inbox that is mirrored on your e-mail server. This allows you to organize and edit your messages and have the same file folder structure preserved when you access the e-mail server from your desktop computer.

Note

If you move a message into a subfolder using an e-mail service that is not IMAP4, the link to the message will be broken. When using ActiveSync, the message will be deleted from your desktop version of Outlook. For POP3 mail users, the message will be erased from the server.

Synchronization with the server occurs whenever you create a folder, move messages, or exit the Inbox application. If you wish to manually perform an IMAP4 synchronization, select Services ⇨ Synchronize Folders. By default all of the main folders (such as Inbox and Deleted) are designated as offline folders that will be copied to your device and can be viewed even when disconnected from the e-mail server. To mark another folder as offline and download its messages, connect to the IMAP4 service, highlight the folder, and then select Services ⇨ Folder Available Offline.

Perform a quick check of Inbox actions

With the ability to mark messages and attachments for later download or deletion, and with the ability to queue outgoing messages for send off, you might be worried that your Pocket PC will be tied up with the e-mail server for a long time. The Inbox includes a Status window that will show you the upcoming actions that will be performed when you next synchronize with each service. To open the Status window, select Tools ⇨ Status from the Inbox menu bar. Figure 10.3 shows an example Status window for a busy session.

Figure 10.3 The Inbox Status window

The term *copied,* as used in the Status window, is synonymous with downloaded. As you can see, one message and zero attachments will be downloaded at the next connection. Messages and attachments are separate items in the Status window because the attachments are frequently much larger files, indicating a longer download time.

Set Inbox options

Although we have already covered a dizzying number of features in the Inbox application, there are a few simple configuration settings in the program that can make your e-communications a little easier. Open the Options window by selecting Tools ⇨ Options ⇨ Message tab. Figure 10.4 shows the Options window with the features I normally use.

Figure 10.4 The Inbox Options window

If you do not wish to include a copy of the original message when you reply, you can deactivate that feature by deselecting the "When replying, include body" checkbox. If you do include the original message, you can toggle the indenting of the original text and set a leading character, which is a symbol that appears before each line of the original text.

Tip

If you do make use of the "Add leading character" feature, you should keep the default character that Inbox has been preprogrammed with: the > symbol. Most Web-savvy users recognize this as an indicator that you have included the original text, and some software programs are designed to remove the symbol if the user finds it visually unpleasant.

One odd feature that I have permanently changed in the Inbox on the Pocket PC and Outlook on my desktop is the "After moving/deleting a message" feature. Although the default is "Show the next message," I have always preferred "Return to the message list." When I delete a message, it is a much more comforting feeling to see the message window disappear and to return to the Inbox, rather than having another e-mail pop up on the screen. Although the Delete button and Next Message buttons are not adjacent to each other, I think making this change on every Pocket PC would make things less confusing for most users.

Summary

The Inbox is the final application of the Pocket Outlook suite. By this point, you should have an expert's knowledge of how to exploit the entire line of personal information management tools to their fullest potential. The following chapter will help you gain the same level of expertise in the Pocket Office Suite, a line of applications designed to provide the connection to your workplace anytime and anyplace.

Pocket Office: Desktop Applications To Go

IN THIS CHAPTER • Using Pocket Word and Notes

• Learning Pocket Excel and Calculator

• Working with Pocket Money

While the Pocket PC is not designed to replace your desktop computer, it performs splendidly as a temporary stand-in while you are away from the office or when traveling. In fact, your Windows Powered device contains scaled-down versions of the Microsoft Office Suite applications right out-of-the-box. Pocket Word, Pocket Excel, and Pocket Money are all compatible — and able to communicate — with their desktop counterparts.

Additionally, the Pocket PC contains some specialized applications that work in tandem with the Pocket Office programs to help those programs work more efficiently on a small screen. Notes and Calculator provide fast and effective solutions when weighed against Pocket Word and Pocket Excel. However, the complete collection of software is much more powerful when combined.

Putting Pen to Paper . . . Or Stylus to Screen with Pocket Word and Notes

A versatile feature of the Pocket PC is its capability to store and retrieve text information. I say versatile because the device has two applications dedicated to viewing, editing, and creating documents that can then be transferred via desktop synchronization, e-mail, or infrared with another Pocket PC. At first sight, Pocket Word and Notes appear to be identical software applications that can be used interchangeably. The similarities, however, are only skin deep.

Word versus Notes

Pocket Word is designed as the Pocket PC's documentation powerhouse, providing advanced text editing, more methods of entering data than the Notes application supports, and built-in file management functions. Text-editing features in Pocket Word include font formatting, paragraph spacing and alignment, and date insert. The popular Find and Replace feature from the desktop version of Microsoft Word enables you to quickly search and substitute text across the entire document. Figure 11.1 shows a document using bullets and multiple font styles. It is important to observe how Pocket Word differentiates between the written signature and the smiley face drawing. The drawing is indicated by a gray outline that is labeled Drawing, while the written text simply stands alone. This functionality is possible due to Pocket Word's adaptable entry methods.

Pocket Word offers four methods of entering information into a document: typing, recording, writing, and drawing. These entry methods should not be confused with entering text using the Pocket PC Input panel. Pocket Word entry methods are only available on the View menu while a document is open. By default, opening a new document activates the typing mode, which uses the Pocket PC Input panel to enter information using the keyboard, Character Recognizer, or Transcriber. The Recording mode enables you to annotate a document with spoken messages. Select View ➩ Recording and then position the cursor in the document where you would like the recording to appear. Figure 11.1 shows how the voice annotation is indicated as a small speaker icon. Detailed information on embedding voice notes appears later in this chapter.

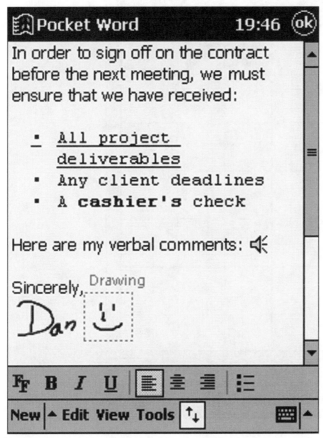

Figure 11.1 A document developed entirely in Pocket Word.

Switch to the Writing mode (choose View ⇨Writing) and you can enter text in your own handwriting, just like writing on a notepad. Written text will not be recognized until you select Tools ⇨ Recognize. Writing mode is very effective when fast note taking is required. When Drawing mode is activated, typed characters and written text are faded out, the document is zoomed in to 200 percent magnification, and a grid appears. Figure 11.2 illustrates Drawing mode using the same document as in the previous example. Again, notice that Pocket Word differentiates between the signature and the drawing. This mode may be useful in creating illustrations that require straight lines, as well as in distinguishing written text from drawings that will be unaffected by the Recognize command. Information entered as writings or drawings appears as bitmap (picture) images when the document is opened on the desktop computer.

Figure 11.2 Pocket Word Drawing mode

Tip

Pocket Word contains a dynamic toolbar that customizes itself for each viewing mode. Activate the toolbar by pressing the Up/Down arrow button on the Pocket Word toolbar (while viewing a document) and then watch the toolbar change by selecting View ➪ Writing/Drawing/Typing/Recording. Figure 11.1 displays the Writing toolbar and Figure 11-2 shows the Drawing toolbar.

Last, Pocket Word has built-in file management features that enable you to revert the document back to its original saved form or to delete or copy the current document while you are viewing it. Furthermore, the application is automatically activated when you attempt to open a Microsoft Word file received via e-mail. Double-click on the Word icon in the e-mail, and Pocket Word displays the file without any hesitation or file conversion. And, when you are ready to forward a document, to someone else you can save it as a Pocket Word, Word 6.0/95/97/2000, Rich Text Format (.rtf), or plain text (.txt) document, as well as a Word 6.0/95/97/2000 template.

Tip

By default, Pocket Word automatically names your files using the first text entered into the document and saves it to your My Documents folder in Pocket Word format. To give the document a personalized name, custom location, or unique file format, select Tools ⇨ Save Document As and edit the fields as necessary.

Light on features but heavy on ease of use, the Notes application is a very different creature. It synchronizes with the Notes section of Microsoft Outlook on the desktop to provide an automated union between computer and Pocket PC. Information in this simple application is entered either by typing or by writing. A unique feature to Notes is that you can set which method you prefer to use by selecting Tools ⇨ Options and changing the default mode field. The Insert Date feature is also available, but only if you tap and hold inside the document while in Typing mode.

Note

If you turn on ActiveSync's file synchronization feature, Notes and voice recordings will be copied to your desktop as individual files in your My Documents folder. However, once you activate Notes synchronization, text and voice notes are synchronized with the Notes folder of Outlook on the desktop. After this occurs, you can only access these items as individual files using ActiveSync's Explore feature to manually copy them to your desktop.

Notes also hosts the Pocket PC's powerful voice recorder feature, which enables you to record spoken reminders to yourself while driving or engaged in another activity in which writing a note might not be safe. Unlike embedded voice annotations, voice recordings are designed to function as stand-alone reminders that do not need any text or drawings to make the point. This is also a wonderful replacement for the executive who carries a cassette recorder to log mental notes throughout the day. If you use the voice recorder so frequently that you find yourself with a list of files named Recording1, Recording2, and so on, try renaming the files to something more intuitive right after you make them.

Both applications support standard editing features (Undo, Redo, Cut, Copy, Paste, Clear, and Select All), five different zoom levels, and the transferring of the current file via infrared or e-mail. Pocket Word and Notes also feature document templates for meeting notes, office memos, phone memo, and to-do lists. You can select which template each program uses when you press New, by selecting Tools ⇨ Options and altering the default template field. It is a good idea use different default templates for each application. For example, set Pocket Word to open the meeting notes template and set Notes to open the to-do list. You can also open templates manually by changing the file folder to Templates when in the File List mode of Notes and Pocket Word.

Cross-Reference

For information on how to quickly choose a template each time you create a new document, read the "Power Pack Your 'New' Menu" section of Chapter 17.

How Pocket Word can become your personal secretary

Anyone would welcome the luxury of a personal secretary who would take dictation on request and who would then type the entire dialog and file it for your later reference. Although the cost of having a personal secretary on-call 24 hours a day would be astronomical, the Pocket PC can function as an inexpensive alternative. To begin, run Pocket Word and select View ⇨ Writing. Now quickly jot a lengthy thought down the page. When you reach the bottom of the page, lift the stylus and pause for a moment and Pocket Word will quickly scroll down so that you have additional room to write. Continue in this manner until you have completely transferred your concept onto the Pocket PC and then select Tools ⇨ Recognize.

Cross-Reference

To learn how to significantly enhance the Pocket PC's handwriting recognition accuracy, read the opening section of Chapter 17: "Advanced personalization for your faithful companion."

In a manner of seconds, you can see your thoughts magically transform from written text to typed characters before your eyes. Pressing Ok to close the document files this thought away using the first few words in the document and adds a time stamp so that you can also locate it later based on the date of inception. Being able to jot an entire idea onto the Pocket PC without having to wait for the device to translate your handwriting enables you to pour out your thoughts unrestrained by a mistyped character or an unrecognized word. This feature alone makes Pocket Word an invaluable companion but as with all things on the Pocket PC, there is much, much more to love.

Make corrections quickly and easily

Like a good secretary, the Pocket PC is very forgiving of mistakes. Although the recognition system is top-quality, occasionally it incorrectly deciphers your handwriting or does not recognize a word. The Pocket PC not only enables you to correct the mistake, but also offers guesses on the correction. Using the stylus, tap and hold the word that was incorrectly translated and then select Alternatives from the pop-up menu. Figure 11.3 is an example of Pocket Word's Alternatives menu. Its most commendable nuance is that the original written word is displayed above all of the recommended options, giving you a chance to compare your handwriting to the program's best guess.

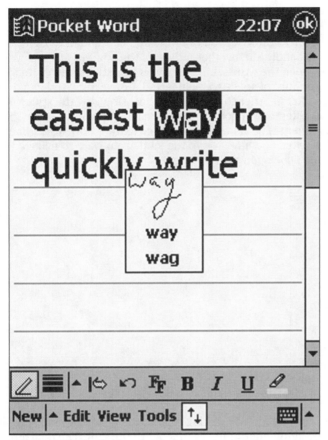

Figure 11.3 The Alternatives menu

Tip

If you want to enter an illustration, symbol, or anything that you do not want translated into text, select View ⇨ Drawing and then sketch the object. Pocket Word will not attempt to translate ink that is entered in Drawing mode when you activate the Recognize command.

Pocket Word has a special toolbar for Writing mode. This toolbar is invaluable for making quick corrections to written text. Activate the toolbar by pressing the Up/Down arrow button at the bottom of the screen. The toolbar is shown in Figure 11.4, which demonstrates how a thin box around the pen highlights the Pen icon when you are in Writing mode. When you want to perform cut-and-paste functions or move the cursor, you can deactivate Writing mode by tapping the icon. The second icon on the toolbar, Pen Weight, enables you to change the width of the ink.

If you write two words too closely together, the Add/Remove Space icon on the toolbar can insert a space. Simply press the icon and then tap-and-hold the stylus between the two words. As you drag the stylus from left to right, Pocket Word displays an expanding arrow that indicates the amount of space you are about to insert between the words. Lift the stylus from the screen when you are satisfied with the amount of space to be inserted. Conversely, you can drag the stylus from right to left in order to remove a space. Dragging the stylus up or down while the Add/Remove Space icon is activated adds or deletes carriage returns in the document. The Add/Remove space feature only works one time, so after you drag the stylus you have to tap the icon again want to make additional modifications to the spacing in the document.

Figure 11.4 The Pocket Word Writing mode toolbar

After you have converted your writing to text, the next four icons provide formatting, bold, italic, and underlining treatments to the font. The final icon is a highlighting pen that can, delightfully, highlight both written and converted text. This is a very powerful tool to use in business and personal communications, as the yellow highlighted text brilliantly illuminates text on a Pocket PC (however, the yellow highlight does not appear when transferred to a desktop computer). To perform highlighting or any of the font formatting functions, select the text by tapping and holding directly in front of the text you wish to highlight. When you see the cursor appear on screen, continue to hold the stylus on the screen and drag across the text that you wish to highlight.

Tip

You can recognize a section of text separately by selecting the word or phrase and selecting Tools ⇨ Recognize. The selected ink is converted to text and the rest of the document remains in its original written form. This is an effective way to correct a word that you know will not be recognized accurately because it is an unusual word or it is poorly written. As soon as you recognize the rest of the document, the previously converted word appears in the correct position amongst the newly recognized text.

Give Voice Recorder a tune up

The Notes application contains the functional and handy Voice Recorder feature. By default, however, the voice recording system on all Pocket PCs is set to conserve device memory. The consequence of this setting is that recording quality is nearly unacceptable or the recording format is incompatible with other Pocket PCs or the desktop computer. To change this setting, access the global Input options applet by selecting Start ⇨ Settings ⇨ Input ⇨ Options tab. (You can also quickly arrive at this screen by opening Notes and selecting Tools ⇨ Options ⇨ Global Input Options hyperlink.) Although other Pocket PCs have unique recording formats, the first three formats in the following list are standard across Windows CE devices:

- Mobile Voice (.7KB/second): Low quality and only compatible with Windows Powered devices.

- GSM 6.10 (2KB/second): Medium quality and compatible with all Windows-powered devices, all Windows desktop computers, and embedded Notes and Word documents.

- HP Dynamic Voice (1KB/second): High quality recording, but only compatible with the HP Jornada line of Pocket PC devices. This is the default for the Jornada Pocket PC.

- PCM (8 to 43KB/second): Highest quality available and compatible with all Windows-powered devices, all Windows desktop computers, and embedded Notes and Word documents. In addition, this format offers mono and stereo recording formats.

Tip

Because it doubles the amount of memory needed, only use the stereo format if you plan to transfer voice recordings to the desktop for professional use. Because the HP Jornada only has a single (mono) speaker, the stereo format is ineffective on the device. Most voice recordings transferred to the desktop work adequately when recorded in mono.

Each of the listings show the amount of memory (in kilobytes) that a particular format will use per second of recording time, the quality of the recording, and the format's compatibility with other Pocket PCs, desktop computers, and embedded Notes and Word documents. After you have selected a format that works best with your needs, select Ok to save your changes. Next, test the system by pressing and holding the recording hardware button for a few seconds. After you hear the beep, which indicates that the voice recorder is activated, speak a few words into the device. Replay the recording that you just made using maximum speaker volume to ensure that you are satisfied with the recording quality.

Fast Voice Recorder file-naming technique

By default, Voice Recorder names each file you create as Recording and appends a sequential number to the end of the filename. If you delete a file, the application fills in the gaps in numerical order when you create new voice recordings. This is important to remember when searching for new recordings, because the highest number may not always be the most recent voice note. When you launch Voice Recorder (Start ⇨ Notes) you will see that the file folder display defaults to All Folders, as shown in the upper-left corner of Figure 11.5.

Tip

For a faster method of launching Voice Recorder, depress the Voice Recorder button quickly. If you release the button fast enough, the Voice Recorder application loads without creating a recording.

Notes		1:19p
All Folders ▾		Name ▾
DataCD1	1:00 p	1.4s
DataCD2	1:08 p	1.4s
My Library1	11:55 a	2.4s
My Library2	1:06 p	1.4s
Note1	11/26/00	1020b
Recording1	1:12 p	2.6s
Recording2	12/5/00	2.6s
Recording3	1:06 p	1.4s

New ▴ Tools

Figure 11.5 The Voice Recorder file folder

This All Folders feature searches main memory and any inserted memory card for voice recordings (and notes) in the My Documents folder and subdirectories within My Documents. After you tap the drop-down menu and select a specific directory, Voice Recorder changes its file-naming convention for new voice recordings. Pressing the Voice Recorder hardware button while in a specific directory creates a file with the same name as the directory. Voice Recorder affixes a number at the end of the file name, starting with 1. Figure 11.5 illustrates the results of creating two voice recordings in the DataCD and My Library folders. Figure 11.5 also shows how voice recordings saved to a memory card are recognizable by a memory card graphic superimposed on the speaker icon (as shown on the files My Library2 and Recording3).

Note

If you set Voice Recorder to save to a memory card (choose Tools ➪ Options ➪ Save to: Storage Card 1) and switch to a subfolder in Pocket PC memory (as described earlier), Voice Recorder automatically saves the voice recording to the storage card if a folder with the exact same name resides within \Storage Card\My Documents\. Otherwise, the file is saved to the folder in main memory.

If you wish to create a set of voice recordings with a specific filename and sequential numbers, you can create a new folder by tapping the file folder drop-down menu in the upper-left corner and selecting Add/Delete. The pop-up window enables you to create a new folder by pressing the New button; it also enables you to rename and delete existing folders. Tap the New button, type **Voice**, and then press Enter to save the changes. When you press Ok, the pop-up window closes and Voice Recorder displays the folder you just created. Pressing the Voice Recorder hardware button or the onscreen record button creates a voice memo named Voice1.

Note

The Add/Delete feature only enables you to make subfolders one level beneath My Documents. Folders that reside within another folder (\My Documents\Voice Recordings\Year 2001\, for example) are not recognized by the Voice Recorder application and, therefore, cannot be created by using the Add/Delete utility.

When you have finished making the voice recordings with matching filenames, tap the file folder drop-down box in the upper-left corner and select All Folders. Voice Recorder will display all of the voice recordings on your device and return to naming new voice memos with the Recording prefix. If you do not return Voice Recorder to the All Folders setting, it will remember the last folder that you had open in the application and continue to save new voice memos in this directory. This is an excellent way to neatly and consistently store the files in a subdirectory of My Documents.

Embedding voice notes

Now that you have successfully modified the Voice Recorder format to support compatibility with the desktop and other Pocket PCs, it is time to learn about the power of embedded voice notes. The spoken word is a powerful tool in business and personal communication. Using a verbal example to explain a complex theory, or attaching the sound of your baby's coos to a birth announcement can make the difference between a good communiqué and a spectacular one.

Voice notes can be embedded into Pocket Word documents or Notes. Figure 11.1 at the beginning of this chapter shows a voice note embedded in a Pocket Word document and Figure 11.6 reveals multiples voice notes embedded in a single Notes file. Figure 11.6 also shows that increasing the document magnification increases the size of the voice recorder icons, making them far easier to select, even if they are close together or embedded next to other objects.

Figure 11.6 A Notes file with voice annotations

Pressing the Voice Recorder hardware button while inside a Notes or Pocket Word document will add a voice annotation where the cursor is. Alternately, you can select View ⇨ Recording in Pocket Word or press the cassette recorder icon in Notes to activate the voice recorder navigation bar. Once activated, the onscreen record button will create a voice note at the cursor's present location. To delete a voice recording from the document, place the cursor directly ahead of the voice recording speaker icon, activate the keyboard in the soft input panel, and press the backspace key. This permanently removes the voice annotation without any confirmation. After you are satisfied with your voice annotations, you can send the document via synchronization, infrared, or as an e-mail attachment. Recipients of the document will be able to listen to your comments by clicking on the icons — just as you can.

Send v-mail from your Pocket PC

Another incredibly novel approach for utilizing the Pocket PC's audio features is to send voice-based e-mail (v-mail). Because you can speak much faster than you enter text on the Pocket PC, v-mail is a quick way to compose a message and you can use it while driving or talking on the phone. To send an e-mail using only your voice, exit out of any Pocket Word or Note document you may be viewing. Now, press the Voice Recorder hardware button or activate the Voice Recorder navigation bar in the Notes application by the cassette recorder icon and press Record. When you have finished recording your message, it should appear as a file in the Notes application. Tap and hold the filename and select Send via E-mail from the pop-up menu. In-box automatically loads and creates a new e-mail message with your voice recording already attached. Address the message and enter a subject or quick explanation in the e-mail to entice the addressee to read the message. In a few seconds, you have created a powerful message in a way that only a Pocket PC user can.

Playing the Numbers Game with Pocket Excel and Calculator

Accountants and those who are pencil pushers at heart beware; the Pocket PC provides a complete spreadsheet solution that will satisfy all of your computational needs. Pocket Excel and the Pocket PC calculator are built-in to the Pocket PC and make excellent companions for any mathematical challenges that may arise. Pocket Excel operates like the desktop version of the application, and — like Pocket Word — enables you to open Excel documents that are sent to you as e-mail attachments. Of course, when copying Excel files from the desktop, there are a few important caveats to remember.

What works best when converting Excel spreadsheets from the desktop

According to the information gleaned from numerous Help files in the Pocket PC and the ActiveSync application, a number of features are not supported in Pocket Excel and are automatically stripped from Excel files when they are copied to the Pocket PC. Chart objects, cell notes and cell patterns, vertical alignment, hyperlinks, scenarios, embedded OLE objects, add-ins, data consolidation/validation, text boxes, drawings, pictures, and controls are automatically removed from the workbook on synchronization. Meanwhile, a placeholder sheet that informs you of their omission replaces visual Basic Application modules and chart/macro/dialog sheets. Pocket Excel does not enable links to cells beyond row #16384 or to other documents. Cells that contain these calls return the code #REF! to indicate a reference that it cannot support.

Excel functionality that is not removed but is permanently modified in the workbook includes the following: custom borders are all changed to a single line, vertical text is changed to horizontal text, hidden sheets and names in the Excel workbook are unhidden, and formulas not supported by Pocket Excel are converted to the final value before copying the document to your Pocket PC (including formulas containing an array or pivot table data). Cell shading, although not supported in the Pocket PC, is correctly displayed when the file is copied back onto the desktop.

Of course, if you created the Excel document and do not understand any of the terminology used here, you probably do not need to worry about any functions being stripped from your Excel documents. As always, however, the best way to test it is to copy an Excel document from your desktop to your Pocket PC and back and then open it to see if all of the calculations still work.

Tip

If you are viewing a large spreadsheet, select View ➪ Full Screen to remove the scroll bars, command bar, and column and row headers. Pocket Excel places a Restore button at the top of the screen to return to the standard view when you complete your work.

Password protect your Excel data

After you have honed a workbook to operate flawlessly on your Pocket PC, you will undoubtedly want to protect the information. Like the desktop version of Excel, Pocket Excel supports password protection that requests the user to enter a secret code before being able to open the document. To require a password for a document, open the document in Pocket Excel and select Edit ⇨ Password. The application will request that you enter the password twice to ensure that you've input it accurately. Select Ok twice to close the password window and save the file. Every successive attempt to open the file will activate the password prompt and require that the code be correctly entered before displaying the Pocket Excel workbook.

Warning

Excel documents on the desktop must have the password protection removed before downloading them to a Pocket PC. Attempting to copy a password-protected Excel workbook to the Pocket PC will result in a synchronization error. Alternatively, when transferring Excel files with a password from the Pocket PC to the desktop, ActiveSync will prompt you to enter the workbook password. Doing so removes the password protection from both versions (desktop and Pocket PC) of the document automatically.

To remove password protection from a Pocket Excel workbook, open the file on your Pocket PC and select Edit ⇨ Password. The existing password will appear (in asterisks) in the top field. Erase all of the asterisks and press Ok twice to close the password window and save the file. The document is now freely accessible with no password required.

Pocket Excel formulas made easy

If you have read this far, you are probably familiar with spreadsheet formulas. While volumes could be written on how to use specific Pocket Excel formulas such as =SQRT(144), most humans would probably prefer a shortcut rather than having to memorize Pocket Excel formulas. Thankfully, Microsoft did not cut corners in this area. Highlight any cell in a spreadsheet and select Tools ⇨ Insert Function.

This feature, shown in Figure 11.7, provides a complete list of Pocket Excel formulas in a convenient scrolling window. The Category drop-down list, shown at the top the illustration, enables you to narrow down the list for easier browsing. In the example, the list is restricted to Math and Trig functions. Scrolling down to SQRT shows us that this is the formula for calculating a positive square root. As you scroll through each formula, the text beneath the window changes to give you a plain-English description of the formula you have selected. Pressing OK inserts the formula into the current cell.

Figure 11.7 The Insert Function feature

Another way to quickly calculate values is by using the AutoCalculate area on the right side of the Pocket Excel status bar. Indicated in Figure 11.8, AutoCalculate displays the answers to the six most-often-used functions on the spreadsheet cells currently selected. By default, AutoCalculate displays the sum of any selected cells as shown in Figure 11.8. Tapping the AutoCalculate bar activates a pop-up menu with Average, Count, Count Nums, Max, Min, and Sum options.

Figure 11.8 Quick calculations in the status bar

The Average feature calculates the numerical average of the selected cells. The Count option tallies the number of cells that you have selected and the Count Nums option tallies the number of selected cells that contain numerical values. Selecting Max or Min displays the highest or lowest value, respectively, from all of the highlighted cells. Although the AutoCalculate feature displays the resulting calculation, the answer cannot be copied or manipulated in any way.

Note

Except for the Count feature, the AutoCalculate feature only includes cells with numerical values. Cells with nonnumeric values, such as titles, cells with symbols, or blank cells, are ignored.

Using symbols in your Pocket Excel spreadsheet

Pocket Excel includes a quick and easy way to insert hundreds of symbols, including copyright symbols, accented letters, and foreign characters, into your spreadsheet. To insert a symbol, highlight any cell, or insert the cursor where you would like a symbol to appear, and select Tools ⇨ Insert Symbol. In the window that appears, select a font family and a subset, and then choose from the symbols that appear on screen. When you tap a symbol, the program provides an enlarged preview. Tapping the Insert button places the symbol in your document.

In many cases, however, the symbol does not correctly display on the spreadsheet. To resolve this problem, highlight the cell that contains your symbol and select Format ⇨ Cells. From the drop-down font list, select the name that matches the font that you chose your symbol from. When you press Ok, the symbol should display properly in the cell of your spreadsheet.

Tip

If you plan to include text with your symbols, do not use a symbol from the Bookdings font, as it does not have an alphabet character set.

In addition to the four font files that come with your Pocket PC, you can copy font files from your desktop. To copy symbols from your desktop computer, locate the font files on your desktop (usually stored in C:\WINDOWS\FONTS) and open the ActiveSync window. In ActiveSync, select File ⇨ Explore and navigate to \My Pocket PC\Windows\Fonts. Drag and drop the files from your desktop fonts folder into your Pocket PC. Standard Windows symbol font files that you can copy include symbol.ttf, symbole.ttf, webdings.ttf, and wingding.ttf.

The Paste Special command

After you have created the perfect cell with a formula, font formatting and border treatments, you will probably want to include some facets of that cell in many different areas on your spreadsheet. This can be accomplished with the Paste Special command. While performing a copy-and-paste on any formula will duplicate all of the features of a cell, the Paste Special command enables you to selectively apply specific aspects of a cell to other areas. To access this feature, copy any cell on your spreadsheet and select Edit ⇨ Paste Special. The window offers you five options:

- **All:** This copies all of the font formatting, cell border treatment and reconstructs the formula of the original cell based on its new location. This command is equivalent to a copy and paste.

Tip

To copy a formula exactly (so that the origin cells that make up the formula do not move as a consequence of you moving the formula) enter dollar signs in front of the column and row designations (for example, "=$B$2+$B$3").

- **Formulas:** This option inserts the computations from the copied cell without changing any formatting and is ideal for duplicating a formula on a spreadsheet that has already been meticulously well designed with font formatting and borders.

- **Values:** This command pastes the result of the copied cell. Instead of inserting the formula, it pastes the numerical value of the original cell. This is an excellent way to quickly copy a value to another cell; however, any updates to the original cell formula will not be reflected in the pasted value.

- **Formats:** Duplicates the formatting of the original cell while leaving the cell's mathematical functions intact. An excellent way of quickly copying good design elements from a single cell.

- **All except borders:** Copies everything from the original cell except for the border treatments. Equivalent to the Formats option but without copying border formatting.

Selecting any of these options and then pressing ok immediately pastes the features to the cell or range of cells you had previously selected.

Create a sequential list in seconds

Have you ever had to enter a continuous series of numbers or dates in an Excel spreadsheet? Pocket Excel makes this extremely simple. Start by entering a number or date where you would like Pocket Excel to begin the series. Figure 11.9 uses the date 1/1/01 as the beginning of the series.

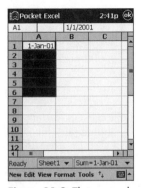

Figure 11.9 The groundwork for creating a series

Tip

If you enter a date in formal text, such as 'January 1, 2001, Pocket Excel automatically converts it to the numeric equivalent (1/1/2001) and displays it in the cell as 1-Jan-01 to conserve space. To change the way the date is displayed in the cell, highlight the cell and select Format ⇨ Cells Number tab.

Next, tap-and-hold the cell that you just entered the date into and drag the stylus down or across to highlight all of the cells you wish to populate. Figure 11.9 has the first six cells selected. From the Pocket Excel menu, select Edit ⇨ Fill to activate the Fill options screen. The first option, Direction, enables you to designate whether the list you are about to create is ascending or descending. The second feature, Fill type, enables you to copy the current cell, or to create a series. Select series and you activate the third section of the Fill tool, Series type, which has three options:

- **Autofill:** If the first cell is a day of the week, a month, or a number preceded by text (a1, for example) Pocket Excel automatically calculates the progression of the series and fill the remaining cells. There are no additional options for this feature.

- **Date:** If you have entered a date, as we have in our example, Pocket Excel can create a sequential list in daily, monthly, or yearly increments. Select from these three options and then enter a number in the step value field, to designate how many days, months, or years it increases in each cell.

- **Number:** Entering a number in the first cell, and then selecting the number series type creates a numerical list. The step value specifies how much the value increases in each subsequent cell.

To complete our sample list, select Date, change the increment to Month, and set the Step value to 1. When you press Ok, Pocket Excel will calculate the series and enter it into the highlighted cells. Figure 11.10 illustrates the results of this example and should match your results exactly.

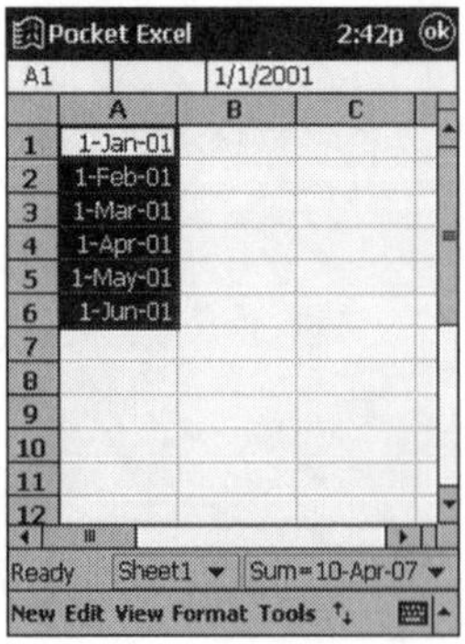

Figure 11.10 The final Pocket Excel series

Tip

The Fill feature can be used on multiple columns or rows simultaneously.

Using the sheets feature to tidy up the spreadsheet

As with spreadsheets on your desktop, Pocket Excel can create documents with infinite sheets. Adding a new sheet creates another spreadsheet page inside the same file. This enables you to perform complex calculations or to create long lists on one sheet while only displaying the totals on the top sheet. To create a second sheet in a Pocket Excel document, select Format ⇨ Modify Sheets.

By default, every Pocket Excel document includes three sheets, named Sheet1, Sheet2, and Sheet3. Figure 11.11 shows the Modify Sheets screen for a new document. To rename any of the sheets, highlight the name that you wish to change and press Rename. Pocket Excel will prompt you for the new designation. Other buttons on the Modify Sheets screen include Insert, which places a new sheet directly above the item you have selected, and Delete, which erases the currently selected sheet. Once you have more than one sheet in your Pocket Excel file, you can rearrange the order of the sheets, by selecting one and pressing Move Up or Move Down.

Figure 11.11 The Modify Sheets screen

Tip

If you are creating an elaborate Pocket Excel document with many sheets, take the time to individually name each sheet with a clear and concise title. This will make the document easier to navigate instead of having to remember what information you entered on Sheet54.

Naming one or more cells

Pocket Excel enables you to define a name for a single cell or a range in a spread-sheet. This is a convenient way to refer to data using plain English, rather than a cell number or cell range. To name any area, highlight it using the stylus and then select Tools ⇨ Define Name. Figure 11.12 shows the Define Name screen. Note that the window displays all of your preexisting names so that you do not duplicate a moniker.

Figure 11.12 The Define Name screen

To name your cell, enter a title in the top window (MaintenanceTotal in our example) and press Add. After you have created the name, you can refer to the cell using a formula value of =MaintenanceTotal instead of B4. And when referring to the cell on a different sheet, you again enter the name, instead of having to refer to a page name, followed by an exclamation point and the cell name. (For example, =!MaintenanceTotal works on any sheet, rather than =Car Maintenance!B4)

Tip

After you have named a cell, you can locate it quickly by selecting Tools ⇨ Go To and entering the cell name. Alternately, you can paste a complete list of named cells and their locations directly on your spreadsheet by selecting Tools ⇨ Define Name ⇨ Paste List.

Supercharge the mileage log template

Pocket Excel contains a built-in mileage log to record travel expenses when using your personal automobile for business purposes. Using the information that you learned in this section, you can create a substantially more powerful mileage log that can track the fuel efficiency and operating costs of your vehicle, display the automobile's maintenance schedule, and show you your current mileage expense tax rebate (if you are an entrepreneur).

Note

The procedures documented in creating this spreadsheet are similar to creating a spreadsheet on your desktop computer, but if you travel frequently, you may find it helpful to record this information while you're on the road. Furthermore, this procedure will take a while, but reinforces the information learned about Pocket Excel while creating a better template for tracking vehicle information.

To begin, copy the Pocket Excel mileage log by launching Pocket Excel and selecting Templates from the file folder drop-down box in the upper-left corner. Tap-and-hold the file named Vehicle Mileage Log and select Create Copy from the pop-up menu. Pocket Excel will create a duplicate of the template in the same folder. Open the duplicate file by tapping it.

The vehicle mileage log file that came with your Pocket PC is a single-sheet spreadsheet and, on its own, works rather well. In fact, you only need to make a single refinement to this sheet to begin developing a supercharged automobile information reference. Highlight the cell that displays the total miles driven (cell B3) and select Tools ⇨ Define Name. Enter **MileageTotal** as the cell name, press Add to name the cell, and press Ok.

The automobile maintenance sheet

Next, create a new sheet to track automobile maintenance by selecting Format ⇨ Modify Sheets ⇨ Insert and entering Maintenance. In the first row, enter **Service**, **Mileage**, **Date**, and **Cost**. These will be the column headers for the maintenance data. After you have entered the titles, highlight the four cells and select Format ⇨ Cells. On the Align tab, change the horizontal alignment to center and then switch to the Borders tab to select a Gray 50% fill from the Fills drop-down box. Now, select the Font tab and change the font to Tahoma size 8 bold. Press Ok to save your changes and apply the formatting to the row. Now that you have a maintenance schedule sheet, you need to populate it.

Find the manual for your automobile and enter one schedule item at a time. For example, start in cell A2 and enter **oil change**. In the second column (cell B2), type in the odometer reading at which the next oil change will be required. Highlight cell B2 using the stylus, and then drag down so that you select the next nine rows. You should have ten cells selected (you can confirm this by tapping the AutoCalculate bar and selecting Count). When you have highlighted ten cells, select Edit ⇨ Fill from the Pocket Excel menu and create a downward, series, number fill that has a step value equal to the number of miles between oil changes. So, for example, if you change your oil every 3000 miles, enter 3000. Press ok and Pocket Excel will calculate your mileage for the next nine oil changes. Tap cell A2 and drag down nine more rows until you meet the end of the calculated mileage numbers. Select Edit ⇨ Fill, and press ok to have Pocket Excel quickly copy the text into all of the selected cells. Move to cell B12 (the cell directly below your last oil change entry) and create a new entry for check up. Follow the process that you used on the oil change records to create ten entries for this item and then repeat any upcoming service for which your automobile is scheduled.

When you have finished your list, you will have a complete itinerary of scheduled maintenance that is sorted by item name, rather than by chronological order. You can quickly rearrange the order so that it appears in the order that the maintenance should occur. Tap-and-hold the title of column A, and then drag your stylus over to column B to select the first two columns of the spreadsheet. Select Tools ⇨ Sort and set the application to sort by column B ascending and check the Exclude header row from sort option. When you check this option, Pocket Excel recognizes that the top row is a header, and resets the Sort by window to Mileage. Press ok and Pocket Excel will rearrange the list of maintenance items in the sequence that they should be performed based on your car's odometer.

At this point, your maintenance sheet is complete. The date and cost fields are designed to record the charges and day of service for each maintenance item that you have performed on your vehicle. These should be entered when each service is performed to provide a complete service record. Figure 11.13 is an example of a complete maintenance sheet with three of the first services performed on the vehicle. I used the full screen feature (View ⇨ Full Screen) to display all of the spreadsheet details in this illustration.

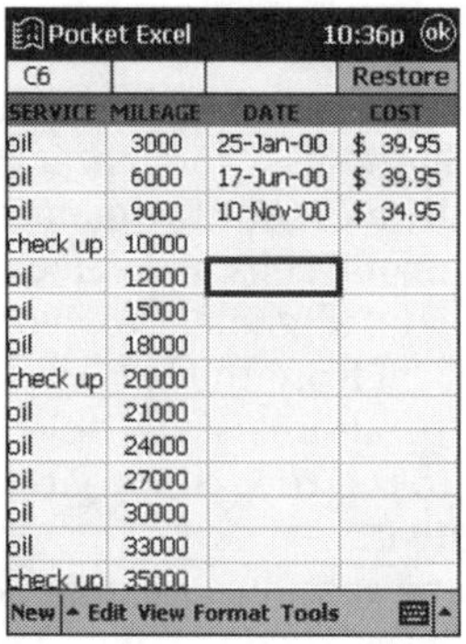

Figure 11.13 The completed maintenance sheet

The fuel economy sheet

Create another sheet (Format ⇨ Modify Sheets ⇨ Insert) called Fuel to track the refueling costs and frequency. After the sheet is created, return to the maintenance sheet (View ⇨ Sheet ⇨ Maintenance) and highlight the headers in the top row. Select Edit ⇨ Copy and then return to your fuel sheet (View ⇨ Sheet ⇨ Fuel). Use the stylus to select the first four cells in row 1 and select Edit ⇨ Paste Special. Because we want to duplicate the design of the previous sheet, but not the cell text, select Formats and press Ok. This will create the gray-filled cells at the top of the screen. From left to right, enter **Date**, **Gal**, **Price**, and **Odometer** as the titles in each cell. Next, format the third column (starting at C2) for currency by selecting Format ⇨ Cells ⇨ Number tab ⇨ Currency.

That is all you needed to do to create a fuel economy entry sheet. Now, every time you fill up your car, quickly record the date, the number of gallons, the price, and the car's odometer reading. Figure 11.14 shows a finished and populated fuel economy sheet. Again, I used the full screen feature to display all of the columns.

Figure 11.14 The fuel economy sheet

The summary sheet

Now that you are tracking all of this information, you will probably want to pull it all together on to one screen that sums up your vehicle usage habits. To do so, create another sheet (Format ➪ Modify Sheets ➪ Insert) called **Summary**. Use the Move Up button on the Modify Sheets screen to push the summary page to the top. This will place Summary first on the list when you change sheets.

Note

Pocket Excel remembers the last worksheet you were viewing and automatically loads that page the next time you open the file.

Because this sheet will be used extensively, it will be set up with a clean and simple style of organization. To begin, create titles for the data in column A by entering these titles into the following cells:

- Cell A1: **Fuel efficiency**
- Cell A2: **Miles per gallon**
- Cell A3: **Number of fill-ups**
- Cell A4: **Cost per mile**
- Cell A5: **Service**
- Cell A6: **Total maintenance**
- Cell A7: **Since**

- Cell A8: **Mileage tax write-off and rebate**
- Cell A9: **Deduction (per mile)**
- Cell A10: **Business miles**
- Cell A11: **Total deduction**
- Cell A12: **Tax bracket**
- Cell A13: **Effective rebate**
- Cell A14: **% used for business**

Next, format row 1 as a title by tapping the row heading on the left side of the screen and selecting Format ➪ Cells. Activate the Bold checkbox on the Font tab, and set the fill to Gray 50% on the Borders tab. When finished, press Ok to apply the formatting. Then select Edit ➪ Copy to paste it to the clipboard. Select row 5 by tapping the row heading and select Edit ➪ Paste Special ➪ Formats to apply the bold font and fill styles to the Service header without deleting the text from cell A5. Repeat this procedure for row 8.

Now that you have set up the text descriptions for the summary page, it is time to create the calculations. To quickly organize the calculations on the summary sheet, you need to define a set of names on the various sheets we have just created. Using names will enable you to quickly refer to entire sets of data, without having to enter a page name or locate the specific cell range. First, ensure that you still have the MileageTotal name that you created earlier by selecting Tools ➪ Define Name and checking for the name in the list.

Switch to the Maintenance sheet and highlight column D by tapping its heading at the top of the page. Select Tools ➪ Define Name and then enter **MaintenanceCost** (without a space) and press Add. Switch to the Fuel sheet and follow the same instructions on columns B, C, and D to create ranges named **Gallons**, **FuelCost**, and **Odometer**. If you would like to check your work, create a new sheet (Format ➪ Modify Sheets ➪ Insert) and then paste all of the names onto the new sheet (Tools ➪ Define Name ➪ Paste List).

Your list should match Figure 11.15 precisely. Note how Pocket Excel includes page and cell references for each name. This enables the application to locate the original data, no matter where you use the name alias. That will come in handy on our summary page, because Pocket Excel will be traveling across all of our sheets to obtain the information.

Note

If any of your names are followed by "formula error!" you may have made a mistake when you created the name. Repeat the process in the text for selecting and creating the name for the ranges.

Now that you have all of your names prepared, it is time for the most exciting part of this exercise: the finale. All you need to do is enter a few formulas and format the cells to complete the Pocket Excel spreadsheet. To prepare the sheet, enter your tax-deductible per-mile expense (usually $0.325) and your tax bracket as decimals (.32 for a 32 percent bracket) in cell B9 and cell B12, respectively.

Figure 11.15 The complete name list

Tip

If you work for a corporation and plan to expense all of the mileage, simply enter the amount that your company pays per mile in cell B1 and you can instantly see how much money you will receive back when your expense check arrives.

The list below contains a complete set of Pocket Excel formulas for the summary sheet. Enter them into the cells as listed, taking special care to include the equals sign and parentheses as noted.

- Cell B2: =(MAX(Odometer)–MIN(Odometer))/SUM(Gallons)

- Cell B3: =COUNT(Gallons)

- Cell B4: =SUM(FuelCost)/(MAX(Odometer)–MIN(Odometer))

- Cell B6: =SUM(MaintenanceCost)

- Cell B7: =Maintenance!C2

- Cell B10: =MileageTotal

- Cell B11: =B9*B10

- Cell B13: =B11*B12

- Cell B14: =B10/(MAX(Odometer)–MIN(Odometer))

Finally, modify cell B4 to display totals in dollar amounts by highlighting it with the stylus, selecting Format ⇨ Cells ⇨ Number tab, and changing the Category to Currency. Leave the decimal places set at 2 and press Ok to apply the formatting. While the cell is still selected, choose Edit ⇨ Copy, tap cell B6, and then select Edit ⇨ Paste Special ⇨ Formats to copy the currency formatting you just created. Repeat this procedure on cells B9, B11, and B13. After that, format cells B8 and B10 to display as percentages.

When you finish this formatting, you should have one of the most impressive automobile tracking spreadsheets ever developed, and have gained — by experience — a thorough knowledge of just how powerful Pocket Excel can be. Figure 11.16 is an example summary sheet created by following the previous instructions. You may want to customize the screen to fit your personal information needs or spend some more time formatting the headers or text to meet your taste. Do so as you wish, and then go to the next section to learn to save the file as a template.

Pocket Excel				6:32p (ok)
C1				Restore
Fuel efficiency				
Miles per gallon		19.78214245		
Number of fill-ups		3		
Cost per mile	$	0.14		
Service				
Total maintenance	$	151.85		
Since		1/25/00		
Mileage tax write-off & rebate				
Deduction (per mile)		$0.32		
Business miles		6888		
Total deduction		$2,204.16		
Tax bracket		32%		
Effective rebate		$705.33		
% used for business		66.66%		
New	▲ Edit View Format Tools			

Figure 11.16 The summary sheet

Save as a template

Now that you have created a spreadsheet masterpiece, you should save it so that it is available in Pocket Excel for future use. Select Tools ⇨ Save Workbook As. You should differentiate it from the Vehicle Mileage Log by giving it a different file name. I recommend Automobile Compendium because it represents all of the powerful features of your new vehicle-tracking spreadsheet and it sounds cool. In the Folder drop-down box, select Templates, and then change the Type to Pocket Excel template and press Ok to save the file.

When loaded, Pocket Excel templates will prompt you for a new filename once you start to enter data into them. If you have more than one automobile, you should create a new spreadsheet for each car. I recommend using a naming convention such as carname_yr2001 so that you can track your car's maintenance costs and fuel efficiency for each year.

Tip

After you have created this spreadsheet, feel free to beam it to friends that own Pocket PCs to show them how adept you are with Pocket Excel!

The Calculator: A no-frills freebie with a priceless feature

Not to be neglected, the Pocket PC's simple but elegant Calculator is a great tool for straightforward math problems. Accessible via Start ⇨ Programs ⇨ Calculator, the program is undoubtedly the quickest to load and the easiest to use. However, one feature that most users unknowingly overlook is its capability to copy the answer to a calculation. For example, if you are writing a contract in Pocket Word and want to quickly calculate tax on merchandise, activate the calculator, quickly punch in the cost of the merchandise, and then multiply it by your state tax percentage. Now, most people would simply memorize this number, switch back to Pocket Word, and enter the number manually. But there is a faster way: Select Edit ⇨ Copy in the Calculator and the answer is automatically stored in Pocket PC memory. When you switch back to Pocket Word (or whatever application you may have been using) select Edit ⇨ Paste. The answer to your calculation is quickly inserted where the cursor is positioned.

Learning Common Features in Pocket Word and Pocket Excel

Because Pocket Word and Pocket Excel are document creation and viewing applications, they share some common features that deliver the power of the desktop versions of Microsoft Office to your handheld. First, both applications can open and save files in desktop formats. This means that you can receive files as e-mail attachments from desktop users and open them without any conversion utility; conversely, you can send files to desktop computer users in a format that they can open. In addition to their native Pocket Format, the applications can save to these file formats:

- **Pocket Excel:** Pocket Excel v1.0 (Handheld PC), Microsoft Excel v5.0/95/97/2000 workbooks, and Microsoft Excel v5.0/95/97/2000 templates
- **Pocket Word:** Plain text (.txt), Rich Text Format (.rtf), and Microsoft Word v6.0/95/972000

To save a file in an alternate format, open the document and select Tools ⇨ Save Document As in Pocket Word, or select Tools ⇨ Save Workbook As in Pocket Excel. The Type drop-down box offers the various file formats, but be sure to change the name of the file before you save it so that you do not overwrite your original document.

Tip

If you are trying to send a word document to someone that does not own Microsoft Word, use Rich Text Format (.rtf) if they own a competing word processing application or use plain text (.txt) if they do not own a word processing application.

In addition to the file formats, Pocket Excel and Pocket Word have advanced file management options available in each application's toolbar. While working on any document, you can return the document to its original saved version by selecting Tools ⇨ Revert to Saved. This enables you to erase any changes you have made and returns the document to the state it was in when you first opened it. Alternately, you can delete a file when the document is open and you select Tools ⇨ Delete Document. This is an extremely fast way to delete a document after you have opened it to ensure that you no longer need it. The Revert to Saved and Delete options both have a confirmation dialog that appears before performing the permanent action.

Tip

An excellent way to free memory on your device is to sequentially open documents and to select Tools ⇨ Delete Document when you encounter files that you no longer need.

Open documents can also be transmitted via infrared and e-mail with two quick taps of the stylus. Tools ⇨ Send via Infrared establishes an infrared communications system with another Pocket PC and transfers the open file without any further interaction from the user. Tools ⇨ Send via E-mail creates a new e-mail with the open file as an attachment and places the cursor in the e-mail's To: field. You can also enter a subject and message to the recipient and press Send to dispatch the message. Both options save the file on your local device before transmitting it.

Last, but certainly not least, both applications sport a Find and Replace feature that enables you to quickly search a document for a phrase or variable. Settings enable you to match the case and to return only responses what contain the entire search criteria. Pocket Excel also lets you distinguish between values and formulas when you perform a search. You can access this feature in both applications via Edit ⇨ Find/Replace. After you enter search criteria and launch the feature, a special toolbar is inserted at the bottom of the application window. Figure 11.17 shows the toolbar during a Replace event. When you perform a Find function, the Replace and Replace All buttons (shown in Figure 11.17) are grayed out and nonfunctional. Pressing Next moves you to the next instance of the item you searched for.

Figure 11.17 The Replace feature in Pocket Word

Working With Pocket Money: Throw Away Your Check Register

Pocket Money is a little sibling to the desktop application Microsoft Money. Designed to be capable of functioning single-handedly as a personal finance manager, Pocket Money will help you track your expenses, balance your checkbook, and monitor your investments from anywhere in the world. When combined with the desktop version of Money, Pocket Money synchronizes account balances, updates portfolio values, and transmits any expenses entered on the Pocket PC into the desktop for permanent storage, saving space on the handheld device. But regardless of how you use the Pocket Money application, there are a couple of features that equate this application to the best financial advisors money can buy.

Warning

If you plan to synchronize your financial data with the desktop version of Microsoft Money, be sure to set up synchronization before using Pocket Money. Synchronization can be established by inserting the ActiveSync CD-ROM into your desktop's CD-ROM drive and running the synchronization set up program (\Extras\MSMoney\pocketpc\setup.exe). Synchronizing after you have already entered data into Pocket Money may erase that data.

Managing accounts

While synchronization from the desktop is the easiest way to set up accounts on Pocket Money, you can create, edit, and delete accounts on your Pocket PC. To create a new account, select Account Manager from the Pocket Money drop-down box in the upper-left corner and tap New. The default tab, Required, provides fields for the account name, type, opening balance, and interest rate. Pocket Money supports cash, checking, credit card, line of credit and savings accounts. If you select credit card or line of credit as the account type, you can also enter the credit limit. The Optional tab, in the Account Details window, stores your account number, institution name, contact name, and phone number.

Tip

If you fill out the information in the Options tab when setting up the account, you will have the complete account details available should you lose your checkbook or bankcard while traveling.

To edit the information in an existing account, select Account Manager from the Pocket Money drop-down box in the upper-left corner, tap-and-hold the account you wish to edit, and select Edit Details from the pop-up menu. If you synchronize with the desktop version of Money, any changes you make to the account details will be copied to the desktop on your next synchronization. You cannot change the account type on accounts that synchronize with the desktop version of Money; accounts that have online banking features enabled on the desktop version of Microsoft Money should not be edited on your Pocket PC.

If you use Pocket Money as a stand-alone financial manager, you can delete accounts from your Pocket PC. When you delete an account, all of the transactions within that account are erased. To delete an existing account, select Account Manager from the Pocket Money drop-down box in the upper-left corner, tap and hold the account that you wish to edit, and select Delete Account from the pop-up menu. To permanently delete an account from a device that is synchronizing Money data, open Microsoft Money on the desktop and delete the account. At the next synchronization, the account will be erased from Pocket Money.

If you want to remove an account from Pocket Money, but not permanently delete it from the desktop version, open the ActiveSync window on your desktop and select Tools ⇨ Options. Double-click the Microsoft Money Data item and uncheck the accounts that you wish to remove. The accounts will be removed from Pocket Money at your next synchronization.

Enter transactions 90 percent faster with AutoComplete+

One of the coolest features of Pocket Money is AutoComplete+. When activated (select the Use AutoComplete+ checkbox in Tools ⇨ Options), Pocket Money compares the payee name that you are currently typing in with all past transactions. If it finds a match, it completes the name and automatically enters the last amount you paid, the category and subcategory for the transaction, and it enter the next check number if the last transaction was paid by check.

Figure 11.18 shows AutoComplete+ finishing Safeway, a grocery store where I shop. On the Payee line, you can see that I have typed the first three letters of the store name, and AutoComplete+ has already entered the rest of the name, along with $100.70 in the Amount line, from my previous purchase at the store. If I switch to the Optional tab, you would see that the Category (Groceries) is already filled in and Pocket Money has already entered in the next check number from my register because it knows I always pay by check.

Figure 11.18 The AutoComplete+ feature

Note

If AutoComplete+ is displaying an incorrect listing for the payee, simply keep typing the name of the person to whom the check is being written. After you enter in a character that is different than the payee AutoComplete+ has entered, it clears all of the fields and enables you to manually enter the amount and category information.

Update your portfolio value while on the go

Whether you are a daytrader or a casual investor, Pocket Money can track your entire portfolio from the palm of your hand. Pocket Money has the capability to download the stock prices from the desktop computer and to gather the current investment prices (delayed by 20 minutes) directly from the Internet. To begin, make sure that you have set up an Internet connection on the Pocket PC.

Cross-Reference

For complete information on how to set up a connection to the Internet, refer to the "Online Services and the Internet" section of Chapter 16.

Next, select the Investments option from the drop-down menu at the top of the Pocket Money application. Figure 11.19 displays the Pocket Money Investments window. If a list of your current investments already appears similar to the example, you are all set. Otherwise, press New and enter the name, symbol, and number of shares that you currently hold for each stock (do not worry about the stock price; Pocket Money will get that the next time you connect). After you have entered all of your investments, connect to the Internet and press the Update Quotes button on the Pocket Money tool bar. The application will display a message notifying you that it is connecting to the MSN MoneyCentral Web site. After the connection is completed, the individual stock price, total value, and your portfolio market value are all automatically updated to give you an at-a-glance view of your financial holdings.

Figure 11.19 The Pocket Money Investments feature

If you do not have an Internet connection, or if you have an employee stock option that is not traded on one of the major markets, tapping an individual stock and entering the new per share price in the last price field will manually update the stock price. Pocket Money automatically multiplies the price times the number of shares you own and update the total value and your portfolio value after you press Ok.

Tip

Even if you don't use Pocket Money to track expenses, you can still use the Investments section to monitor your stocks.

Password protection

Because of the confidentiality of financial information, Pocket Money enables you to password protect the entire application. While running the application, select Tools ⇨ Password, enter the same password twice, and press Ok to save your changes. Pocket Money will not request a password for access to the application until you have closed the program and reopened it. This means that to activate the password feature you must completely exit the program (switching to another application does not exit the program) or perform a soft reset on the device. To exit the program select Start ⇨ Settings ⇨ System ⇨ Memory ⇨ Running Programs, highlight the Money application by tapping it, and then press Stop.

Tip

For a much faster way to close Pocket Money, activate the keyboard and press Ctrl+q.

To remove Pocket Money's password protection, open the application and select Tools ⇨ Password. The existing password will appear (in asterisks) in the top field. Erase all of the asterisks and press Ok to save your changes. The program is now freely accessible with no password required.

Summary

By now, you should have extensive knowledge of how to put the Pocket Office suite to work for you in a corporate or personal setting. In addition, you have learned a few special techniques that enable you to use professional tools such as the Voice Recorder and Calculator in an innovative and exciting way.

In Chapter 12, we explore the advanced features of the applications dedicated to leisure-time activities such as reading and listening to music.

CHAPTER 12

Media Player and Reader: Satisfy Your Senses with Personal Content

IN THIS CHAPTER
- Learning the Media Player
- Customising your tune machine
- Supercharging Pocket Reader
- Highlighting, commenting, and bookmarking your e-books
- Getting customized content from Slate
- Managing e-books on your device
- Developing e-books of your own

Until now, this book has focused on the professional uses for the Pocket PC. But the Pocket PC is far more than just a business tool. Because it will quickly become your constant companion, the Pocket PC helps to satisfy your entertainment and information needs as well. Media Player and Reader offer music and literary refinement anytime and anywhere.

Tip

If you find yourself using the audio features of the Media Player or Reader application often, consider purchasing a cassette adaptor for your car stereo. Available from Radio Shack and most electronics stores for under $10, the cassette adaptor plugs into your Pocket PC audio jack and enables you to listen to music and audio books through your home or car stereo's cassette player.

Getting More Bang for Your Buck from the Media Player

Designed to play the popular MP3 music that is available over the Internet, the Pocket PC Media Player application primarily functions as a replacement for a portable CD player. Music, once downloaded to your desktop computer, can be copied to the device using ActiveSync, just as any other file is copied. But a more compelling method is to use the desktop version of Microsoft's Windows Media Player (version 7.0 or above) because it provides an automated method of selecting and copying music to your Pocket PC. Figure 12.1 shows the portable device tab of the Windows Media Player. As you can see, the audio files on the desktop computer and the Pocket PC are displayed in separate windows, with a meter displaying the available Pocket PC memory directly below. Drop-down boxes above each window enable you to select the music listed in the desktop window by genre (in this example, Rock) or CD title, or to change to a different device if you have more than one Pocket PC connected to your computer. This application also reveals the actual size of each file on the Pocket PC and enables you to delete them individually.

Tip

If you do not want to use the desktop version of Windows Media Player, but want an automated way to conserve memory and transfer music files, install the Windows Media Manager (available in the ActiveSync CD \Extras\Media folder). It converts MP3 files to the Windows Media Audio (WMA) format and copies them to your device. Plus, it's free, and you already have it on a CD-ROM that came with your Pocket PC!

Figure 12.1 Windows Media Player (desktop version)

Before copying the files to the Pocket PC, Windows Media Player automatically converts MP3 music to Microsoft's proprietary WMA format. The WMA format offers higher compression, which, in plain English, enables you to fit more music on your device and to conserve memory. Naturally, people planning to use the Pocket PC Media Player extensively should invest in a high-capacity memory card to store their music on and they should use the WMA format for higher compression. Because the conversion process considers the available space on your device it will, occasionally, compress a file to a quality that music purists may find substandard. Should this occur, open the desktop Media Player, select Tools ➪ Options ➪ Portable Device tab, and then choose the "Select quality level" radio button. Now you can manually control the quality of the conversion by moving the slider from smallest size to best quality.

Cross-Reference

For a power-saving Pocket PC Media Player tip only available to HP Jornada users, see Chapter 21.

If, for some reason, you wish to forgo the use of automated MP3 installation programs, you can manually copy MP3 or WMA files directly to your Pocket PC using ActiveSync. Dock your Pocket PC with your desktop, open the ActiveSync window, and select File ➪ Explore. If you are copying the music files to main memory, you can drag and drop files directly into the window that appears, which is the My Documents folder on your Pocket PC, or create a subdirectory within that folder. If you wish to copy the songs to a memory card, double-click the My Pocket PC icon in the pop-up window and select Storage Card from the list of folders. If the My Documents folder appears in the resulting window, open it, otherwise select File ➪ New Folder in this window to add a folder named My Documents. Copying the music to this folder transfers the files directly to your device's storage card.

Note

Music files must be stored in the My Documents folder or in one subdirectory in the My Documents folder in your device's main memory or the memory card. If you have copied songs to your Pocket PC and they do not show up in your All My Music playlist (see "Create Customized Playlists" later in this chapter), check to make sure that the songs are in the My Documents folder or inside a file folder that resides within My Documents.

Creating digital music from your own CDs

If you do not have a high-speed connection to the Internet, you may wish to convert your existing CD music collection to WMA format, rather than spending hours downloading music from the Internet. Because you can legally make a copy of music that you have purchased, this is a lawful and moral way to compile music on your Pocket PC. To copy an audio CD, insert the disc into your computer's CD-ROM drive and launch Windows Media Player on your desktop. Select the CD Audio option. If you are connected to the Internet, Windows Media will attempt to download the track titles and artist information for the CD in the drive. By default, it automatically selects all of the tracks for conversion. Deactivate the checkboxes of the CD tracks that you do not wish to copy to your computer and then click on the Copy Music button. This will begin converting the tracks on your CD to WMA format. Most computers support the capability to listen to the audio tracks while the music is being recorded to the hard drive.

When the music has been copied to your desktop computer, Windows Media Player automatically makes it available in your music library. You may now use the method described earlier to copy the digital music to your Pocket PC. It is important to note that electronic music files created using this method have a digital license attached to them that permits you to play them on the single desktop computer and the Pocket PC that you have a partnership with. In other words, you will not be able to trade these files between Pocket PCs via infrared.

Create customized playlists

After you have digitized and downloaded your entire music collection to your Pocket PC, you undoubtedly need a way to manage your electronic concert hall. The Media Player includes a Playlist feature that enables you organize files into music sets that you can play and organize onboard your Pocket PC. To compile a new set of music, select Playlist from the Media Player command bar. By default, Media Player creates an All My Music playlist that contains every song on your Pocket PC.

To create a custom playlist, tap the All My Music drop-down menu in the upper-left corner of the screen and select All Playlists. Although not intuitive, this option takes you to the screen for creating a new playlist or for renaming and deleting existing ones. Tap the New button and Media Player prompts you to enter a name for the new playlist you are about to create. After you enter the name, Media Player automatically provides a complete list of all of your music. Activate the checkboxes for the songs that you wish to add to the new playlist and press Ok. After you have selected songs, you will be returned to the Media Player Playlist screen, where you can arrange the order of the songs in your playlist.

Tip

While the playlist is open, you can tap and hold any song to activate a pop-up menu with options to play, to move the track up or down in the playlist, or to delete the song from the playlist (this feature does not delete the file from your Pocket PC).

Working with memory cards and digital music

If you have a playlist that contains songs in main memory and on a memory card, the Media Player will automatically detect when the memory card is inserted. If the card is not installed, the application will automatically skip songs on the memory card. In addition, when you open the list by selecting Playlist from the command bar, Media Player will identify which songs are not available by graying out their filename. Should you insert the memory card into your Pocket PC while viewing the playlist, Media Player will detect the song and instantly reset the song's font to black. This can be useful in locating a particular song if you have many identical memory cards and do not know on which one a particular song resides.

Note

If the first or last song in a playlist is on a memory card and the memory card is not inserted, Media Player will not be capable of play on continuous play.

Sharing playlists

After you have created a playlist, you can share it with other Pocket PC users. Although the other users do not need to have all of the songs on your playlist installed on the second device, at least one music file must be in the identical directory on their Pocket PC and have the same filename for this option to work. To transfer your playlist, launch File Explorer by choosing Start ➪ Programs ➪ File Explorer and locate the playlist in your My Documents folder. The playlists are easily identifiable in the file listing because the filename is the playlist name, and all playlists have a musical note superimposed on a page icon. Tap and hold the playlist that you wish to send and then select Send via Infrared. When the recipient activates infrared receive on their Pocket PC, the file is automatically downloaded to the appropriate directory.

To activate the playlist on their device, your friends will need to launch Media Player, select Playlist ➪ All My Music ➪ All Playlists, and then highlight the name of the playlist. When they tap the Ok, the playlist is imported into Media Player and all music installed on their device appears in black type. Music not available appears grayed out. Selecting the first available song and pressing the Play icon in the command bar will start the music. This technique is a great way to create a mix of music for friends. One step better is to quickly beam them your playlist and insert the card into their device. Now your friends can enjoy your entire song collection on their device in just moments!

Note

If you have activated File Synchronization on your desktop, ActiveSync will copy the playlist to your desktop computer when you synchronize. This makes a backup copy of your music sets should your device ever lose data. The playlist files can be identified on your desktop computer by the .pmp file extension.

Customizing Your Tune Machine with Skin Chooser

After using the Pocket PC Media Player for awhile, you will probably become bored with the bright rainbow-colored interface. The Skin Chooser application enables you to customize the look and feel of the Media Player quickly and easily. Skins (a cool term for the different styles that you can give to the Media Player) are available, for free, in the "download" section of www.pocketpc.com. After you have found and downloaded an individual skin, double-click the file to open it and extract the contents (by default, skins usually extract to a folder named c:\skins\[*skin name*]). Connect your Pocket PC to the desktop and copy the entire folder to the Pocket PC's \ Program Files\Windows Media Player\ folder so that it creates a subdirectory within the Windows Media Player folder.

After you have copied one or more skins to the Pocket PC, activate the Skin Chooser, which is shown in Figure 12.2. The drop-down menu enables you to select a skin by name, and the left and right arrows scroll through all of the skins installed on the device. The application offers a preview of what Media Player will look like with the skin applied. When you have found the skin that you would like to use, press Ok. Skin Chooser will employ the new skin the next time that Pocket PC Media Player is run. To remove the skin, activate the Skin Chooser application and select Original Skin (factory default) from the drop-down list and then delete the entire skin folder from the \Program Files\Windows Media Player\ directory.

Figure 12.2 The Skin Chooser

Note

If on startup of the Skin Chooser application you receive a message that states "the selected skin can not be found, the default skin will be used instead," simply press Ok to dismiss the message. This is a standard error when the application is first run or if a skin has been removed from the system that Media Player was previously using.

> ## Get the Skin Chooser
>
> The Skin Chooser is available as a free download on www.pocketpc.com in the PowerToys software section. It is also included in the Pocket PC Fun Pack, available from www.pocketpc.com. You should obtain and install this application before using the instructions in this section to install a skin. For more information on PowerToys, see Chapter 15.

Upgrade Media Player for Streaming Audio and Video

A new version of the Microsoft Windows Media Player for Pocket PC that supports streaming audio and video is available. This means that while connected to the Internet, you can listen to audio and video as it downloads to your device. This method is far superior to downloading the entire file to your Pocket PC before you can listen to it. The addition of video capabilities makes this upgrade a must-have software application. The upgrade for Media Player is available at no charge from www.microsoft.com/mobile/pocketpc/downloads/.

After you have downloaded the application to your desktop and installed it on your Pocket PC, Media Player will automatically launch if you click on a link to a Windows Media file in Pocket Internet Explorer. Files can also be copied from your desktop to your Pocket PC for repeated playback. Windows Media files can be identified on Web sites and your local hard drive as files with .wma, .asf, and .wmv extensions. The File ⇨ Open command enables you to browse your Pocket PC memory for video files, and File ⇨ Open URL enables you to enter a URL if you happen to know the Web address of a Windows Media file.

Note

For an extensive list of video and audio files in the correct format, surf to www.windowsmedia.com.

Figure 12.3 is an example of streaming video on the Media Player application. Notice that the large controls that are normally available have been replaced with VCR-style buttons at the bottom of the screen. The upgraded version of Media Player enables you to jump to a specific location in the video by moving the slider (called a *tracker bar*). It also adjusts the volume with slider and mute (by tapping the speaker icon) controls. In addition to Play, Pause, and Stop, you can skip between sections of the program or to the beginning and end of the video using the forward and back controls.

Figure 12.3 Streaming video on Media Player

To maximize your viewing experience, each of the controls can be removed from the screen in piecemeal fashion. Media Player also has a full screen display option that removes all of the onscreen controls, including the menu bar, and expands the video to fit the width of the Pocket PC screen. Tapping the screen anywhere restores the controls. A repeat play feature rolls the video in a continuous loop, which is excellent for showing off to your friends as you hand the device around, or at a trade show.

Note

Even if you set the Windows Media Player to repeat play, the Pocket PC is smart enough to automatically turn off the device after the preset delay. If you wish to disable this feature so that you can continuously playback video, select Start ➪ Settings ➪ System tab ➪ Power and deactivate the turn off device checkbox.

If you have downloaded a Moving Pictures Experts Group (MPEG) video file to your desktop computer, you can convert it to Windows Media Video format by downloading the Microsoft Windows Media Encoder or by purchasing Windows Movie Maker. When converting video, compress the video portion of the files to 128 kbps total bandwidth, 240×180 resolution, and 15 frames per second. The audio settings should be adjusted to 22 KHz and 22 kbps mono, and the file should be saved in Windows Media Video version 7 format.

Cross-Reference

For information on how to play MPEG video on your Pocket PC without any file conversion, read about PocketTV in Chapter 18.

Supercharging Pocket Reader

Although one of the greatest strengths of the Pocket PC is that it works perfectly right out-of-the-box, there are a few features in the Pocket Reader application that require a little preparation to get the full benefit from your e-book experience.

Naturally, this can be accomplished without purchasing any extra accessories. All you need is a little time and the ActiveSync CD that came with your Pocket PC.

Fine-tune the text readability

Pocket Reader uses ClearType, a technology that enhances the readability of the text in an e-book. To make the ClearType text display as crisp and clear as possible, the Pocket PC must be set to a precise contrast setting. To begin, launch Pocket Reader (Start ➪ Programs ➪ Microsoft Reader) and open an e-book. Scroll to a page that is filled, from top to bottom, with text. Take a moment to examine the text, specifically studying characters with diagonal strokes such as v and w. These characters should not appear light or blurry when compared to other letters on the page.

Cross-Reference

For complete information on how to develop an e-book that specifically takes advantage of the ClearType technology in Pocket Reader, read the "Tips for designing an eBook for optimal viewing on Pocket PCs" section of Chapter 20.

If the diagonal characters do not appear clear, or if you would like to change the settings to suit your personal taste, perform the following steps:

1. Select Start ➪ Settings ➪ System tab ➪ Contrast.

2. In the Contrast applet, make a note of the current slider position so that you can return the Pocket PC to this setting should changing the contrast adversely affect the ClearType text.

3. If the diagonal characters appeared lighter or blurrier than the other characters, move the contrast slider seven clicks to the right. If all text on the page appeared too bold, or the e-book page show signs of gray vertical lines running down the screen on top of the text, move the slider seven clicks to the left.

4. Press Ok to save the changes. Next, tap the Start menu and select the Pocket Reader icon from the Start menu shortcut bar. When you switch to Pocket Reader, you will instantly see the difference in the text clarity.

Repeat the process above, decreasing the number of clicks that you adjust the contrast slider each time until you have found the optimal contrast setting for reading e-books. It is important to know that the best contrast setting for reading e-books may not be different than the optimal contrast for regular Pocket PC use.

Cross-Reference

Using the HP settings feature, users can create a customized scheme that includes contrast settings that can be activated when reading an e-book and then reset to a different scheme for normal Pocket PC use. For information on this feature, see Chapter 17.

Install a free e-book dictionary and audio book player

The Pocket PC Reader has a number of surprising features hidden inside of the application. One of the best features is the context-sensitive Encarta Pocket Dictionary, which instantly looks up a word while you're reading any e-book. Figure 12.4 shows the Dictionary Lookup feature activated within the Two Fairy Tales novel. Particularly important is that you need not avert your eyes from the book text to find a definition.

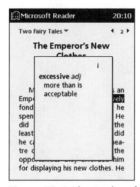

Figure 12.4 The Lookup feature

To install the dictionary, insert the ActiveSync v3.1 CD-ROM that came with your Pocket PC and open the \Extras\MSReader\books\ folder. Copy the msebdict.lit file to your My Documents folder in the Pocket PC or onto a My Documents folder on a memory card. Now activate the Reader application and open an e-book. When you tap and hold any word and select Lookup from the pop-up list that appears, a complete dictionary definition will appear before your eyes. Alternately, you can select Encarta Pocket Dictionary from the list of books that appear in your library. This provides a 90,000-word dictionary at your fingertips without having to lug around a phone-directory-sized book.

Tip

In addition to the Encarta Pocket Dictionary, the ActiveSync CD-ROM comes with almost 30 novels that you can download to your Pocket PC. Open the \Extras\ MSReader\books folder to find them all!

Playing audio books on the Media Player

A secondary and even lesser-known feature of the Pocket PC Media Player is its capability to play audio books (also known as books-on-tape). Popular with commuters and the visually impaired, audio books are an excellent alternative to reading novel-length stories on the small Pocket PC screen. Instead of using a cassette tape, the audio books are downloaded to the Pocket PC electronically via the Internet. An additional benefit of the electronic format is that more timely information is available, such as daily news from *The Wall Street Journal* or *The New York Times*. Figure 12.5 shows the out-of-the-way Reader audio book screen with an e-book from *The Wall Street Journal* that delivers the morning news and information. Controls at the bottom of the screen offer Play, Pause, Rewind, and Fast-Forward features, similar to VCR controls.

Figure 12.5 The Audio Book feature

Tip

Holding down the Fast-Forward or Rewind buttons when an audio book is loaded moves through the programming in increasing increments as you continue to press the buttons. An audio voice announces the increments once you have pressed the button long enough to reach one minute, and will continue to verbally guide you until you have reached the end of the audio file.

Like the music files, the audio books have a desktop companion that aids the purchase, download, and transfer of the files to the Pocket PC. The software is available from www.audible.com and can be downloaded or mailed to you (via USPS mail to U.S. residents only) free of charge. As you might expect, audio content is available separately for a fee. Electronic audio books cost significantly less than their cassette-tape counterparts and daily news and information services offer subscriptions at a discounted rate.

Highlight, Comment, and Bookmark Your E-books

Have you ever wanted to write or draw in the sidebar of a book to make notes you could refer to later? How about highlighting a section of text or being able to type entire text messages that you can scroll through after you have finished the book? Well, Microsoft Reader for the Pocket PC accommodates all those needs and more. Highlight a word, phrase, or entire paragraph using the stylus, and then tap and hold the selection. Options on the pop-up menu include adding a bookmark, highlight, note, and drawing.

Bookmarks, as you might expect, are simply the equivalent of a dog-eared page. When you create a bookmark, a colored square icon is added to the right column of the e-book. Figure 12.6 shows an e-book with three bookmarks. If you look closely, you will notice that the center bookmark in the screenshot has lines and an arrow icon on it. This is to indicate that you are on the page represented by that bookmark icon. Bookmarks are listed in the order in which they appear in the book and each bookmark appears in a different color. Also shown in Figure 12.6 is highlighting, which enables you to indicate important text with a bright yellow emphasis over the text.

Figure 12.6 Annotations in Pocket Reader

The notes feature in Pocket Reader is roughly equivalent to inserting a sticky note into a book. When selected, a pop-up window appears that only accepts text entered using the soft input panel. While the notes window is open you can jump to the previous or next note with a touch of the button, making it a great method to quickly refresh your memory if you summarize sections of the book in notes. However, the notes window can only accommodate nine lines of text, so notes should be short and concise. A circle with the letter T in the left column identifies notes placed in an e-book. Figure 12.6 shows an example of a note at the top of the page, and an example of drawing at the bottom.

Drawing enables you to create any freeform idea directly over the page of an e-book. When you select Add Drawing from the Reader pop-up menu, an option bar appears at the bottom of the screen as shown in Figure 12.7. The first option on the bar enables you to select from 12 different colors of ink. The second option is Undo, which erases the last drawing stroke you made with the stylus. The third option, Done, closes the option bar and returns you to the e-book. Note also the pen icon in the bottom-left corner of the e-book page. When tapped, this icon hides all of the ink drawing on that page. Tapping and holding this icon displays a menu that enables you to delete or edit the drawing or navigate to the previous or next drawing in the book.

Figure 12.7 Pocket Reader Drawing options

After you have begun using the highlight, comments, and drawing features, you might find yourself with an e-book that is so marked up that it is impossible to read without being distracted. To combat this situation, and to enable you to locate and manage all of the various modifications you can make to an e-book, Microsoft includes an Annotations Index. This index, available from the cover page of each e-book, lists all of the various annotations contained within the tome. Figure 12.8 shows an Annotations Index for the book we were marking up in previous figures. Notice how icons on the left side of the screen enable you to quickly identify bookmarks, text notes, drawings, and highlighting. Annotations are erased from this screen by tapping and holding the item and selecting delete from the pop-up window. Annotations can also be renamed (although the new name will not be shown on the page where the annotation appears, but only in the index) with by tapping and holding an annotation and selecting rename from the pop-up menu.

Figure 12.8 The Annotations Index

Tip

After bookmarking a page, tap the book title at the top of the screen and select Annotations Index from the drop-down list. Find the bookmark you just made and tap and hold that item. Select rename from the list, and enter the current date and time. This way, you will have an easy way to see where you last finished reading, and you will have an entire set of bookmarks that show how quickly your reading has progressed.

If you wish to keep the annotations in an e-book, but would like to turn them off temporarily, open the Microsoft Reader Guidebook and select Quick Settings. In this window, you can individually activate and deactivate bookmarks, notes, drawings and highlights. Quick Settings also enables you to hide the visual guides (the arrows surrounding the page numbers, the down arrow on the book title indicating a drop-down menu, and underlined text to indicate hyperlinks) although I strongly recommend leaving this option on. Hyperlinked text is sometimes difficult to recognize by only a slight difference in color; keeping the Visual Guides options on ensures it will always be underlined. Moreover, the arrows that indicate page turning and drop-down menus do not take up any additional space on the screen. The final feature in the Quick Settings window is the Use Large Font feature. Activating this feature automatically increases the text size by almost 75 percent, and makes the text readable for users with poor eyesight. Try doing that with a paper book!

The other options on the Pocket Reader pop-up menu are Find and Copy Text. The Find feature is extremely useful for quickly locating sections of a book when you can recall partial passages. When you select Find, Reader automatically pre-populates the Find window with the text that was highlighted when you performed the tap-and-hold. Entering text over it using the soft Input panel will erase this text.

One little-known feature is that tapping what appears to be the window title (Find Exact) changes the search to Find Approximate. This searches for words or phrases similar to the one in the search box. Pressing Find First starts the search from the beginning of the e-book, and Find Next begins searching from the current page.

Tip

Open the Encarta Pocket Dictionary and use the Find feature to quickly look up word definitions.

The copy text feature enables you to copy an excerpt from an e-book into the Pocket PC clipboard. This text can then be inserted into an e-mail, a Word document, or a Notes file. The Pocket Reader application will not enable you to copy text that spans more than a single page.

Acquiring Customized Content from Slate

One Web site offering free content in e-book format is Slate, Microsoft's quirky news webzine dedicated to clever commentary on politics and pop culture. Interested readers can download the last seven days of Slate articles at `http://slate.msn.com/e-book/` and uncover special edition e-book compilations on popular topics such as "Sons" (Nicholas Lemann's profiles of George W. Bush and Al Gore that originally appeared in *The New Yorker* in 2000). Moreover, the Slate Web site enables you to create your own customized e-book by selecting individual articles using the My Slate feature of the site and saving them to a single e-book. This advanced feature requires signing up with the Web site and obtaining a Microsoft Passport, which can be accomplished at `http://slate.msn.com/myslate/`. All of the e-books should be copied to the Pocket PC's My Documents folder using ActiveSync.

Managing E-books on your device

Depending on the content in your e-book, the file sizes can range from 20KB to nearly a megabyte per e-book. Obviously, this can wreak havoc on your Pocket PC's memory. Avid readers who are quickly running out of memory because of all the e-books stored on their device should invest in a memory card. The only rule of thumb for storing e-books is that they must reside in the \My Documents\ folder or in a folder created within the \My Documents\ folder. This applies to e-books both in main memory and on a memory card.

Tip

Your entire collection of e-books does not have to reside in the same directory. For example, you could keep your favorite e-books in the Pocket PC's main memory, while storing an alternate set of e-books on the memory card. Likewise, you could create different storage subdirectories for fiction, nonfiction, and reference. All of them will show up in the Reader Library as long as the memory card is installed.

The easiest way to install an e-book is to automatically copy the file from the desktop during synchronization. To do so, activate file synchronization (Tools ➪ Options ➪ Files checkbox) in ActiveSync on your desktop computer. A directory will be created on your computer hard drive within the My Documents folder. This directory will be your Pocket PC's name followed by My Documents. The first time you activate file synchronization, ActiveSync places a shortcut to this folder on the desktop of your computer. This shortcut is the key to quick e-book installation.

If you are installing an e-book from the ActiveSync CD-ROM (as discussed earlier in the "Install a Free E-book Dictionary and Audio Book Player" section), simply insert the CD-ROM and open the \Extras\MSReader\books directory. Resize the file folder window so that you can see the shortcut on your desktop to the Pocket PC file synchronization folder. Now drag the e-book files that you wish to copy to your Pocket PC from the CD-ROM folder to the desktop shortcut. When you release the mouse button, copies will be created in your file sync folder that will be transferred to your Pocket PC upon synchronization.

If you download e-books from the Internet, activate file synchronization as described above and surf to your favorite e-book Web site. After you have purchased a book or found a freeware book that you would like to read, begin the download process in your Web browser. When the browser presents the option of where you would like to save the file, navigate to the Pocket PC file synchronization folder inside My Documents. When the file finishes downloading to your desktop, it will be automatically copied to your Pocket PC.

Tip

Three great Web sites for downloading e-books for the Pocket PC are http://ebooks.barnesandnoble.com/pocketpc/index.asp, www.pocketpcpress.com, and www.dotlit.com.

Removing e-books

Warning

Before removing an e-book from your device, you should ensure that you have a copy of the file on your desktop, especially if you paid for the volume. On the desktop, e-books have an .lit extension to make them easier to identify.

After you have read an e-book, you can delete it in several different ways.

The fastest way to delete an e-book is to tap and hold the book name in the Pocket Reader library. A pop-up menu with only one option appears: Delete. Select this option and Pocket Reader presents you with a delete confirmation dialog box. If you confirm that you want to delete the e-book, Pocket Reader will permanently remove the e-book from your device. An alternate way to remove an e-book from your Pocket PC is to delete the file using File Explorer. This is a more effective method to use when trying to free up memory on the device because you can see how large each file is, and whether it resides in Pocket PC memory or on a memory card. Navigate to your e-book directory, tap and hold a file, and select delete from the pop-up menu. This method also enables you to quickly delete volumes of books by selecting multiple files at one time and deleting them.

From the desktop, you can remove files from the Pocket PC main memory by deleting them from the Pocket PC file synchronization folder when file sync is activated (see the previous section). At the next synchronization, the deleted e-books will be removed from your device. If you do not use file synchronization or store your e-books on a memory card, dock your Pocket PC and select Explore from the ActiveSync window on your desktop. Navigate to the file folder where you store your e-books and delete each file just as you delete items on your desktop.

Note

The Microsoft Reader Guidebook and Two Fairy Tales e-books cannot be deleted from your Pocket PC library. They are burned into the ROM memory on your device.

Exchanging e-books

Transferring e-books between Pocket PCs is even easier. Open File Explorer (Start ➪ Programs ➪ File Explorer) and navigate to your e-book directory. Locate the file that you wish to transfer. If you cannot recognize the e-book by its file-name (some e-books are cryptically named) tap the filename and Pocket Reader will launch and display the cover page for the file that you tapped. Return to the File Explorer by opening the Start menu and selecting the program's icon from the shortcut bar at the top. Tap and hold the file that you wish to transfer and, as with all files on the Pocket PC, the pop-up menu enables you to transfer the file via infrared or e-mail.

Alternately, you can copy the file using a memory card. To do so, select Copy from the pop-up menu. Tap the upper-left drop-down box in File Explorer and select My Device from the directory list. If a memory card is inserted, you should see a directory named Storage Card in the program window. Tap it and paste the e-book (Edit ➪ Paste) into the main directory of the storage card. Now insert the memory card into the second Pocket PC and launch File Explorer. Navigate to the memory card and copy the file (tap and hold ➪ Copy) from the directory. To return to your Pocket PC main memory, tap the upper-left drop-down box in File Explorer, select My Device, and then select the My Documents folder. Insert the e-book in this directory (or any subdirectory within My Documents) by selecting Edit ➪ Paste.

Share annotations via infrared

Just as e-books can be traded, annotations made in the e-book can also be transferred to another Pocket PC. This makes a convenient way to share notes on a book that a friend is reading, or to copy some annotations that you may have jotted down on a friend's device. Although annotations can be transferred using e-mail, or a memory card, this section will explain how to do it using infrared as an example. The steps are essentially the same, regardless of which transfer method you use. To copy annotations to another Pocket PC:

1. Open File Explorer (Start ➪ Programs ➪ File Explorer).

2. Navigate to the directory where your e-books are stored.

Note

Files for the annotations made to the Microsoft Reader Guidebook and Two Fairy Tales books can be found in the Windows directory as files named guidebook and hcaft10, respectively.

3. Locate the e-book filename.

4. If you are sorting by name — tap the upper-right drop-down list in File Explorer and select Name from the sort methods — you should see two files with the same name as shown in Figure 12.9. One file has the Pocket Reader "r" icon (this is the e-book file) while the other has a nondescript Windows logo within a page icon, as highlighted in Figure 12.9. This file contains the annotations.

5. Tap and hold the annotations file and select Send via Infrared.

6. On the receiving device, activate Infrared Receive (Start ⇨ Programs ⇨ Infrared Receive) to capture the file and then launch File Explorer.

7. By default, the file will be deposited in the My Documents folder. Because File Explorer opens that directory when launched, scroll down to locate the file.

8. Tap and hold the file and select Cut from the pop-up menu.

9. In File Explorer, navigate to the directory in which you store your e-books.

10. Tap Edit ⇨ Paste to place the annotations file in this directory.

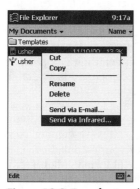

Figure 12.9 Transferring the annotation file

Now, when you launch Pocket Reader, select the e-book title from the library, and open the Annotations Index, you should see a complete list of all of the notes, drawings, bookmarks, and highlighting that was created on the other device. Any annotations that you make to the e-book will be appended to the same file on the Pocket PC. Using this technique, an entire group or class could comment on a writing, one at a time, to create a collaborative annotation volume with everyone's comments.

Tip

If you are running low on memory, you can delete the e-book but save your annotations. Open File Explorer, navigate to the e-book directory, tap and hold the e-book file (denoted by the Pocket Reader "r" icon), and select Delete. You will free up the memory that the e-book was occupying; later, you can reload the e-book from your desktop computer and retain all of the annotations. Deleting the e-book from the Pocket Reader Library erases both the book and the annotations.

Developing E-books of Your Own

If nothing thus far has excited you about the opportunities that the Pocket PC Reader offers, there is one last feature that is sure to provoke enthusiasm from even the most indifferent user. In addition to downloading e-books, audio books, and customized content, you can create your own electronic books for the Pocket PC Reader in just minutes! Using nothing more than your desktop computer and a free application available on the Internet, you can download company guideline manuals and personal information resources, or publish your own novel in Microsoft Reader format.

OverDrive Incorporated has developed an application called ReaderWorks, which converts HTML and Microsoft Word documents into fully functional e-book documents in the Pocket PC's .lit file format. The free version of the application includes a fully functional e-book builder plus a wizard that creates a table of contents automatically. The professional version, named ReaderWorks Publisher includes the capability to add cover art, digital copyright, and marketing information for commercial e-book distribution, and is available for purchase on the company's Web site www.overdrive.com.

To begin, download the ReaderWorks Standard application at www.overdrive.com and install the application on your desktop. Start the application, select the Source Files icon, and add an HTML, MS Word, or text document. Next, select the Properties icon and enter a title and author for your e-book. Now, select File ➪ Build e-book to save your first potential bestseller in .lit format. Microsoft Word documents can also be converted to e-book format easily by selecting File ➪ Print to Microsoft Reader once ReaderWorks has been installed.

Tip

Personalized e-books can be copied to the Pocket PC's My Documents folder using ActiveSync and can be shared with other Pocket PC owners using the Send via Infrared command in the File Explorer application.

Summary

By now, you should have great appreciation for the robust functionality in the Media Player and Reader applications in the Pocket PC. Rather than merely providing entertainment or information, these applications are full-featured resources for personal education and leisure time distraction.

Next, you will learn how to use another free application that is concealed on the ActiveSync CD-ROM to navigate your way around unfamiliar cities and to provide a complete itinerary for friends and family

Pocket Streets: Get Around Town and Give Your Friends the Lay of the Land

IN THIS CHAPTER • Find food, transportation, and ATMs with a few taps of the stylus

• Create a custom itinerary in minutes

• Pushpin Explorer

• Configure Pocket Streets to your needs

• Create customized maps

Tucked away on the Microsoft ActiveSync CD is an application that will delight even the casual traveler. The application, called Pocket Streets, is an offspring of another successful Microsoft desktop product, Streets & Trips. Pocket Streets enables you to carry a section of the nationwide map and location database on your Pocket PC, providing information on food, transportation, and financial centers within the immediate area.

To begin, synchronize your Pocket PC with the desktop and insert the ActiveSync CD. Navigate to the \Extras\PStreets\PocketPC folder and double-click the setup.exe file to install the Pocket Streets application on your device. Next, open the \Extras\PStreets\Maps folder on the CD and copy a map to the Pocket PC using ActiveSync. The CD-ROM contains 14 major metropolitan area maps: Atlanta, Boston, Chicago, Houston, Los Angeles (East and West), Las Vegas, Miami, New York, Philadelphia, Phoenix, San Francisco, Seattle, and Washington, DC. Additional locations (including Dallas, London, Paris, and Munich) are available in the downloads section of www.pocketpc.com.

 Warning

If you have a Pocket PC that uses a processor other than the MIPS or SH3 chips, you should download the Pocket Streets application from www.pocketpc.com (you can check which processor your Pocket PC uses in Start ⇨ Settings ⇨ System ⇨ About). The HP Jornada Pocket PC users need not download this update because it uses the SH3 chip.

If none of the above cities are close to your locale, purchasing the desktop application, Microsoft Streets & Trips, enables you to create custom U.S. and Canada maps (of your hometown, for example) that can be copied to your Pocket PC. International readers and users planning a trip abroad should consider Microsoft AutoRoute, an application that enables you to create Pocket Streets maps for more than 2.6 million miles of European streets. Both applications enable you to export sections of the map by highlighting an area, right clicking the mouse, and selecting the Export Map for Pocket Streets command. The file created can be used on any Windows-powered device, so you can share your maps with fellow Pocket Streets users.

Finding Food, Transportation, and ATMs with a Few Taps of the Stylus

After you have the application installed and a map copied to the device, run Pocket Streets and open the map file. You now have a bird's-eye view of the immediate area, as you would expect from a map. But the features in Pocket Streets surpass paper maps and rival many of the Internet mapping programs. Choosing Tools ⇨ Find Address pinpoints a location by the street address, but the Tools ⇨ Find Place feature is a far more powerful tool. Using the Streets & Trips database of more than 600,000 locations, the Find Place option enables you to enter the name (or even a partial) name of a business or government office and return results in almost any category. For example, select Tools ⇨ Find Place and enter the **ATM** or **bank** and select Ok. Pocket Streets will return a list of the financial institutions on the currently loaded map almost instantly. Most locations will also display an address enabling you to distinguish between ATM locations and to select the one nearest you.

Tip

If you enter an exact name for a location and there is only one match in the database, Pocket Streets will take you directly to the location on the map, rather than making you pick the location from the Find Place list.

An alternate way to locate companies is in relation to your current position. This is an effective method if you are in unfamiliar territory or simply want to patronize a new business. Select Tools ⇨ Points of Interest and press Uncheck All to conceal all icons on the map. Now scroll through the points of interest and select the type of establishment that you are trying to locate. Figure 13.1 illustrates a search for hotels and motels.

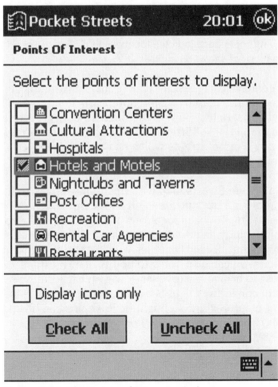

Figure 13.1 The Points of Interest window

As the figure indicates, leave Display icons only deactivated, so that you can evaluate your options by company name. Press Ok to close the Points of Interest window, select Tools ⇨ Find Address, and enter your current location. Depending on the density of your location, you may already see icons that represent the type of business that you are searching for. If not, zoom out by pressing the magnifying glass with the minus sign inside of it until you notice icons. These are the nearest businesses fitting the criteria you set in the Points of Interest window.

Creating a Custom Itinerary in Minutes

While being able to navigate on your own is a great feature of Pocket Streets, there is nothing more inspiring than being able to show your friends around town with the Pocket PC. Pushpins enable you to easily customize any Pocket Streets map with locations not in the map's database (such as your home) and add comments to existing locations. To add a pushpin, tap the Pushpin icon on the Pocket Streets menu bar, and then tap a precise location on the map where you wish the pushpin to appear. A Properties window pops up that enables you to enter a name and notes and to select the map symbol for the pushpin.

Tip

The Pushpin feature includes arrow symbols that point in every possible direction. Use them to create a driving route or to indicate locations that are positioned off the viewable area of the map (as shown in Figure 13.2).

Pushpins can also be created from existing map icons. For example, a hotel may already be designated on the map by a blue hotel icon. If you tap the symbol, the name of the hotel appears in a pop-up text box. To convert it to a pushpin, tap the Pushpin icon in the Pocket Streets menu bar and then tap the hotel name in the pop-up text box. Pocket Streets will keep the blue hotel icon as the pushpin's symbol, but you will now be able to change the name and add a description for the pushpin.

Figure 13.2 illustrates a Pocket Streets map with pushpins applied to it. The use of an automobile symbol for a parking area and a fork and knife symbol for a restaurant make differentiating between locations much easier, and also give your map a more professional look. In addition, the use of the notes fields (shown in Figure 13.2 as text which is not bolded) enables you to provide additional information about each location. You can add notes to points of interest locations by tapping on point of interest to bring up a text window with the location name, and then selecting the Pushpin icon in the menu bar and tapping the text window. This will convert the point of interest into a pushpin. Pushpins can be edited or deleted by choosing Tools ⇨ Pushpins from the Pocket Streets menu.

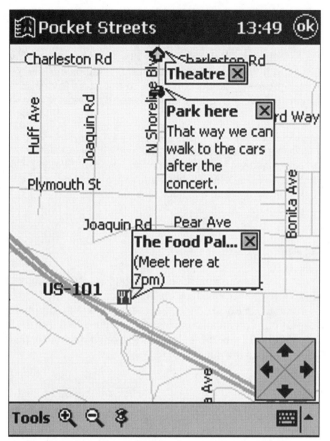

Figure 13.2 Pushpins in a Pocket Streets map

After you have created a customized itinerary like the one shown in Figure 13.2, you can share the information with your friends a number of ways. If you can fit the information in one screen (as shown in the figure above) with all roads and event locations clearly identifiable, select Tools ⇨ Map ⇨ Copy Map. This takes a snapshot that you can paste into a Pocket Word or Notes document. If you plan to e-mail the itinerary to your friends, paste it into a Pocket Word document. If you plan to send the itinerary via infrared, paste it into a new Notes file. Optionally, add written or typed text to the message to further describe your plans for the evening.

If the locations are distant, or if the instructions are too complex to fit in a single Pocket Streets screen, you can send the entire map to your fellow Pocket Streets users complete with your customized pushpins and comments. Before you send the file, press Ok while viewing the map to save all of your pushpins. Pocket Streets will return you to the file-viewing menu when you have saved changes. Tap and hold this file and select Send via E-mail or Send via Infrared to transfer the map to your guests. After you have successfully sent the map, you must send the separate file that contains all of your custom pushpins and comments. Open the Pocket PC File Explorer and navigate to the location where your Pocket Streets maps reside. You will now see a file with the exact same name as your Pocket Streets map, but with a blue Pushpin icon preceding it. Tap and hold this file and send it using the same method (e-mail or infrared) you previously used, and instruct the recipients to save it to the same folder as the map you sent earlier. They now have a dynamic itinerary of the evening's festivities!

Note

If you are using a map that you know your friends already have installed on their Pocket PC, you can save time by just sending them the customized Pushpin file. However, you need to ensure that they give the Pushpin file and the map the same filename so that Pocket Streets will know that the files are linked.

Pushpin Explorer

With all of the different uses for pushpins, your Pocket Streets map may quickly become overcrowded with symbols and notes. To help manage the clutter, Pushpin Explorer is included in Pocket Streets. Select Tools ⇨ Pushpins to open Pushpin Explorer; your screen should resemble Figure 13.3. Naturally, your pushpins will be different from mine, but aside from a dissimilar pushpin list, the window should appear the same.

Figure 13.3 Pushpin Explorer

The checkboxes to the left of each location indicate that the pushpin is viewable on the Pocket Streets map. If you deselect a checkbox, Pocket Streets will temporarily hide the icon and text balloon for an individual pushpin. This can be very helpful when trying to create a screenshot for an itinerary or if you are trying to locate a business but it is surrounded by the pushpins you have made. After you have found the location, or taken the screenshot, you can display the pushpins again by reactivating their checkboxes.

Find, edit, and remove pushpins

The three buttons at the bottom of the screen enable you to find, edit, and remove the pushpins in your list. Go To returns to the map and jumps to the selected pushpin's location on the map. However, the pushpin's checkbox must be activate for Go To to work (otherwise the map would open and you would just see an unlabeled expanse of land). Properties enables you to edit the pushpin's name, note, and symbol.

Note

Pushpins can only be deleted one at a time using Delete. If you wish to remove all of the pushpins from your map quickly, close the map and exit Pocket Streets, load File Explorer (Start ⇨ Programs ⇨ File Explorer) and delete the Pushpin file.

Reopen text balloons with Pushpin Explorer

If you have closed the text balloon on a pushpin, you can reactivate it using Pushpin Explorer, instead of trying to tap the pushpin's tiny icon on the map. The procedure for opening a text balloon is as follows:

1. Select Tools ⇨ Pushpins.

2. Locate the pushpin in the list and highlight it. Ensure that its checkbox is activated.

3. Press Go To.

Tip

Double-tapping the text balloon of any pushpin opens Pushpin Explorer's Properties window for that item. This is a faster way to edit the title, note, or symbol for a pushpin that you see on the map, instead of opening Pushpin Explorer, highlighting the object, and selecting Properties.

Configuring Pocket Streets to Meet Your Needs

Although Pocket Streets is a well-designed product, there are a few changes that you might want to make after you have used the product for a while and created a few customized itineraries. Your personal style and experience of what works best when copying maps to other applications dictates which features you activate in customizing Pocket Streets.

Enhancing your view with Map Styles

Because the product is visual in nature, Microsoft has created several options for adjusting the graphical nature of the maps. Select Tools ➪ Map ➪ Map Styles to access two options that enable you to customize the way that maps display in Pocket Streets. The first option, Dark or Light Background, enables you to set the background color level in Pocket Streets. I prefer the dark background because the colors look more robust and realistic; however, Pocket PC users with grayscale displays or users creating itineraries that will be printed on black and white printers should leave the setting on light background, which is the default.

The second option, Less or Full Street Detail, enables you to display street-level features on the map, even when zoomed out. Activating Full Street Detail offers a more complete map picture, but causes a slower response when opening and scrolling around the map. Figure 13.4 illustrates the differences in map details. The image on the left uses the default settings of light background and less street detail; the image on the right shows the map with a dark background and full street detail. Notice how much darker the waterways are and how the city street features are included in the landmasses.

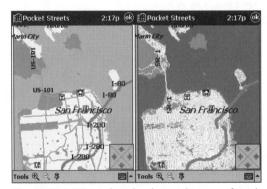

Figure 13.4 Normal and enhanced views of Pocket Streets

Tip

To quickly zoom out for a view of the entire map, select Tools ➪ Map ➪ Zoom Full.

Toggle on-screen controls and remove Points of Interest icons to reduce clutter

In addition to the Map Styles feature, Pocket Streets enables you to deactivate the navigation arrows on the map and quickly remove all of the Points of Interest icons from the map. To remove the navigation arrows, select Tools ➪ Map ➪

Pan Arrows. When the arrows are disabled, the only way to move around the map is by activating the soft keyboard and tapping the up, down, left, and right arrows. The Pocket Streets navigation arrows may be restored by selecting Tools ➪ Map ➪ Pan Arrows again.

Note

When copying a map (Tools ➪ Map ➪ Copy Map), Pocket Streets automatically removes the navigation arrows from the screenshot. Thus, you do not have to worry about deactivating the arrows before taking a screenshot.

To disable the Points of Interest icons on the map, select Tools ➪ Points of Interest and press Uncheck All. This effectively hides the icons on the map. If you want to display the icons (to create landmarks to navigate by) select Check All or activate the checkboxes of Points of Interest that you want to display. Deselect the Display icons only option, so that the titles of the Points of Interest will be labeled with the name of the location.

Creating Customized Maps

At the beginning of this chapter, I mentioned the capability to create a custom map based on your local territory. This is a key feature for many Pocket Streets users because you can either create one huge map that encompasses all of the areas you frequent or you can create a number of smaller maps that can be copied to your Pocket PC as you need them. The single, larger map is more convenient to create and store, but the smaller maps enable you to get more information on a memory-constrained device.

To create a customized map for Pocket Streets, follow these steps:

1. Install Microsoft Streets & Trips, MapPoint, or AutoRoute (for international maps) on your desktop computer.

2. Launch the application and navigate to the region of the map that you would like to copy to your Pocket PC.

3. Click and drag with the left mouse button to select the area.

4. Right-click within the selected area; your screen should resemble Figure 13.5.

5. Select Export Map for Pocket Streets.

6. The application will calculate the approximate file size of the resulting Pocket Streets map, so that you know how much free memory will be required on your Pocket PC before you create the map. Press Ok to make the map. This process may take several minutes, depending on the speed of your computer and the size of the area you selected.

Warning

The file size estimate is only a rough calculation. Be sure to check the actual file size of the map before copying it to your Pocket PC.

7. When the map has been built, locate the file on your desktop and open the ActiveSync window.

8. Press Explore in ActiveSync and copy the map into the pop-up window that appears.

9. Launch Pocket Streets.

10. If the application loads with a map already displayed, press ok to return to the file menu.

11. Select your new map from the file menu.

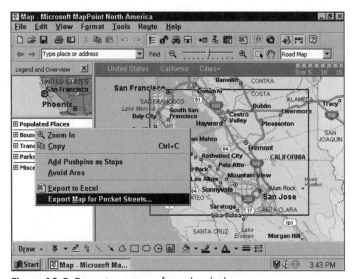

Figure 13.5 Exporting a map from the desktop

If you convert a large area into a Pocket Streets map, you should install it directly onto a memory card. To save a map on a memory card, repeat the process above, but when you reach Step 8, press Explore, double-click the My Device icon, and open the Storage Card folder. Create a My Documents folder inside of the Storage Card folder, or open it if it already exists. Copy the map into this folder.

Cross-Reference

For complete information on how to prepare a memory card for use on the Pocket PC, see Chapter 21.

Summary

After completing this chapter, you should be able to find your way out of foreign lands and to provide a stunning electronic invitation for your next party or business function. In addition, you discovered an application that came with your Pocket PC but was hidden on the ActiveSync CD.

In Chapter 14, you will discover a set of utilities called PowerToys. They are available free of charge on the Microsoft Web site and they add many of the features that users want in their Pocket PC but did not get when they received their device.

PowerToys: Work Like a Pro

Shortly after the release of each new Windows Powered device, Microsoft developes and releases a set of PowerToys for that platform. These add-ons take care of all of the little trouble spots that the software developers did not address in the built-in software, and usually include a few "power user" applications that provide more functionality than one would normally expect in the Pocket PC. Best of all, these applications are always available free of charge. More power at no cost — who could resist such an offer?

Warning

Although developed by Microsoft, the PowerToys are free applications that are not as well refined or tested as commercial products. As a result, Microsoft offers PowerToys to the public "as is" and does not provide any technical support for these add-ons.

You can attain these powerful accessories in the "downloads" section of www.pocketpc.com. Each application is available as a separate download, so you can pick and choose which PowerToy features you would like to install on your system. If you do not know which applications you are interested in, read this chapter before downloading the PowerToys.

Cross-Reference

The Media Skin Chooser PowerToy, which enables you to customize the appearance of the Pocket PC's MP3 player, is covered in Chapter 12, "Media Player and Reader: Satisfy Your Senses with Personal Content."

Power Contacts

Because communication is a major focus of the Pocket PC, the Power Contacts PowerTop unites several applications with one simple but incredibly useful menu in the Contacts application. Available by tapping and holding any contact, Figure 14.1 shows the three new menu items available once Power Contacts is installed. Create Appointment, Create Task, and Open Web Page all activate other Pocket PC applications by using information in the selected contact to prepopulate the new item.

Selecting Create Appointment from the menu opens a new calendar item with the contact as an attendee. By default, Power Contacts schedules the appointment for the next 60 minutes (starting at the top of the hour), but leaves the calendar item open so you can quickly change the appointment's date and time. If a contact does not have an e-mail address, Calendar cannot notify them of the meeting and will not add them to the recipients list, but will notify you of this in the appointment item window. Once you enter all of the details for the appointment and press Ok, you automatically return to the Contacts application and the Calendar program closes to preserve memory.

Figure 14.1 New Power Contacts menu items

Tip

The Power Contacts features can be applied to more than one contact. For example, if you have a meeting with multiple attendees, highlight all of the people in your Contacts list, tap and hold a single contact, and then select Create Appointment. A new appointment is created with all of the contacts as invitees.

As with the Create Appointment item, Create Task generates a new task item with the selected contact's name and primary phone number prepopulated in the subject field. This is an excellent way to quickly create a reminder to call a friend or coworker. When the task is created, all the information you need is available in the task item, which eliminates the need to look up their phone number. It is important to note that Power Contacts enters the work number by default, or the home phone if no work number exists. If you need to reach a contact on their cellular phone or pager, you will have to manually replace it yourself. If you attempt to create a task for contact with no work or home phone number, the subject will only contain the subject name.

The Open Web Page option, as you can probably imagine, opens the URL listed in the contact's Web Page field. Pocket Internet Explorer is activated and automatically surfs to the Web address. There are two important caveats to using this feature: You must be connected to the Internet when you select this option and if the contact does not have a URL entered in the Web Page field, nothing will happen when you select this option.

Tip

If you have an HTML file or a picture (in jpeg or gif format) in the My Documents folder on your local device, you can enter the location of that file in the contact's Web Page field using the following formula: file://\My Documents\[file name]. Now, when you select the Open Web Page feature for that contact, it will load the local file without having to connect to the Internet. You also can save family photos and frequently referenced HTML documents.

Internet Explorer Tools

Available at Start ⇨ Programs ⇨ Internet Explorer Tools, this PowerToy enables you to quickly modify many advanced settings for Pocket Internet Explorer (IE). Figure 14.2 demonstrates the IE Tools window with the default settings activated. The JavaScript options available at the top of the screen include Enable, Disable and Enable Jscript, and show JScript errors. This last alternative is useful for developers who are experiencing difficulties creating pages that contain JavaScript for the Pocket PC. The Disable JavaScript feature is available for users who want to prevent any JavaScript code from running in their browser for security or for faster Internet access.

Next, the PowerToy enables you to set the maximum amount of space that Pocket Internet Explorer will use for caching Web pages. This is a vital setting to conserve memory if you spend a lot of time surfing the Web on your Pocket PC. If you visit many different Web sites, and do not visit the same site more than once, select a very low value for the cache. If you frequent the same Web sites often, set the cache higher. Here are some typical cache space values for various usage scenarios based on the amount of memory you have on your device and your surfing habits:

- 16MB RAM Pocket PC and never visit the same site a second time: 0.00 MB

- 32MB RAM Pocket PC and never visit the same site a second time: 0.00 MB

- 16MB RAM Pocket PC and return to the same sites over and over: 2.75 MB

- 32MB RAM Pocket PC and return to the same sites over and over: 5.50 MB

- 16MB RAM Pocket PC and repeatedly visit a large number of sites: 5.50 MB

- 32MB RAM Pocket PC and repeatedly visit a large number of sites: 11.00 MB

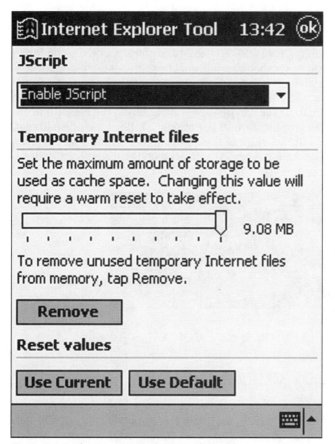

Figure 14.2 The Internet Explorer Tools window

Remember that this feature sets the maximum amount of space *available* to Pocket Internet Explorer for caching data. That means that the memory will not be used until Pocket IE has information to store in it. Cached information includes graphics (such as navigation bars and logos on Web pages) in addition to the actual HTML page information, so you are accelerating the load time of all of the constant elements of the page by using the caching feature, even if you download a new page of information.

To delete all of the files currently stored in Pocket IE's cache, press the Remove button. Although this feature appears to be already available in Pocket Internet Explorer (choose Tools ➪ Options ➪ General tab ➪ Delete Files button) occasionally files elude Pocket Internet Explorer's Delete Files function and stray files remain in the cache. The Remove button seeks out these files and deletes them so you can regain the memory. Finally, the two buttons at the bottom of the screen enable you to reset the window to display the values currently in use and the system defaults.

Today Screen Image Tool

The Today Screen Image Tool adds the ability to display a picture on the Pocket PC Today screen and has a special additional benefit: a hidden application launcher. When installed, this PowerToy adds an Image option to the Today screen settings applet (Start ⇨ Settings ⇨ Today ⇨ Image item) as shown in Figure 14.3. Any jpeg, gif, or bitmap image can be picked by entering the file path or browsing to the location of the graphic file and selecting it. Options include automatically resizing the image to fit the width of the Today Screen window and centering it horizontally, both of which have been activated on the example in Figure 14.3.

Figure 14.3 An image on the Today screen

The hidden application launcher is accessible by entering a file path for an application in the "Run this when tapped . . ." window. Once filled in, the program is launched when you tap on the picture in the Today screen. Power users can create an unconventional shortcut menu with customized graphics by making the most of this feature. The "New Image Item. . ." button makes a duplicate image item in the Today screen Settings applet so that more than one image can appear on the navigation bar at one time.

Warning

Selecting the "New Image Item. . ." button creates a duplicate item inside the Today screen Settings applet in the control panel. These cannot be removed from the control panel without uninstalling the Today Screen Image Tool PowerToy. You can easily disable them from the Today screen by unchecking each item, but clean freaks might not enjoy the unalterable presence of extra items in the Settings applet window.

Password for Pocket PC

If you are concerned that a four-digit password is not enough security for locking your Pocket PC, you should consider installing the Password for Pocket PC Power Toy. Although it deactivates the HP security features (which include a password hint and logging all access attempts to the device), this application enables you to use letters, numbers, and some symbols in your password and extends the size of the password from four to an unlimited number of characters.

Note

All letters entered into the password screen are converted to lowercase, so codes created in the Password for Pocket PC PowerToy are not case sensitive.

After you have downloaded and installed the PowerToy, password setup is moved from HP security to Start ⇨ Settings ⇨ Password. When the applet is launched the new Password window, shown in Figure 14.4, appears. Enter the same password into the first and second fields and then check the "Require password when device is turned on" option if you would like the Pocket PC to prompt you for a password every time the device is activated.

Figure 14.4 Setting up the password

In addition to prompting you for the password each time the device is powered up, ActiveSync requires that you enter the password before desktop synchronization can commence when the "Require password when device is turned on" option is activated. Naturally, access to the Password for Pocket PC Power Toy applet in Settings always requires entry of your secret code. To temporarily stop password protection, select Start ⇨ Settings ⇨ Password and erase the password from the first field, which is labeled Enter Password, Figure 14.5.

Figure 14.5 The new password entry screen

Tip

Because you cannot see the characters you are entering into the password field, always use the soft keyboard to enter your password. It shows you which characters you have selected by reversing out each key when the screen is tapped.

To permanently remove the PowerToy (if you prefer the original HP security screen with the numeric touchpad), there is a very quick method that must be followed in order to uninstall the Password for Pocket PC PowerToy. To return your device to the original HP security settings:

1. Select Start ⇨ Settings ⇨ Password and enter your password.

2. When the setting menu appears, erase your password (indicated by asterisks) from the field labeled Enter Password. When you do, the second field should automatically erase itself and the "Require password when device is turned on" option should gray out. This indicates that you have deactivated the Password for Pocket PC PowerToy.

Note

If you do not erase the password completely from the Password for Pocket PC PowerToy screen, the Remove Programs program will not permit to you uninstall the application.

3. Press Ok to close the Password for Pocket PC PowerToy applet and select the System tab in the Settings window.

4. Tap on the Remove Programs icon and scroll down to the Microsoft Password for Pocket PCs option. Highlight the option and press the Remove button.

5. Perform a soft reset on your device.

6. Select Start ⇨ Settings ⇨ Password and set a four-digit numeric password on your device. Press Ok and answer yes when the applet asks you if you want to save your changes.

Warning

At this point, do not activate the "Require password when device is turned on" option. This may prevent access to your device if the removal procedure is not successful. Once you have completed Step 7, you can activate the power-up password from the HP security applet.

7. Tap the HP Security icon. A pop-up window requesting your password should appear. Enter the four-digit password you just created in the previous step. You should once again be able to access the HP Security applet.

Summary

Through PowerToys, advanced users can get more advanced functionality and better performance from the Pocket PC. This chapter has simplified the installation and application of each of the PowerToys available for the device at the time this book went to press. However, Microsoft may release more PowerToy applications in the coming months. Visit the "downloads" section of www.pocketpc.com often to keep an eye out for new releases.

The final chapter of Part II of the handbook focuses on ActiveSync, the computer application designed to provide a connection between your Pocket PC and the desktop. This chapter concentrates on the three major connection factors: speed, security and synchronization.

ActiveSync: Desktop Communications for Maximum Speed and Security

IN THIS CHAPTER
- USB port versus serial port
- Get maximum speed connections
- Speedy alternative: infrared synchronization
- Customize the synchronization process
- Synchronize your Pocket PC clock with the atomic clock
- Sync with other desktop applications besides MS Outlook
- Sync the Contact list with your cellular phone

The Pocket PC's connection with the desktop computer is similar to the connection between mother and child. The Pocket PC learns from the desktop by downloading information and installing programs, is protected through desktop backups, and sees the real world (well, the Internet) through the desktop's Internet connection. The program that manages this maternal communication is called ActiveSync and ships with the Pocket PC. Because so much information is funneled through the ActiveSync program to the Pocket PC, it is critical that the connection be as efficient as possible.

USB Port versus Serial Port

All Pocket PC devices connect to the desktop using a cable or a cradle. Some devices (such as the HP Jornada 545 and 548) ship with a universal serial bus (USB) cradle and serial port cable. The USB system has a square connection port at one end that plugs into the USB port on your computer. USB ports are commonly available on newer desktop and laptop computers. The serial port is a rectangular-shaped plug with 9 holes in it. This is commonly referred to as a communications (COM) port. The serial port is available on almost every PC ever made, although a computer mouse or external modem sometimes occupies the port. Before continuing any further, inspect your computer and the connection cables that came with your Pocket PC and figure out which options are available to you.

Whenever possible, use the USB cable to connect with your desktop. According to Microsoft, USB cable connections are up to 6 times faster than serial ports connections. If you synchronize your device frequently, but your Pocket PC did not come with USB connections, you should consider purchasing the USB port cradle or cable, as most hardware manufacturers offer as an accessory. If own an older device for which a USB accessory is not available, Socket Communications (`www.socketcom.com`) manufactures a USB synchronization card that plugs into the Pocket PC's CompactFlash port and offers approximately twice the speed of the serial port connection.

Get Maximum-Speed Connections

If you must use the serial connection because of a lack of USB ports on your computer or if USB connectivity is unattainable, here's a quick trick that will significantly increase your synchronization speed: After you have successfully synchronized your Pocket PC with your desktop computer, select Start ⇨ Settings ⇨ Connections tab ⇨ PC icon on your Pocket PC. Figure 15.1 shows the PC Connections applet with the drop-down list activated. Select `115200 Default to connect to the desktop at the fastest possible speed and press Ok to save the changes.

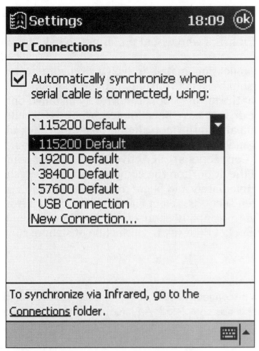

Figure 15.1 The PC Connections applet

Immediately after saving the changes, dock your Pocket PC and ensure that the device successfully connects with the desktop. Older computers may not be able to handle the high-speed connection. If the Pocket PC fails to connect and synchronize, repeat the previous steps, this time setting the connection speed to 57600. Test the connection again by docking your Pocket PC and then continue reducing the connection speed until you find the highest possible speed that your computer can handle. If the system fails to synchronize, return the speed setting to 19200, which is the Pocket PC default.

Speedy Alternative: Infrared Synchronization

Another alternative for desktop synchronization is available via the infrared (IR) port on the Pocket PC. An infrared port is a standard feature on modern laptops; Extended Systems (www.extendedsystems.com), a third-party hardware vendor, offers an accessory to add infrared communications capabilities to the desktop computer. Although many might view the use of infrared light as a slow method of data transfer, connections with the Pocket PC are established at a blazing

115,000 bytes per second. And, more importantly, a synchronization cable is not required once infrared transfer is set up, making this an ideal method of synchronization to a work computer for users who would prefer not to have to purchase a second cable.

To establish infrared communication, install ActiveSync on your desktop computer and establish a partnership by synchronizing through a synchronization cable or cradle. Make sure that the infrared port is correctly installed on your computer and that the proper drivers have been loaded. Windows should have an Infrared eye icon in the taskbar and the icon should be graphically pulsating to indicate that it is activated and searching for infrared signals. On your Pocket PC, select Start ➪ Programs ➪ Connections ➪ IR ActiveSync and then point the IR port on the Pocket PC toward the IR port on the computer. ActiveSync should recognize the signal almost immediately and begin the synchronization process. If this does not occur within ten seconds, select File ➪ Get Connected from the ActiveSync window to attempt to manually connect. To disconnect from the computer, simply move your Pocket PC away from the line of sight of the computer's infrared port.

Tip

Whenever possible, try not to disconnect the Pocket PC from the desktop computer until the synchronization process has completed. An interrupted synchronization can result in duplicate items or even corrupted data.

Customize the Synchronization Process

Once you've maximized your synchronization speed, the next step is to protect and augment your Pocket PC by customizing the synchronization process. By default, the ActiveSync software is programmed to download only a subset of your Outlook data. All contacts and notes are downloaded, but only the past two weeks and all future Calendar items and incomplete tasks are copied to your device. E-mail, while not synchronized by default, only syncs the first 100 lines of messages received in the last 5 days. To change any of these settings, open the ActiveSync window while your Pocket PC is connected and right-click the individual item. Select Settings from the pop-up menu and modify the synchronization rules. An alternate way to modify the settings is to select Tools ➪ Options from the ActiveSync menu, highlight the item you wish to change, and press the Settings button.

Warning

If you delete an item on your Pocket PC it is permanently deleted from the desktop the next time you synchronize. To remove items from your Pocket PC, change the synchronization settings in ActiveSync to exclude those items.

Once you have adapted the synchronization system to fit your needs, you should secure ActiveSync so that others cannot connect with your desktop and download your data. In the ActiveSync application, select File ⇨ Connection Settings and deselect the checkboxes for all methods of synchronization, excluding for the port that you are using. This helps prevent others from connecting to your desktop with an alternate Pocket PC over the network (if you computer is on a local area network, or LAN) or with a connection cable from another device. For maximum security, hide the ActiveSync window by doing the following:

1. Select Tools ⇨ Options ⇨ Rules tab and unchecking the "Open ActiveSync when my mobile device connects" checkbox.

2. Next, deactivate the Taskbar icon by choosing File ⇨ Connection Settings and unchecking the "Show status in Taskbar" checkbox.

3. Set the system to manually synchronize by choosing Tools ⇨ Options ⇨ Sync Mode tab and select Manually.

4. Finally, hide the ActiveSync icon elsewhere in your Start menu.

Now, the only way to connect to a device and download information is for you to dock your Pocket PC, locate and run the ActiveSync icon in the start menu, and press the Sync button. This should ward off all but the most persistent thieves.

Tip

If you password protect your Pocket PC (Start ⇨ Settings ⇨ HP Security), ActiveSync will require the password in order to connect with your device. This can be a powerful weapon against data hijacking if you frequently leave your Pocket PC unattended. No one can connect to your Pocket PC on any desktop computer unless they know the password.

The Add/Remove Programs feature

In previous chapters, you learned how to install applications from the ActiveSync CD-ROM that came with your Pocket PC. When you install an application, the set up files are stored on your desktop before being copied to your Pocket PC. This enables you to quickly reinstall the application on your device without having to locate the original CD-ROM or keep track of software that was downloaded over the Internet. To access this feature, open ActiveSync and select Tools ⇨ Add/Remove Programs. Figure 15.2 shows the Add/Remove Programs window for a Pocket PC displaying files with symbols that indicate each application's installation and backup status:

■ A checked item indicates software that is installed on the Pocket PC and has setup files available on the desktop for backup. Unchecking this item only removes the application from the Pocket PC.

■ An unchecked item indicates software that is not installed on the Pocket PC but has setup files on the desktop. Checking this item installs the software on the Pocket PC.

■ An item with a grayed-out checkbox signifies software that is installed on the Pocket PC but has no backup file on the desktop computer. This application must be uninstalled on the Pocket PC. You can do this by selecting Start ➪ Settings ➪ System tab ➪ Remove Programs.

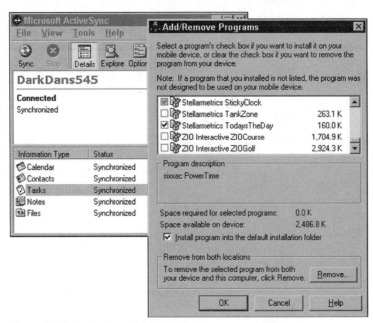

Figure 15.2 ActiveSync Add/Remove Programs window

One of the most impressive features of the Add/Remove Programs feature is that the window displays the amount of memory the application currently occupies (if the application is checked) or will require when installed (for unchecked programs). This provides an excellent indicator of memory-hogging software. Memory requirements for software with grayed-out checkboxes cannot be determined because ActiveSync does not have a desktop file to examine.

As mentioned before, you can remove programs can be removed from the Pocket PC by unchecking the application's checkbox. To remove programs from the desktop and the Pocket PC at the same time, select the application in the Add/Remove Programs window, and push the Remove button. To clear hard drive space on the desktop computer, most applications enable you to remove their backup files by selecting Start ➪ Settings ➪ Control Panel ➪ Add/Remove Programs on the desktop. Each application has its own line item in the window and can be safely removed without affecting the program on the Pocket PC.

Tip

You can set up third-party software to automatically install at the next synchronization. Simply run the software setup program on your desktop while the Pocket PC is not connected. The program runs through the entire set up process but stops when it is time to copy the application to the Pocket PC. The next time you synchronize, the software is automatically installed on the Pocket PC.

Perform instant backups

The ActiveSync application also offers two levels of data protection with manual and automatic backup capabilities built into the software. To perform a manual backup, select Tools ⇨ Backup/Restore and press the Backup Now button. The Pocket PC should not be operated during the backup procedure to prevent data corruption, but the backup can take hours depending on the amount of information stored in your device. Once it is completed, you can reduce the amount of time it takes to copy your data by changing your setup to "Incremental backup." This will copy only the information that has changed since the last backup. To automatically backup your Pocket PC every time you connect to your desktop, select Tools ⇨ Backup/Restore and select "Automatically backup each time the device connects." This archives all of the Pocket PC data upon your next synchronization and then subsequently performs incremental backups of the data that has changed every time you dock your Pocket PC.

Tip

If you don't want to back up your entire device, turn on ActiveSync's File Synchronization feature (Tools ⇨ Options ⇨ Files checkbox) to copy all of the files in the My Documents folder of your Pocket PC. This will ensure the safekeeping of your voice recordings, Pocket Word and Pocket Excel documents, and Notes, as well as any other items stored in that directory or any subdirectory beneath it.

As with all files, the backups made by ActiveSync are susceptible to becoming corrupted. In order to ensure that your backups are safe, change the name of your backup files once every month (I suggest using the current date) and then copy the files to a floppy disk. This will help prevent corruption and provides incremental backups in case you install an unstable program or are infected by a virus.

To restore data to your Pocket PC, dock your device with the desktop, open ActiveSync, and select Tools ⇨ Backup/Restore ⇨ Restore tab. Pressing the Restore Now button overwrites all files on your device with the contents in the backup archive. Once started, this process cannot be stopped and (as with the backup procedure) the Pocket PC should not be operated while files are being copied to the device.

Synchronize Your Pocket PC Clock with the Atomic Clock

It is a well-known fact that all computers drift. *Drifting* is the loss or addition of a few seconds in the onboard clock that eventually can cause a computer to be imprecise by as much as minutes every month. If you count on your Pocket PC to accurately inform you of appointments or to serve as a timepiece in lieu of a pocket watch, you must make sure that the device is accurate. The following three-step prevention system can ensure that drifting never happens to your computer:

1. Synchronize your desktop computer with the atomic clock. Dimension 4, a freeware program available from Thinking Man Software (www.thinkman.com), automatically connects to military time servers via the Internet and sets your PC clock to precise time. Download and install the software (or any application which performs the same function) to correct any drifting that may occur on your desktop clock.

2. Open ActiveSync, select Tools ⇨ Options from the menu, and activate the "synchronize mobile device clock upon connecting" feature. Press Ok to close the window and save your settings.

3. Dock the Pocket PC and its clock is automatically updated to match the desktop's time and date settings. Once set up, having your system periodically connect to the Internet and synchronize your device keeps your clocks accurate to the millisecond!

Sync with Other Desktop Applications Besides MS Outlook

Perhaps the company you work for does not deploy Outlook as the company's desktop Personal Information Manager (PIM) or you simply prefer not to use Microsoft's desktop. Whatever the reason, you need to synchronize your Pocket PC with another desktop PIM application. A duo of third-party applications, discussed in the following paragraphs, enable you to synchronize your desktop computer with a number of other popular PIMs.

Warning

Synchronization with any data files is always a difficult process. I strongly suggest that you take advantage of the free trial versions of these applications to ensure that the synchronization process is performed to your satisfaction before purchasing a full version of the software.

Intellisync from Puma Technologies Incorporated (www.pumatech.com) enables you to synchronize your calendar, e-mail, contacts, and tasks for the following applications:

- Lotus Organizer 4.1/5.0/6.0
- Lotus Notes 4.5/4.6/5.0
- Microsoft Outlook 97/98/2000
- Microsoft Schedule+ 7.5
- Microsoft Exchange 5.0/5.5
- Novell GroupWise 5.2/5.5
- SalesLogix 3.0
- Symantec ACT! 4.02/2000

As with ActiveSync, Intellisync offers customized filtering of synchronized data to control the amount of information being imported, resolve system conflicts, and support multiusers. The application even enables you to synchronize data across multiple applications, which is an invaluable feature if you use different PIM programs for work and home. A free trial download is available from the Puma Web site (www.pumatech.com).

Another third-party application that enables synchronization with non-Microsoft PIM applications is CompanionLink by CompanionLink Software Incorporated. The product is available in a standard version, which enables you to synchronize one desktop PIM to one Pocket PC, and a professional version, which enables synchronization between multiple applications and your Pocket PC. A 15-day evaluation version of CompanionLink is available on the company's Web site (www.companionlink.com) and it supports synchronization with:

- GoldMine 2.5a (or later)/3.0/3.2/4.0/5.0
- Lotus Organizer 97GS/4.1/5.0/6.0
- Outlook 97/98/2000
- Schedule+ 7.x
- Symantec ACT! 3.0.7 (or later)/4.0/4.1/4.2/2000
- TeleMagic 3.5c/4.0+

Remember, both of these applications are developed by third-party companies. Although they enable you to synchronize with other PIM applications, the ActiveSync software must still reside on your desktop in order to install Pocket PC software and backup the device.

Sync the Pocket PC Contact List with Your Cellular Phone

Cellular phones are becoming as popular and ever-present as keys to the office in the modern day workforce. Likewise, the importance of having up-to-date contact information in your cellular phone sometimes surpasses the need for a synchronized personal digital assistant (PDA). Thankfully, a number of companies offer PDA and cellular phone synchronization services and software. All of these services connect to either your Pocket PC or your desktop Outlook application in order to synchronize with your cellular phone. Which synchronization company you select depends mostly on the cellular phone model that you own; many cellular phones require a connection cable (similar to the synchronization cable for your Pocket PC) in order to connect to the service.

FoneSync

FoneSync (www.fonesync.com) by Phone.com Incorporated solves both problems in one simple package. For under $80, you will receive the FoneSync software and either a cable for connecting to your desktop or a desktop SimCard Reader for GSM phones. The connection cable performs as you would expect, synchronizing your cellular phone with the desktop computer Outlook application. The SimCard Reader actually writes the contact information to a GSM card and enables you to quickly copy the information to your cellular phone by inserting the card. Between the SimCard and connection cable methods of synchronization, FoneSync supports hundreds of models of cellular phones.

FusionOne

FusionOne (www.fusionone.com) offers numerous connectivity options for synchronization with your desktop Outlook data and your mobile phone. At press time the company was working to include Pocket PC synchronization support. In the interim, users of this service would have to synchronize their Pocket PC with the desktop, synchronize the desktop with the FusionOne service, and then synchronize their cellular phone. Although this might seem like a tedious process, the service is free and includes a number of other services for synchronizing home and work computers. The FusionOne connects with over one hundred mobile phones via a serial cable. It also connects with Nokia GSM phones via a short messaging system (SMS) and enables you to browse contacts, calendar, e-mail, tasks, and notes from any Web-enabled cell phone. Although Web-enabled phones can access the information without any additional software, all other devices must download and install the FusionOne application to enable synchronization. But, the service is free, and you cannot argue with that.

TrueSync

If you recently purchased a mid-to-high end Motorola cellular phone, you might already have everything you need for synchronizing your cellular's phone book. In an extensive agreement, StarFish Software Incorporated (`www.starfish.com`) has been bundling their TrueSync software with what they report to be millions of Motorola cellular phones. The software, combined with a connection cable available directly from Motorola or your local cellular service provider will quickly get you up-and-running with synchronization of your Pocket PC, desktop and cellular phone, without even requiring the ActiveSync desktop software.

SunnySoft GSM Manager

An application that enables you to manage both your phone book and text messages from the Pocket PC, SunnySoft GSM Manager connects to the GSM phone via serial port (both devices must have serial cables), CompactFlash connector, or infrared ports on the Pocket PC and cellular phone. Once you have installed the software and established a connection, you can download contact information from the cellular phone's main memory or SIM card memory. Figure 15.3 shows a phone list downloaded from the GSM phone onto the Pocket PC. This information can be edited, assigned a new sort order, and uploaded back to your cellular phone. The application also enables you to import phone numbers from the Pocket PC contacts list, or export the cellular phone list for backup purposes.

Figure 15.3 SunnySoft GSM Manager

Additionally, SunnySoft GSM Manager enables you to work with the SMS mail messages by downloading them directly to the Pocket PC. As with contact information, SMS messages can be edited and exported once they have been downloaded to the SunnySoft program. New messages can also be created in the Pocket PC application, saving you the tremendous hassle of trying to compose a message using your cell phone keypad.

Summary

If you have followed every step in this chapter, you have a very fast and efficient ActiveSync connection and the use of a number of tools to protect and correct data on your Pocket PC. Now that you have tuned up your Pocket PC's applications and desktop connection, you have completed Part II of this handbook.

The next section focuses on more advanced uses for your Pocket PC, including Internet and wireless communications, transferring information with other devices (such as scanners and printers), customizing the Pocket interface, and employing third-party applications, which provide additional functionality above and beyond the standard software in the Pocket PC. Before you continue, you should be comfortable with all of the concepts in this chapter, as well as the general nomenclature of your Pocket PC.

Getting More from Your Pocket PC

CHAPTER 16

Exchanging Data and Documents

IN THIS CHAPTER • Online services and the Internet

• Going wireless

• HP Capshare and HP JetSend

Given that you have mastered the use of all of the standard Pocket PC applications, the next logical step is to move into cyberspace, where information is abundantly available and always up to date. The Pocket PC supports universal Internet protocols. This chapter discusses all of the methods for connected your device to the Internet and introduces a number accessories and appliances that will enhance your online and communications experiences.

Using Online Services and the Internet

Although I hope that no one reading this book requires convincing of the power of the Internet, using the Pocket PC to surf the Web often requires a little persuasion. At first glance, a device with such a small screen does not appear suitable for viewing Web sites, but a number of compelling reasons make the Internet a beneficial connection. The software program AvantGo enables you to effortlessly grab news and information from popular Web sites without having to hunt for it. The Inbox application enables you to download e-mail directly to your Pocket PC, Pocket Internet Explorer (IE) supports Web surfing, and you can update your portfolio value in Pocket Money. You can do these things from anywhere in the world, and all this is possible after establishing a connection to the Internet.

Getting online

To connect to the Internet, you first need the appropriate hardware. In addition to the Pocket PC, you must purchase a modem that connects your device to the phone line. One option is to purchase a CompactFlash modem from Pretec Electronics (www.pretec.com) that plugs into the Type I CF slot on the Pocket PC. Later in this chapter you can read about the Psion Travel Modem, which uses Infrared to connect the Pocket PC to a home telephone line wirelessly; you'll also learn several options for remote communications. Once you have the modem, you will need to configure the Pocket PC to connect to the Internet.

Setting up the connection

In order to create your Internet connection, you must first obtain the connection settings for your Internet Service Provider (ISP). This information can usually be found on a desktop computer that is already configured to connect to the ISP (Start ➪ Settings ➪ Control Panel ➪ Dial Up Networking on your desktop) or by contacting the ISP's technical support. Regardless of how you locate the information, you should enter it into the following list for easy reference.

Note

America Online (AOL) users do not need to enter in this information because AOL has a complete software application that sends, receives, and forwards e-mail. For complete information, skip ahead to the "Accessing America Online and MSN" section of this chapter.

Data Bits (circle one): 4 / 5 / 6 / 7 / 8

Parity (circle one): None / Odd / Even / Mark / Space

Stop bits (circle one): 1 / 1.5 / 2

Flow Control (circle one): Software / Hardware / None

IP address: Server assigned / ___ . ___ . ___ . ___

[   ] Use Slip

[   ] Use software compression

[   ] Use IP header compression

Name server: Server assigned addresses, or:

DNS ___ . ___ . ___ . ___

Alternate DNS ___ . ___ . ___ . ___

WINS ___ . ___ . ___ . ___

Alternate WINS ___ . ___ . ___ . ___

Dial-up Phone Number: (_____) _____ - _____

Once you have gathered this information, open the Connections applet in the Pocket PC (Start ➪ Settings ➪ Connections tab ➪ Modem icon ➪ New Connection. . .) and enter it when prompted. Most of the information listed previously is input in the advanced section of the connection setup. If you do not have specific settings for your ISP, leave the Pocket PC default settings in place and attempt to dial your service provider. A successful connection can often be made even if all of the settings are not completely filled in. Once you have successfully connected to the Internet, you can use Pocket Internet Explorer and Pocket Money's Update Quotes feature.

Cross-Reference

For more information on updating your Pocket Money portfolio values over the Internet, return to Chapter 11, "Pocket Office: Desktop Applications to Go."

Setting up the Inbox

In order to download e-mail, the Inbox application needs additional information for contacting the mail server. Designed to support the popular POP3 Internet standard and the IMAP4 corporate standard, setup information differs slightly depending on which protocol your ISP or company is using. Write the setup information into the following list for later reference.

Note

If you use a browser-based e-mail service (such as Hotmail, Excite or Yahoo), you can access your account on the Pocket PC once you have established a dial-up connection. Launch Pocket Internet Explorer and enter the Web address of the e-mail service, and then just log in as you would on your desktop. You now have access to your e-mail from anywhere. In addition, Web sites such as Mailstart.com and Yahoo! enable you to receive POP3 e-mail using your Web browser.

Server: _____

STMP Host: _____

Domain: _____ (required only when connecting to Windows NT networks)

User ID: _____

Password: _____

Return e-mail address: _____

Once you have the preceding information, launch Inbox and select Services ➪ New Service, and then enter the information into the first two screens in the Set up Wizard. The subsequent two screens contain optional settings when establishing an e-mail account on your Pocket PC and can be individually configured based upon your needs. If you have already set up e-mail service on your Pocket PC and wish to modify any of these settings, you may do so by selecting the Tools ➪ Options ➪ Services tab. Double-tap the name of the individual account and use the Next button to navigate to the selection you wish to modify. Review the following options to see which ones are appropriate for your needs.

■ Disconnect service after actions are performed (Use this if you only dial up in order to receive e-mail; the Pocket PC will sever the connection when it has finished transferring mail.)

■ Check for messages every *xx* minutes (This option will schedule the Inbox application to automatically download e-mail at an interval you select. An excellent option if you keep your connection open on a network.)

■ When new messages arrive, notify me (Only available when connecting to IMAP4 servers; the Pocket PC will notify you with an audio alert when new e-mail has arrived in your Inbox. If you connect to the corporate network for an extended period of time, this makes an excellent reminder to check your mail.)

■ Send using MIME format (Exclusively for POP3 mail service, this enables you to send messages with extended MIME characters to mail clients which support the format. I suggest you do not activate this feature, as it also encodes messages that are sent out to the Internet, possibly rendering a message unreadable to some users.)

■ Only display messages from the last *xx* days (Although this feature is designed to conserve memory on the Pocket PC, it is advisable not to activate it unless you download large amounts of e-mail on your device. Otherwise you may lose messages that have been sitting in your Inbox when you have not retrieved messages for a few days.)

■ Get message headers only (and Include *xx* lines) / Get full copy of messages (Again designed to conserve memory, this feature enables you to control the size of the e-mails you download. This should be set to personal preference, as only users who regularly receive extensive e-mails can decide whether or not the information is valuable enough to trim without human intervention.)

■ Synchronize only Inbox folder (Only available to IMAP4 clients, this feature enables you to merely synch the main e-mail folder on your account. This feature should be activated for users with extensive subfolders containing large amounts of e-mail.)

■ Get meeting requests (Because meeting requests are incredibly small in size and are deleted automatically when you respond, all attendees should activate this feature so that everyone can receive scheduling information via Pocket PC.)

■ Get file attachments (This feature is the most important choice that a Pocket PC user can make when setting up an e-mail account. If this feature is activated, you will be able to open Word, Excel, and HTML documents on your device by double-tapping the attachment that is automatically downloaded to your device. Users who receive many attachments of a large file size, or in file formats that the Pocket PC cannot open, may wish to deactivate this feature to save memory on the Pocket PC.)

■ Get attachments/meeting requests, only if smaller than *xx*K (Available only for IMAP4 server users, this feature enables you to control the size of the attachments being downloaded to your device. This feature should be customized to the preference of the individual user but makes a great compromise when the "Get file attachments" feature is activated.)

Once you have established an e-mail account on your Pocket PC, you can download messages by activating the service as shown in Figure 16.1. A bullet next to its name in the Services menu denotes the active service. To make another account active, choose it from the menu; otherwise select Connect to download e-mail from the selected account.

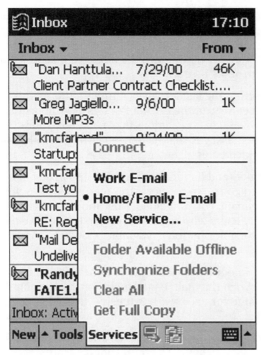

Figure 16.1 Selecting the active E-mail account

Cross-Reference

For more information on using the Inbox application refer to Chapter 10, "The Inbox: Your One-stop Information Repository."

Setting up dialing locations

Once you have configured your Internet connection and your e-mail account, you will probably want to connect to the Internet from as many different locations as possible. The Pocket PC enables you to configure the device to recognize different dialing locations so that you can quickly switch between a setup for work that dials 9 to get an outside line and your home configuration that cancels out the call waiting service.

Note

At least one dialing location must be set up in order to connect to an ISP. By default, the Pocket PC has been preprogrammed with Home and Work locations, but their local area code is preset as 425. This means that unless you live in Seattle, Washington, your Pocket PC will always attempt to dial the full ten digit number for your ISP, which most often results in dialing errors.

Creating a location

Setting up a dialing location consists of two separate processes, creating a location and creating a dialing pattern. To enter a location, complete the following steps:

1. Select Start ⇨ Settings ⇨ Connections tab ⇨ Modem ⇨ Dialing tab.

2. Select Home or Work from the Location drop-down box at the top of the screen. (Figure 16.2 shows the Dialing tab with the Home option selected).

3. Enter the correct area code for your home or work, select Tone or Pulse dialing, and then activate the Disable Call Waiting feature if you have subscribed to the call waiting service on your telephone.

   In Figure 16.2, you can see that I have set up the Home location in the 650 area code, chosen tone dialing, and disabled call waiting. If you are a traveler who frequents the same destinations, take a few minutes to create dialing locations on your Pocket PC for each destination. To create a new dialing location, press the New. . . button on the Modem Connections Dialing tab, enter a name for your new location, and then repeat the preceding steps.

Figure 16.2 Setting up a dialing location

Creating a dialing pattern

Once you have set up the Pocket PC to dial from different locations, you need to create a dialing pattern for each location. Dialing patterns detail how local, long distance, and international calls are made from each location. While on the Dialing Location screen (Start ⇨ Settings ⇨ Connections tab ⇨ Modem ⇨ Dialing tab), select a location from the drop-down Location menu and then tap the Dialing Patterns. . . button.

   The pop-up Dialing Patterns window has three sections: local calls, long distance calls, and international calls. Each of these sections has a text field where character codes are entered to determine how the program will dial the respective number. Figure 16.3 shows the window with the most common settings for a household telephone. Also note that the Dialing Patterns window lists the three most common character characters that can be used: local number, area code, and country code. For the expert user, a complete list of dialing pattern codes is available in the following sidebar.

Figure 16.3 The Dialing Patterns window

Because most readers would prefer to have the dialing patterns interpreted into plain English, I have created a several sample locations. Enter the characters, exactly as they appear in the following list, into the three fields on the dialing patterns window.

Warning

These settings are based on the most common dialing settings for each locale. You should research the dialing strings for each location that you set up to ensure that these settings are correct.

Home:

- Local calls: G
- Long distance calls: 1FG
- International calls: 011,EFG

Work:

- Local calls: 9,G
- Long distance calls: 9,1FG
- International calls: 9,011,EFG

Dialing Pattern Codes

Area code: F

Country code: E

Country code (GSM phones only): +

Dial the subsequent numbers with tone dialing: T

Dial the subsequent numbers with pulse dialing: P

Local number: G

Pause (2 seconds): ,

Flash (hang up for .5 seconds): !

Tone-dialing controls: ABCD *#

Wait for credit card tone (used with calling cards): $

Wait for next tone (used with $, above): W

Wait for "quiet answer": @

Hotel telephone:

- Local calls: 9,G
- Long distance calls: 8,1FG
- International calls: 8,011,EFG

Cellular phone:

- Local calls: G
- Long distance calls: FG
- International calls (GSM phones only): +,EFG
- International calls (all other cell phones): 011,EFG

In-flight telephone:

- Local calls: 1FG
- Long distance calls: 1FG
- International calls: 011,EFG

Once you have finished entering the dialing pattern, press the Ok button to save your changes. If you have created more than one location, select another location from the Location drop-down, tap the Dialing Patterns. . . button and enter the correct dialing codes for the second location. Repeat this procedure until you have correct dialing patterns established for each of your locations.

Connecting to the Internet

After all this work, you are ready to connect to the Internet. To begin an Internet session, ensure that your modem is securely inserted in the Pocket PC and then select Start ⇨ Programs ⇨ Connections folder. Tap the connection you created earlier in this chapter and the Connect To window appears, as shown in Figure 16.4. Enter your password if necessary and tap the Dial from drop-down window to select your current location. Figure 16.4 reveals the options that would be available if we had created locations for home, work, Chicago hotels, and New York hotels. Press the Connect button to initiate a call to your ISP.

Figure 16.4 The Connect To window

Note

If you are having trouble connecting to your ISP, visually inspect the Phone field in the Connect To window (shown in Figure 16.4). This line displays the actual number that will be dialed when the modem is activated. Try dialing this exact string of numbers with a regular telephone. If you cannot connect using the phone, your dialing pattern is incorrect. Check to make sure you have selected the correct location in the Dial from drop-down window.

The Pocket PC will command the modem to dial and initiate the Internet session. When the device is connected, you will hear an audio sound (if you have your volume turned up). The Log In pop-up window quickly flashes a success message and then it disappears. To end the session, you must select Start ⇨ Today and tap the connection icon at the bottom of the screen. Select Disconnect from the pop up menu and wait a few moments while the device concludes the session.

Tip

If you need to make an urgent Internet connection with your Pocket PC at work or in an office building, unplug the fax machine and use its phone cord. Fax machines use an analog line (digital phone lines can damage your modem) and the dialing instructions (whether or not to dial 9 to get out) should be printed on or near the fax.

Once a connection is established, this tiny icon is available on the Today screen (Start ⇨ Today). Tapping on the icon delivers a pop-up window with details about the connection method and data transfer speed and includes buttons to hide the window or terminate the connection.

Accessing America Online and MSN

If you are fortunate enough to use one of the major commercial online services, you can connect using a customized application that saves you from entering most or all of the complex server information that the Pocket PC requires. In fact, America Online has designed a beautiful customized client for connecting to their server that automatically detects your modem settings and gets you online in just minutes. MSN, on the other hand, has a special application that configures your Pocket PC to download mail from their secure server system.

America Online service on the Pocket PC

The CD-ROM that ships with the HP Jornada includes an application that automatically sets up the AOL service on the Pocket PC. Install the AOL set-up application on your Pocket PC and then attach a modem to your device. When you launch the application, the software dials in to AOL and downloads the latest version of the software. To install the America Online software on any other brand of Pocket PC, log into the AOL service on your desktop computer and visit keyword: Anywhere. Download the AOL Client for the Pocket PC and launch the application while your device is connected with the desktop. The first time you run the application, it will configure itself and establish a set of local numbers for regular connections.

Once you have the program properly configured, it will appear as shown in Figure 16.5. All of the major features of the online service are available from this screen including Auto AOL, a feature that enables you to download e-mail from the America Online service at scheduled intervals. This is a great way to make sure you have the latest e-mail on your device and provides an automated way to send any e-mail that you have created while away from a phone connection.

Figure 16.5 The America Online program

Note

If you install the AOL software on your Pocket PC and your screen does not have as many icons as Figure 16-5, you may have version 1.0 of AOL installed on your device. In the application Command bar, select File ⇨ About AOL to ensure that you have version 2.0 or higher. If you do not, visit "AOL keyword: anywhere" to download the newest version of the AOL software for your Pocket PC.

To set up Auto AOL, select a screen name from the drop-down box in the upper-right hand corner and tap the Auto AOL icon. The first two features, "Send 'Waiting' mail" and "Put unread mail into 'Saved'", send all of the outgoing messages to the Internet and download all your new messages from the AOL service. The third option, "Keep all mail received as new" keeps the downloaded messages on the AOL server so that you can also access them from your desktop. I highly recommend activating this feature (which is off by default) so that you have a back up copy of your e-mail should anything ever happen to your Pocket PC. Last, "Stay online when finished" enables you to keep the connection open so that you can quickly reply to any new e-mail. Once you have configured the Auto AOL options to fit your needs, select the Begin icon to start the connection to AOL and transfer the messages.

Tip

If you have more than one America Online account or are traveling with a friend who would like to check their AOL e-mail, select the "Guest" account name (as shown in Figure 16.2) in the drop-down box at the top of the screen and AOL will prompt you for the account name and password before logging in.

When traveling, you can use AOL for Pocket PC to locate local numbers. In addition to reducing the phone bill as you travel, you can set up each city in AOL so that it becomes an option in the Location drop-down shown in Figure 16.6. Notice how each city is selectable — this provides a quick way to change locations just before dialing into the AOL service. Select Edit ➪ Locations ➪ +Loc to create a new city and the application will walk you through the set up. To add additional dial-up numbers to an existing location, highlight the location name and press the +Num button.

Figure 16.6 The Location drop-down

Tip

If the hotel you are staying in charges an exorbitant amount of money for telephone calls, or if no local number is available in your immediate area, consider using AOL's toll free service. Although a fee applies based on the amount of time you use the service, it may be cheaper than using the hotel phone or paying long distance rates. In the AOL application, select Edit ➪ Locations ➪ Anywhere (surcharge). The drop-down menu displays the various toll-free phone numbers available to you and their respective fees, based on an hourly rate.

The AOL for Pocket PC software enables you to connect to the AOL service using a modem or over the Internet, if your Pocket PC is connected to an Internet-connected corporate network. To connect over a network, select Edit ➪ Locations and select TCP/IP LAN Connection from the list of locations. In addition to the e-mail service provided by the AOL for Pocket PC client, version 2.0 supports instant messaging, e-mail file attachments, Internet Explorer Web surfing, and Transmission Control Protocol/Internet Protocol (TCP/IP). This means that AvantGo channels (discussed later in this chapter) can be updated while you're connected to AOL and your favorite Internet applications can be launched while connected to the Internet with the AOL for Pocket PC software.

Cross-Reference

For a list of TCP/IP compatible applications, check out the "Internet Applications" section of Chapter 18.

The Microsoft Network E-mail service

Users of the popular MSN service can set up their Pocket PC to download e-mail from the online service using a special application called "MSN e-mail for Pocket PC". Available for free download at www.pocketpc.com, this application provides the Secure Password Authentication feature that the MSN e-mail server requires in order to download e-mail from an MSN account. Install the application on your Pocket PC and then return to the "Setting up the Inbox" section of this chapter to configure the Inbox application using the following server information:

- Server: pop3.email.msn.com
- STMP Host: secure.smtp.email.msn.com
- Domain: [leave blank]

Once configured using the preceding information, the Inbox will download MSN mail in the same way as any other e-mail service on the device. And, because the MSN service uses the same Inbox, it can take advantage of all of the same advanced rules, file attachments, and HTML compatible functionality that any other e-mail service can. Read Chapter 10, "The Inbox: Your One-Stop Information Repository," for complete information on these services and more ways to use your MSN E-mail account in powerful new ways.

Free ISPs

If you do not want to pay for Internet service, you might explore using a free Internet Service Provider to connect your Pocket PC to the Internet. Although countless services provide free Internet service on the desktop, finding an ISP that will support a Pocket PC connection is a little difficult. The ISP must support your connection to their service without any third-party software, which means that they cannot advertise to you despite the fact that you are using their free Internet connection.

You can use a search engine to find companies providing free connectivity in your area. A search on Yahoo! for "free Internet access" can provide an extensive list. But remember, you must be able to connect without installing any software (unless it is specifically designed for the Pocket PC) and the ISP must support the common protocols for connecting to the Internet; these protocols include PPP (Point to Point Protocol), SLIP (Serial Line Internet Protocol), and POP3/IMAP4 (Post Office Protocol 3/Internet Message Access Protocol 4) for transferring e-mail.

Note

Be sure to include the company you work for in your search for free ISPs. Many corporations have dial-up access numbers that provide Web and network access for your Pocket PC. Ask the network administrator at your office if this service is available to you.

Accessing the Web: AvantGo versus Mobile Favorites versus Internet Explorer browsing

Now that you have established a connection to the Internet, you probably want to view Web content. The Pocket PC has a number of different tools for browsing the Web, including Pocket Internet Explorer, Pocket Internet Explorer Mobile Favorites, and AvantGo. But which tool you use for viewing Web pages depends on how you plan to access the content.

- **Pocket Internet Explorer:** Designed for Web surfing, where you browse (using a live connection) through many diverse Web pages not all belonging to one Web site.

- **Mobile Favorites:** Created for users that have a constant connection to the Internet (via a corporate network, or a cable modem/DSL connection) to pull down personal content.

- **AvantGo Channels:** Delivers access to ready-made content in the form of channels.

Pocket Internet Explorer

Although the application contains all of the tools mentioned previously, on its own, Pocket Internet Explorer really only works for live Web surfing, where you have a modem (or network) connection directly to the Internet. As with Internet Explorer on the desktop, entering a Web address into the Address bar at the top of the application sends Pocket Internet Explorer off to retrieve the information, as shown in Figure 16.7.

Figure 16.7 Pocket Internet Explorer

Amazon.com's Pocket PC Shopping Site

Amazon.com has created a special Web site specifically for browsing on your Pocket PC. The Web site is light on graphics so that you can surf it quickly to find what you need. You can also log in using your desktop Amazon.com account to receive buying recommendations and make one-click purchases. To visit the store, point Pocket Internet Explorer to www.amazon.com/pocketpc/.

The Web page shown in the screenshot appears a little compressed because, by default, Pocket IE is programmed to compress a page in order to fit everything on it's screen. If you find the view objectionable because it makes the text too small, increase the font size by selecting View ➪ Text Size ➪ Largest. If you still have an aversion to the display, deactivate the feature by selecting View ➪ Fit to Screen.

Tip

Pocket IE has the ability to e-mail Web site addresses to your friends. If you find a Web page you would like to share, select Tools ➪ Send Link via E-mail, and Pocket IE will create a new message with the Web page's URL in the body.

Once you visit a Web page, the content (including graphics and sounds) is stored on the mobile device for a limited time in a *cache*. By default, Pocket Internet Explorer automatically checks to see if a page is cached if you enter a URL into the browser while disconnected from the Internet service. If the content is not available in the cache, you can set Pocket Internet Explorer to automatically dial a connection. Select Tools ➪ Options ➪ Connections tab and select a connection type from the drop-down list.

Separately, you can view the contents of your cache by selecting View ➪ History from the Pocket IE toolbar. You can manually control how long the cached content stays on the device or delete all of the Web pages and Mobile Channels that have been downloaded by selecting Tools ➪ Options. Pocket Internet Explorer also enables you to control the downloading of cookies (and clear the cookie cache), sounds, and images, and it notifies you when it changes from a secure Web site to an insecure one. These settings are all available in Tools ➪ Options ➪ Advanced tab.

Cross-Reference

Return to Chapter 14, "PowerToys: Work Like A Pro," to learn about the Pocket IE PowerToy that enables you to better manage the cache and other Pocket IE settings.

Mobile Favorites

Created on the desktop, Mobile Favorites are a unique Pocket Internet Explorer feature that enables you to quickly download Web content to your device. Mobile Favorites are best suited for content that does not change very often because you can only update them when you are synchronizing with the desktop, not when you connect directly to the Internet using a modem. More importantly, Mobile Favorite items become unavailable if there is ever any difficulty synchronizing the data. Figure 16.8 shows the Mobile Favorites folder (available by selecting the folder icon on Pocket Internet Explorer) with a few pieces of synchronized content. The last item on the list appears grayed out because there was a problem synchronizing this favorite. Problems can occur if you attempt to synchronize your Mobile Favorites when you're disconnected from the Internet or if the Web site that hosts your Mobile Favorite is unavailable when you synchronize.

Figure 16.8 A Mobile Favorites list

Note

When you install ActiveSync from the CD-ROM that came with your Pocket PC, a "Create Mobile Channel" icon (shown previously) is added to Internet Explorer on your desktop. This button enables you to copy any Web page to your Pocket PC. One click and the Web page will be transferred to your device at the next synchronization.

Tip

Although it does not appear so, you can download entire sections of Web sites in one Mobile Favorite. After you have created the Mobile Favorite, select Favorites ➪ Mobile Favorites on Internet Explorer on your desktop and right-click the item you wish to modify. Select Properties from the pop-up menu and the Download tab from the pop-up window that subsequently appears. The first item, "Download pages *xx* deep from this page," enables you to specify how large a section of the Web site you would like to store on your Pocket PC.

AvantGo

Because of the many difficulties I have experienced using Mobile Favorites, I highly recommend that users instead take full advantage of AvantGo for all of their Internet content needs. Designed as an information hub for all personal digital assistants (PDAs), AvantGo provides mini-portals of data via online subscriptions. Users can subscribe (for free) to thousands of channels developed by *The Wall Street Journal*, C I NET news, and many other top media and Internet companies. These channels are automatically downloaded to your Pocket PC every time you synchronize. In addition, you can update AvantGo Channels by connecting directly to the Internet using a modem or network connection; this is a feature that Mobile Favorites does not support.

Tip

User of any first-generation Pocket PC (HP Jornada 540 Series, Compaq Aero 1550, iPAQ 3650, and the Casio E-115/125/EM500/EG800) should immediately upgrade their AvantGo software by visiting `avantgo.com/help/pocketpcsetup.html`. The new version of the software vastly improves the synchronization speed and makes the channel update process much smoother and more trouble-free.

To access AvantGo Channels, click the AvantGo logo on the Pocket Internet Explorer homepage, or tap the folder icon in the toolbar and select AvantGo Channels from the window that appears. Figure 16.9 shows the AvantGo main menu. The list of channels shown are ones to which I have personally subscribed. The Add link at the bottom of the AvantGo page enables you to subscribe to some of the most popular channels directly from your device, but you must visit `www.avantgo.com` from the desktop to select from the thousands of channels available for subscription. The Remove link enables you to mark channels for deletion the next time you synchronize with your desktop computer.

Figure 16.9 The AvantGo main menu

In addition to the channels offered on the AvantGo Web site, you can create channels of any Web page, such as your favorite news Web site, a personal Web page, or even Intranet content from your company. I download the company phone list from our Intranet so that I have a continually up-to-date version of our employee's cellular phone numbers. To set up your desktop computer so that you can automatically create your own AvantGo channels, select My Account" while logged in to AvantGo on your desktop computer and scroll down to the Channel Tools. I use the AvantGo AutoChannels feature, which enables me to create an AvantGo channel by choosing a bookmark from my favorites.

Tip

To save connection fees, set up all of your favorite Web sites as AvantGo Channels and then as soon as you connect to your ISP, perform a modem sync. When AvantGo is finished downloading your channels, hang up. You now have an entire sphere of Internet content waiting for your review in AvantGo.

Performing a modem sync and using tools

To update your AvantGo channels using a modem, connect to your ISP, and then open Pocket Internet Explorer. To do this, tap the AvantGo icon, scroll to the bottom of the AvantGo channel Web page, and then select tools ⇨ Modem Sync. The device displays a Progress bar while the channels are being downloaded. When complete, all of your AvantGo channels will contain the newest content. This is a great way to keep yourself in the know with news, weather, sports, and other information while on the go.

Note

The Tools option mentioned in this section is a hyperlink on the AvantGo main menu page, not the Tools item in the Pocket Internet Explorer Command bar. The Tools option can be seen in Figure 16.9, to the left of the Add and Remove options.

Two other important features on the AvantGo Tools page include Channel Manager and Forms Manager. Opening the Channel Manager page displays a list of each channel you are subscribed to and the amount of memory that the channel is using on your device. If you need to temporarily regain memory, visit this page, activate the checkboxes of the channels using the most memory, and then press the Clear button. The channels will be removed from your device immediately but, when you synchronize next, they will be copied back onto your Pocket PC.

The Forms Manager page enables you to see what information you have sent to the channels to which you have subscribed and the results of this information. For example, if you subscribe to the Weather Channel's AvantGo page, you have probably submitted a form with your ZIP code so that you can receive local weather information. This information can be helpful when troubleshooting applications that seem to be giving you incorrect information based on data that you entered into a specific form.

Tip

If you have recently deleted a large number of channels, select Tools ➪ Forms Manager on the AvantGo Web page and inspect the list for channels you have removed. Activate their checkboxes and tap the Delete button. This removes the cached forms and responses and clear up memory.

The Choose Server and Server Options in the "Server & Connection" section of the AvantGo Tools page are best left unused. If you need to reestablish a connection to an AvantGo server, here is the most effective way set up your Pocket PC using www.avantgo.com:

1. Dock your Pocket PC with the desktop and wait until the device has completed synchronization.

2. Log onto www.avantgo.com/channels/ and tap the My Account text above your personalized list of channels.

3. Select Software Setup from the My Account menu.

4. Select Configure Mobile Link and follow the on-screen instructions.

Once you've completed these steps, the AvantGo server settings are transferred to your Pocket PC. These steps can be repeated as often as necessary and may be required if AvantGo changes their server settings.

A few "must have" AvantGo channels

Once you start using AvantGo, you will find that information is far easier to obtain when you can automatically download it instead of having to surf the Web for answers. Although everyone will have their own favorite AvantGo channels, a few channels should be on everyone's subscription. They provide news, weather, and travel information but, best of all, these channels are all free of charge. You can subscribe to channels on the AvantGo Web site or by surfing on your desktop to the URLs provided.

Naturally, one of the oldest search engines on the Internet has one of the coolest AvantGo channels. If you have a My Yahoo! account, you can automatically download the content on your handheld by subscribing to the Yahoo! Channel. With personalized news, sports scores, stocks, movies and weather, there is plenty of reading material to get you through a boring meeting or a short flight. The channel works even if you do not have a My Yahoo! account by delivering default news and sports information to your Pocket PC. Complete information and a subscription link is available at mobile.yahoo.com/wireless/home/.

The Weather Channel offers a self-titled AvantGo page that delivers a seven-day weather forecast to your Pocket PC. Enter your ZIP code and the top of the page offers a current temperature based on the time that you synchronized, followed by a seven-day forecast. A link to national weather news that has been downloaded to your device is available at the bottom of the Web page. You can subscribe to the Weather Channel at `www.avantgo.com` or learn more about it at `cgi.weather.com/custom/wireless_splash/`.

For frequent or infrequent business or casual travelers, one of the best channels to subscribe to is Expedia To Go, from Microsoft's Expedia travel Web site (`www.expedia.com`). Shown in Figure 16.10, Expedia To Go stores all of the travel arrangements that you have made on the Microsoft Expedia Web site, and it is designed to function as your travel liaison. Complete itineraries including flight information, hotel reservations, and car rentals are organized by trip with confirmation numbers and contact information. Expedia To Go even provides you with turn-by-turn driving directions from the airport to the hotel if you have made flight and lodging reservations on their Web site. Other routes can be set up on Expedia.com and downloaded to your Pocket PC, complete with graphical maps. In addition to the itinerary and trip planning features, Expedia To Go stores all of your frequent flyer, hotel membership, and car rental account numbers along with more than 50 telephone numbers for the top airline, hotel, and car rental organizations. And finally, wireless PDAs can access flight status and airline timetables to track flight arrivals and departures as well as search for a new flight if your travel plans change. Expedia To Go is available at `www.expedia.com/togo/`.

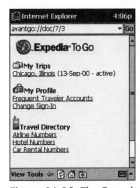

Figure 16.10 The Expedia To Go channel

Customize your home page in Pocket Internet Explorer

The Web page that opens when Pocket Internet Explorer is launched is called the *home page*. You can customize Pocket IE to display any Web page you want as the home page, including Mobile Favorites, AvantGo channels, and regular Internet addresses. To set the home page on Pocket IE, complete the following steps:

1. Open Pocket Internet Explorer and navigate to the page you wish to use as a home page.

2. Select Tools ⇨ Options. . .

3. Tap the Use Current button

4. Press the Ok button to save your changes.

When you tap the Use Current button, the Web site address is displayed on screen, as shown in Figure 16.11. Visually confirm that the address is correct, or repeat the preceding steps to correct the entry. Once you have set your own home page, Pocket IE begins at the Web address you have designated every time it is launched. In addition, you can press the Home icon on the Pocket IE command bar to return to your home page. To reset Pocket IE's home page to the original home page, press the Use Default button as shown in Figure 16.11. This will return the Web site address to about:home on the Options page.

Figure 16.11 Configuring the home page

Tip

If you only use AvantGo channels, set the AvantGo channel list as your home page.

Set up Pocket Internet Explorer to connect to the Internet automatically

Once you have set up Pocket Internet Explorer to preload with your favorite Web site, you might want to program the application to automatically dial your ISP. This enables Pocket IE to connect to the Internet whenever you enter a Web page that is not stored in the device's cache. The process is simple:

1. Set up your Pocket PC to dial into your ISP as directed in the "Setting up the connection" segment earlier in this chapter.

2. Select Tools ⇨ Options. . . ⇨ Connection tab

3. From the Type drop-down menu, select your ISP.

4. Check the "Access remove content automatically" option.

5. If you are using a corporate network, enter in the proxy server information, if required.

6. Press Ok to save your changes.

Upgrade Pocket Internet Explorer to 128-bit security

Microsoft has created a patch to support 128-bit SSL (Secure Sockets Layer) security for Pocket Internet Explorer. This is useful if you plan to use your Pocket PC to perform online banking tasks or stock trading. You can obtain the update, free of charge, from the "downloads" section of www.pocketpc.com.

When you have completed setting up the Connections tab, your screen should resemble Figure 16.12. Obviously, your ISP name will be different, but it is important to note that the drop-down window should not say Make new connection. This feature is obviously best suited for users that have the Pocket PC connected to a wireless modem (see the following section of this chapter) or constantly have a modem plugged into their device and connected to a telephone cord.

Figure 16.12 Configuring an automatic ISP connection

Note

If you only use your Pocket PC for mobile channels and AvantGo content, you may wish to disable this option so that Pocket Internet Explorer does not attempt to dial out every time the browser cannot locate Web content.

Create a list of Favorites

In addition to the Mobile Favorites, which consists of Web content that can only be updated from the desktop, Pocket Internet Explorer can maintain a list of Favorites, which are bookmarks that take you directly to Web sites. To help keep them straight, all you need to remember is that Pocket Internet Explorer Favorites are exactly like Favorites on the desktop version of Internet Explorer. But one confusing factor in Pocket IE is that Favorites and Mobile Favorites are available from the same menu.

You can create a Favorite by performing the following steps:

1. Surf to a Web site that you would like to have as a Favorite.

2. Tap the folder icon in the Pocket Internet Explorer command bar, select the Add/Delete tab and then press the Add. . . button.

3. Pocket Internet Explorer will automatically enter the Hypertext Markup Language (HTML) page title from the Web page as the name of the Favorite. Because many Web sites use very long page titles, you might want to shorten the title to something you can quickly recognize.

4. Press Ok to save the Favorite in your list.

Cross-Reference

For instructions on how to make subfolders for your Pocket Internet Explorer Favorites, refer to the "Make any menu your own" section of Chapter 17.

Once you have saved the Favorite, Pocket Internet Explorer returns to the Web browsing window. To surf to one of the Web sites you have saved as a Favorite, tap the folder icon in the Command bar and select the Web site from the list. Pocket IE will return to the Web browsing window and begin loading the page. To delete a Favorite, Tap the folder icon in the Pocket Internet Explorer Command bar and then tap the Add/Delete tab. Tap the Favorite you wish to delete and press the Delete button.

The IEClearTypeUtil freeware application

I have always wished that ClearType technology was employed across the entire Pocket PC platform. Having an PDA with the ability to display super-crisp text at incredibly small font sizes would be an invaluable benefit for scanning long volumes of text in a Pocket Word document or data in a Pocket Excel spreadsheet. While system-wide deployment of ClearType is not yet a reality, Web Information Solutions has created an application that implements ClearType in one of the most important places for reading small text: Pocket Internet Explorer.

Once it is activated, you can launch Pocket Internet Explorer from the Start Menu and you should immediately notice a difference. The text will be bolder and smaller fonts will appear less jagged than normal. This is especially noticeable when Pocket Internet Explorer is set to Fit to Screen mode (View ⇨ Fit to Screen) or Smallest Text mode (View ⇨ Text Size ⇨ Smallest) because the font size is significantly reduced. Figure 16.13 illustrates the difference between regular text and ClearType-enhanced text. On the left is a normal HTML page; on the right is the same page with the ClearType feature activated.

Note

When the IEClearTypeUtil has activated the ClearType feature, the text in the Help application (which is HTML-based) will also be enhanced.

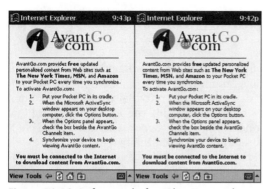

Figure 16.13 Before and after ClearType enhancement

It is important to note that some users do not favor ClearType text because they consider it blurry or illegible. Most often, this is because they have not optimized their screen for viewing ClearType content (see the following Cross-Reference). However, if you prefer viewing HTML with standard text, you can remove the IEClearTypeUtil program from your device as follows:

1. Run the application (Start ➪ Programs ➪ IEClearTypeUtil) and tap the Turn ClearType Off button to ensure that the program will not leave all HTML windows ClearType enabled.

2. Press the Ok button to ensure that the application is completely shut down.

3. Select Start ➪ Settings ➪ System tab ➪ Remove programs.

4. Highlight the WebIS IEClearTypeUtil item in the program list and press the Remove button.

Cross-Reference

For information on how to adjust your screen for optimal ClearType viewing, review the "Supercharging Pocket Reader" section of Chapter 12.

Going Wireless

Now that you have so many reasons to connect to the Internet, it is only a matter of time until you find yourself trying to connect everywhere you go. But constantly carrying phone cords and searching for telephone jacks to connect becomes quickly tiresome. Now, with a number of different accessories, you can connect to the Internet wirelessly and be the envy of all your friends.

Infrared communication with an IrDA-equipped mobile phone

By a long shot, the coolest way to connect to your Pocket PC is by just using your cellular phone. If you have an Infrared Data Association (IrDA) compatible mobile phone, the Pocket PC can connect to it to dial your ISP and communicate wirelessly. Figure 16.14 shows an example using the Jornada Pocket PC and an IrDA-equipped Nokia cell phone. Notice that there are no wires. All that the infrared beam requires is a direct line between the two infrared ports.

Figure 16.14 Infrared communication

Enable wireless communications

To enable wireless communications, follow these steps:

1. Call your cellular service provider and make sure that you have activated the data communications feature activated on your service (there may be a service charge for this feature).

2. Create a new connection on your Pocket PC by selecting Start ⇨ Settings ⇨ Connections tab and tapping on the Modem icon. Name the connection "Cell Modem" and select Generic IrDA modem from the Select a Modem drop-down menu. Set the baud rate as 14,400 (the standard data transfer rate for cellular communications; check with your carrier to ensure they can support this speed) and use the Advanced button to enter your ISP settings from earlier in this chapter.

3. Press the Next button and enter the phone number for your ISP.

4. Press Next to get to the final screen and deactivate the "Cancel call if not connected within" and "Wait for dial tone before dialing" features.

5. Press Finish to save the new connection.

6. When the window closes, you will be returned to the Modem connections window. Select the Dialing tab and press the New button to create a new location. Name the location "Wireless", ensure that the Tone dialing feature is activated and disable call waiting is deactivated, and then press the Dialing Patterns button.

7. Enter **FG** in all three fields so that the phone always dials the area code and phone number of your ISP, regardless of where you are (if your cellular provider requires you to dial a "1" before the area code, enter **1FG**). Press Ok twice to close the Dialing Patterns window and save your new connection.

Now you're all ready to connect wirelessly. Point your Pocket PC's infrared port at the port of your cellular phone and then select Start ⇨ Programs ⇨ Connections ⇨ Cell Modem. When the window appears, enter your account information and ensure that the "Dial from" field is set to Wireless. Press Connect and you will be surfing the Web using your cellular phone.

The Socket Digital Phone Card

If you are not fortunate enough to have an infrared equipped cellular phone, a second option to enable Pocket PC communications over the cellular network is available. Socket Communications (www.socketcom.com) has developed a Digital Phone Card that connects the Pocket PC to many common cellular phones via the CompactFlash port. Figure 16.15 shows the Jornada Pocket PC connected to a Motorola cellular phone. Notice how the connection kit seamlessly connects the two devices using existing ports. This is a fairly inexpensive way to quickly add wireless capability if you already own a compatible cellular phone and a Pocket PC.

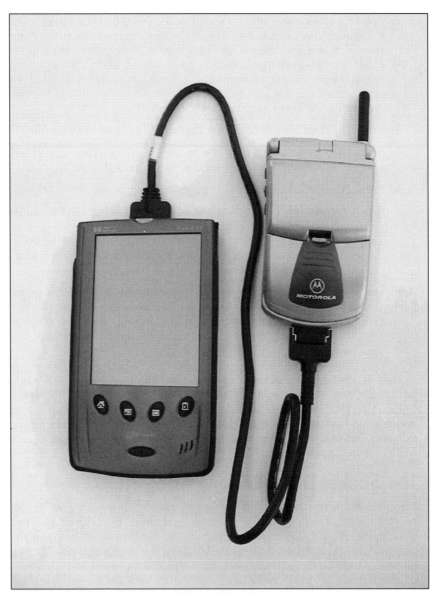

Figure 16.15 The Socket Digital Phone Card

HP Jornada users already have the drivers for the Socket Digital Phone card installed on their device. All other Pocket PC users should install the driver from the CD-ROM that accompanies the Socket accessory. Once the driver is installed, insert the Socket DPC into the CompactFlash slot and connected it to your cellular phone. Next, follow the exact process listed in this chapter's "Enable wireless communications" section to set up the IrDA modem (including calling your cellular carrier to activate data communications service). However, choose "Socket DPC" from the Select a Modem drop-down box instead of "Generic IrDA modem."

The Novatel Minstrel 540 Wireless Sled

One invention created solely for the HP Jornada line of Pocket PCs is the wireless sled from Novatel Wireless (`www.novatelwireless.com`). This accessory is the next step beyond the cell phone-Pocket PC hybrid. Instead, it makes the HP Jornada a completely self-sufficient wireless communications device. Figure 16.16 shows the accessory behind a HP Jornada Pocket PC. Designed to attach to the back of the Jornada with just a few screws, the system is almost undetectable behind the unit, except for a small antenna protruding from the top and an increase in the overall thickness of the device. The screws in the back of the wireless sled permit the accessory to be quickly removed from the Pocket PC

Figure 16.16 The wireless sled

The Minstrel 540 is a Cellular Digital Packet Data (CDPD) modem, which means that it communicates using the same networks that cellular phones do. CDPD modems transfer data at 19,200 Kbps, a speed considerably slower than the 56,600 Kbps available in landline modems, but still acceptable for sending text e-mail and surfing Web sites(such as Amazon.com's special Pocket PC Web site, mentioned earlier in this chapter) that are specifically designed for browsing on a wireless handheld device. Using minimal graphics and keeping the Web page content small streamlines these sites and helps them download quickly using the Minstrel 540.

The Minstrel 540 has a rechargeable lithium ion battery that can operate from six to eight hours on a single charge. When the HP Jornada is docked with the Minstrel 540, a single power cord plugged into the wireless modem will recharge both devices. This means that travelers have one less cord to carry if they take the Minstrel 540 with them on their next trip.

Minstrel 540 Service plans

Just as a cellular phone requires a phone company to provide telephone service, the wireless sled requires a service provider to deliver wireless data. There are a few different service plans you can opt for from the companies that provide wireless service. Your options depend on whether the company provides wireless coverage in your area and on your usage habits. Two companies with vast wireless networks, OmniSky (www.omnisky.com) and GoAmerica (www.goamerica.com), provide service for the Novatel Minstrel 540 wireless sled. Users considering purchasing the wireless sled should consult the both providers' Web sites to check for coverage in their area and review their service plans. Both offer unlimited coverage for a monthly fee, and GoAmerica offers a low-usage plan with lower monthly service fees and per-use charges. The Novatel Wireless Minstrel 540 Sled is a great solution for the constantly connected professional who does not want to relinquish style for communications features.

Tip

If you pay for an unlimited use service contract, consider downloading an Instant Messaging Application such as AOL's Instant Messenger (www.aol.com/AIM/) or BSQUARE Messenger (www.bsquare.com) so that you can communicate with your friends in real time from anywhere in the world.

Wireless portal software

Designed to work specifically with the HP Jornada Wireless Sled, OmniSky has developed an on-device Web portal that preloads content using their wireless service. Upon launch, the software checks for updates to the portal content and then presents a set of categories with drop-down subcategories, as shown in Figure 16.17. Selecting any subcategory delivers a list of Web sites, many of which have content streamlined for wireless viewing. In addition, the software provides appropriate (but not obtrusive) advertising for services related to the current category.

Figure 16.17 OmniSky's customized portal

One innovative option in the OmniSky service is the taxi-cab pick up feature. In the Travel category, OmniSky has partnered with 1-800-TAXICAB to offer you the ability to call a cab from anywhere in the U.S. Users select the 1-800-TAXICAB icon and fill out an order form with basic taxi pick-up information to have their order relayed to the appropriate cab company in their area. Although that sounds like a simple enough task, the compelling wireless feature of the 1-800-TAXICAB service is that users can monitor their request in real time, assuring that a cab company received the order.

Icons on the left of the interface provide quick access to the Inbox and Pocket Internet Explorer favorites, and also provide business and personal phone number searches via InfoSpace and search engine capability using the popular Google engine. At your discretion, the application also places an icon in the Pocket PC taskbar (shown in the upper-right corner of Figure 16.17) to return to the mini-portal with a single tap. The software is available free with OmniSky's Internet service. GoAmerica has a similar browser-based service dubbed "MyGo.Web".

The NextCell Pocket Spider

If you do not own the HP Jornada Pocket PC, or if you are looking for an alternate wireless modem solution, NextCell makes the Pocket Spider wireless modem. The Pocket Spider, shown in Figure 16.18, is a Type I CompactFlash card, which means it will operate in any Pocket PC with a CompactFlash card slot. In addition, the Pocket Spider card has built-in drivers and software that automatically install onto the Pocket PC when the Pocket Spider is inserted into the CF slot.

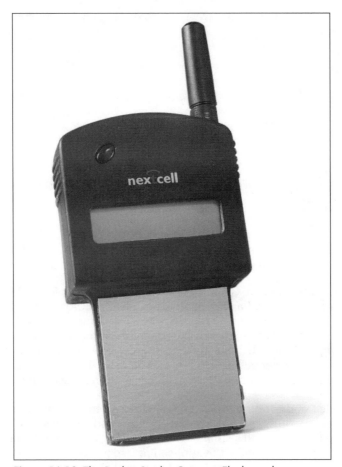

Figure 16.18 The Pocket Spider CompactFlash card

As with the Novatel Minstrel 540, the Pocket Spider is a CDPD modem that transfers data and uses a lithium ion rechargeable battery. In addition, the Pocket Spider has an accessory option to receive Global Positioning System data from satellites so that it can be used with mapping software. Service plans for the NextCell Pocket Spider vary; rebates are available when you purchase the Pocket Spider with a one-year wireless service contract. For more information on the Pocket Spider and available wireless service plans, visit www.nextcell.com.

Infrared communication with the Psion Travel Modem

The final communications accessory for the Pocket PC offers communications over regular telephone lines in a unique and wireless manner. Figure 16.19 shows the Psion Travel Modem, a device that plugs into telephone line in your home and wirelessly connects the Pocket PC to an ISP just as a CompactFlash modem would.

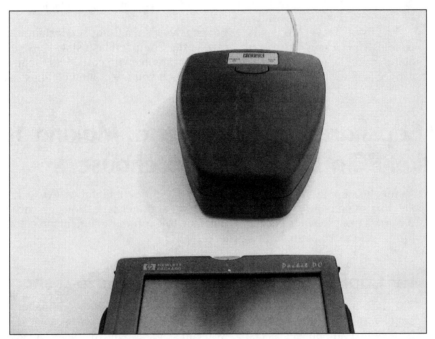

Figure 16.19 The Psion Travel Modem

To set up a communications session with the Travel modem, create a new connection on your Pocket PC by selecting Start ➪ Settings ➪ Connections tab and tapping the Modem icon. Name the connection "Travel Modem" and select Generic IrDA modem from the Select a Modem drop-down menu. Set the baud rate as 115200 and then use the Advanced button to enter your ISP settings from earlier in this chapter. Press the Next button and enter the phone number for your ISP. Press Next and enter any applicable settings for your communications preferences.

Note

Drivers for the Psion Travel Modem are built in to the HP Jornada. Owners of other Pocket PC devices should visit www.psionconnect.com to download the software for your specific brand of Windows Powered device.

Because the Travel modem can use the same location as a regular modem, you are all ready to connect to your ISP. Point your Pocket PC's infrared port at the front of the Travel Modem and select Start ⇨ Programs ⇨ Connections ⇨ Travel Modem. When the window appears, enter your account information and press Connect. The Travel modem's data light should begin to flash and you will be connected within seconds.

The Psion Travel Modem is less expensive than a CompactFlash modem and enables you to keep the memory card in the CompactFlash slot. These benefits alone make the modem worth owning, but anyone who considers themselves a gadget junkie will love how cool it looks when you are communicating!

HP Capshare and HP JetSend: Making Your Pocket PC a Document Warehouse

As much as I regret it, I have to deal with paper documentation every day of my life. It is an unavoidable truth that I simply cannot escape. However, two new products from Hewlett Packard enable me to capture documents in electronic format and store them in my Pocket PC.

HP CapShare 920: copy documents in a snap

The CapShare 920 (www.capshare.com) is an electronic device smaller than a paperback book (4.1"×5.5"×1.5" and weighs 12.5 ounces) that can scan an entire page of text and images as fast as you can swipe it over the page. Once you have scanned it into the CapShare, you can wirelessly transfer the image to anything from printers to desktop computers to PDAs, — even to a cellular telephone. Now, expense report receipts, business cards, paper forms (that can be filled out electronically later), phone book listings, legal documents I signed, and even large flip charts from company meetings are all quickly and easily captured by the CapShare.

In fact, the handheld device can copy a page that is over 13 square feet in size. To explain it on a smaller scale; if you wanted to copy this page out of the book (which of course you wouldn't do for copyright reasons), you'd simply place the CapShare on the upper-left corner of the page, swipe it all the way to the bottom, move it over to the right, and then swipe back up to the top. This U-shape move-ment over the page enables you to get an entire 8½ inches of page content with the CapShare's 5-inch scanner surface. The only hitch is that the device requires that you overlap ½ inch on every pass so it knows where to paste the pieces together. If your document is larger than a piece of paper, you can simply repeat the U-shaped path as many times as you want. And once you've got the data into your CapShare, you'll be amazed with all the things you can do with it.

Tip

You can create instant copies of a document using the CapShare 920. After you have captured the document, press the yellow Transfer button twice and point it at almost any printer with IrDA infrared. The document comes out of the printer in near copy-machine quality (and well above fax quality).

The CapShare device is compatible with Windows Powered, Windows 95/98/NT, EPOC32 (Psion Series 5), and even the Nokia 9000i/9000il/9110 Communicator. A serial cable is provided for connection to your desktop computer, but the device uses its infrared port for connecting to all the other devices. Figure 16.20 shows the CapShare sending a copied document to the Jornada Pocket PC via infrared. HP calls the transfer technology "JetSend," and claims that over 5 million JetSend-enabled devices are already in use today. When you transfer a document to any Windows-based computer, the documents can be stored as PDF (Adobe's Portable Document Format) or TIF (Tagged Image File Format, a standard graphics file format). The TIF file format is available to users of graphics and optical character recognition (OCR) applications WHO want to convert the file to text for editing or pasting into a document.

On a Psion or Windows Powered device, the document is transferred as a TIF file. HP offers a free version of JetSend for Windows CE (described in the next section of this chapter) that enables you to receive, view, and annotate documents received from CapShare. Finally, sending a document to a Nokia Communicator enables you to wirelessly fax or e-mail the document anywhere in the world.

Tip

If you plan on e-mailing the document to other users, PDF should be your file type of choice, as most people have Adobe Acrobat Reader installed on their system, which it keeps the document's file size small.

The device comes with 4MB of memory, which can store up to 150 pages of flip chart data in compressed mode, up to 50 letter-size documents in normal mode, or 15 pages in Graphics (high-quality) mode. Two fully charged nickel metal hydride (NiMH) batteries (4 are included with the device) can copy and send 100 letter-sized, Normal mode pages. Also included with the device is a compact NiMH battery charger, serial cable, capture sleeve, soft cloth carrying pouch, user guide, and a software CD-ROM.

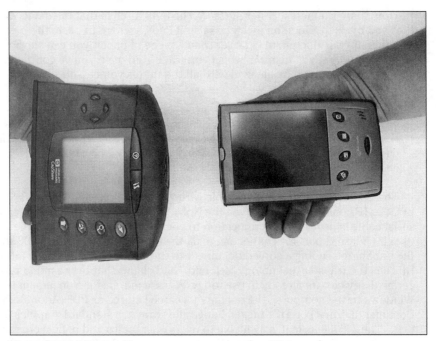

Figure 16.20 The CapShare communicating with a HP Jornada

HP JetSend: the document filing system for Windows Powered devices

Used in conjunction with the CapShare 920, HP JetSend enables you to wirelessly receive scanned documents. However, the software does much more than just link the two devices. For example, users of the HP C500 Digital Camera could send a document or photo to the Windows CE device, and the user can view and annotate it using highlighting or text. Once the user is satisfied with the document, it can be sent via infrared to a laptop or printer, as an e-mail attachment directly from the JetSend application, or copied off the device during synchronization.

Note

The CD-ROM that ships with the HP Jornada Pocket PC includes a full version of JetSend.

The software can be downloaded from www.jetsend.com and can be installed on any Windows Powered device. One ancillary benefit built into the JetSend software is that you can now exchange e-mail with other devices via infrared, a feature previously unavailable in the Pocket PC. Older Windows Powered devices also receive the added functionality of being able to beam appointments and tasks.

Summary

After completing this chapter you should have a thorough understanding of the different ways of collecting Web pages using Pocket Internet Explorer. You should also have a Pocket PC that is now fully equipped to communicate on the Internet. Also, you've learned about the many different accessories that provide wireless communications capabilities to the Pocket PC. And finally, you know that a technology called JetSend expands the number of devices that the Pocket PC can exchange information with.

Now it is time to focus on advanced personalization for your Pocket PC. In the next chapter, you will learn what basic changes should to be made to your device right away, and you'll discover a number of ways to customize the system to reflect your personal tastes and preferences.

CHAPTER 17

Advanced Personalization for Your Faithful Companion

IN THIS CHAPTER
- Supercharge the Pocket PC interface
- Ten things every user should change in the Control Panel
- Customize your Start menu and startup applications

Now that you have learned to skillfully use the interface Pocket PC and applications, it is time to customize the device to meet your needs. After all, a system that is tailored to your personal tastes and needs provides a far more pleasurable experience than one that you must constantly adapt yourself to. This section is for power users who are very comfortable working with the Pocket PC interface and applications. Changes in this section may make your device operate slightly differently than many of the examples in this book. For example, the "Customize your Start Menu" section will instruct you on how to move icons in the Start menu so that your frequently used applications are close at hand. In every situation, instructions for restoring each component to its original default state are provided.

Supercharge the Pocket PC Interface

The Pocket PC interface is best described as the look and feel of the device. The methods that you use to input data and audio responses from the system are two examples of interface elements. They are also two interfaces that you can easily adjust and customize to enhance your overall experience with the Pocket PC. Making modifications to the first interface (data input) allows you to increase the precision of the system's capability to recognize what you are trying to write, and modifications to the second interface makes the device more interesting and enjoyable.

Using File Explorer

Throughout the rest of this chapter, you will be moving files around your Pocket PC. The Windows Powered operating system includes a file-management utility called File Explorer. Although each Pocket PC application can copy, delete, and move files in the program's native format, File Explorer enables you to work with all of the files in your Pocket PC's memory and also provides access to directories that are not otherwise reachable.

To launch File Explorer, select Start ➪ Programs ➪ File Explorer. The program always starts in the My Documents folder. Should you ever launch another program and then return to the File Explorer using the shortcut bar, the application will reset to display the contents of the My Documents folder. If you wish to avoid this, select Start ➪ Settings ➪ System ➪ Memory ➪ Running Programs ➪ File Explorer and press the Activate button. This will return you to File Explorer without resetting the directory.

In nearly every example, you will see a reference to navigate to a subfolder of My Device. Because File Explorer starts in \My Device\My Documents\ you will need to move up one folder before you can progress to any other files inside of the

My Device folder. Consider My Device the equivalent of the root directory, or C:\, of your desktop computer. All other folders spawn from this folder. But because it is generally accepted that 99 percent of all file management is performed within the My Documents folder, the application starts off in that subfolder. To back up one directory, tap the My Documents drop-down box in the upper-left corner of File Explorer and tap My Device. Figure 17.1 shows File Explorer with the drop-down menu activated and My Device highlighted.

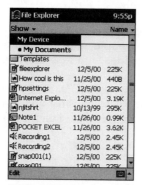

Figure 17.1 Moving to the My Device folder

After you open the My Device folder, you will see four or five folders:

- **My Documents:** The folder where you began. This folder holds all of the documents that you have created on your Pocket PC.

- **Program Files:** This folder is the area where new applications are installed on your device. You can explore this folder if you wish to see how much memory the applications that you have installed are using. In addition, \Program Files\Communication\Mail Attachments\ is where all of the Inbox mail attachments are stored. Browsing to this folder will show you exactly how much memory these files are using.

- **Temp:** A storage space that the Windows Powered operating system uses for temporary files.

- **Windows:** The location for all of the files that run the Windows-powered operating system. Modifications to files in this directory, and to any of its subdirectories, should be performed with extreme caution. (Of course, none of the procedures outlined in this book will cause any harm to your system.)

- **Storage Card (optional):** This folder is only available if you have inserted a memory card into the accessory slot of your Pocket PC. The Storage Card folder takes you directly to the top directory of the memory card.

Warning

None of these folders should be deleted, renamed, or moved. These folders and all of their contents are system folders, which the Pocket PC operating system needs to function properly. Although you may freely explore these folders without any apprehension, you should never delete or move their contents unless you are already know what the effect of doing so is.

Now that you have learned how to launch File Explorer and to navigate to the My Device folder, you can continue to customize your device throughout the rest of this chapter. But while you have File Explorer open, you might want to organize your files in the \My Documents\ folder. For example, consider creating a My Library subfolder for your e-books (which coincides with ReaderWorks, the desktop e-book publishing software).

Other new folder options include a My Music folder for MP3s, My Files for Pocket Excel and Pocket Word documents, and My Recordings for voice memos. Creating these folders now will make the My Documents folder much easier to navigate after your device is packed full of files.

Secret Voice Recorder playback controls

Although File Explorer normally launches the application when you tap a specific file, Voice Recorder files earn special treatment when selected in File Explorer. Launch File Explorer and tap a voice recording. The result should mirror Figure 17.2. As you can see, rather than launching the Voice Recorder application, File Explorer has a set of controls that appear. The Sound file plays once and then can be replayed by tapping the Play button.

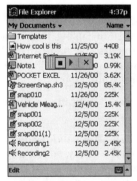

Figure 17.2 Playback controls for voice memos

The three subtle hash marks on the left side of the pop-up controls enable you to move the controls around the screen. Simply tap and hold the hash marks and move the stylus to reposition the controls. The Stop button enables you to discontinue playback of a recording and the X button closes the pop-up window.

Sadly, only one voice recording control set can be active at a time, so you cannot fill the screen with different voice memos. Furthermore, tapping File Explorer or selecting another application closes the pop-up window.

Tip

If you copy a voice recording into the Start menu or Programs menu (see instructions in the "Add Any File to the Start Menu" section later in this chapter) and run it once, the Pocket PC will add the voice recording to the shortcut bar at the top of the Start Menu as shown in Figure 17.3. This is a great way to quickly replay multiple files. Because the icons are not titled in the shortcut bar, you will have to remember what order you played them in.

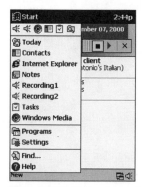

Figure 17.3 Voice Recorder files in the Start Menu

Make room for two more icons on the shortcut bar

The shortcut bar is an invaluable feature of the Pocket PC. By default, the shortcut bar presents the icons of the last six applications that you launched on your device. This is a great way to switch applications quickly and easily. To make the shortcut bar even more useful, you can perform a quick procedure that adds two more icons on the shortcut bar, so that you have eight quick shortcuts.

1. Open File Explorer (Start ⇨ Programs ⇨ File Explorer) and navigate to \My Device\Windows\Start Menu\.

2. Tap and hold any icon in the list and select Rename.

3. Change the item's name so that it contains 21 to 23 characters, including spaces. Two options for possible filenames are changing Internet Explorer to Pockt Internet Explorer or changing Windows Media to Windows Media Player (with two spaces between the words Media and Player).

Note

The number of characters required to extend the shortcut bar is an approximation based on the average width of each character in a filename. If a name is too wide to fit in the Start menu, Pocket PC will cut off the end of the name and add three periods to it. Pocket Internet Explorer name was reduced to Pockt Internet Explorer in the example above to avoid this problem.

Naturally, your filename renaming options depend on which applications you have in the Start menu. But the concept works with any text icons. After you have renamed the file, tap the Start button. You should notice two more icons on the shortcut bar at the top of the screen as shown in Figure 17.4. This feature does not impede or hinder any other functions of the Pocket PC and adds a third more shortcut icons with just two minutes of work.

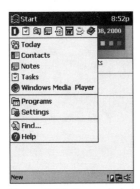

Figure 17.4 Expanded shortcut menu with eight icons

Improve your text entry accuracy

Although your handheld computer is a great product for viewing data, it is equally valuable as a data gatherer. Therefore, to gain complete satisfaction out of using the Pocket PC, you have to master one of the methods of entering text. Moreover, even though I am sure that even identical twins would argue over which method of data entry is best, there are several tips that will improve your accuracy for each method of data entry. If you have already steadfastly decided which method you prefer, skip to that section below. Otherwise, read all of the tips for improving data entry and try them out. You might find that an entry method that you previously shunned is really better for your writing style.

Keyboard

Although few tricks exist for improving your accuracy on the keyboard, there are a number of keyboard shortcuts that will greatly improve your interaction with the Pocket PC. First, use the keyboard *gestures*. Teach yourself to tap and hold a letter, and then to move the stylus toward the top of the screen and lift it off to capitalize a letter. This step alone saves at least one keystroke for every sentence that you type. Next, after you are comfortable using this gesture, learn the gestures for space, backspace, and enter. These will increase your text entry speed because they can be performed anywhere on the keyboard, rather than trying to find the tiny buttons for each command. Finally, use the following keyboard shortcuts to perform high-level functions in applications without accessing the menu:

- **Ctl+A**: Selects all of the text in a file, or all of the items in a list. This is an excellent tool for quickly selecting the entire passage of a document, or selecting all of the files in a folder for copying.

- **Ctl+X/C/V**: The Cut/Copy/Paste commands. These keyboard combinations enable you to edit text and files without accessing the Edit menu or the object's tap and hold menu.

- **Ctl+Z:** The Undo function. Quickly reverses the last change made in a document. This is the exact same function as the Undo command on the Edit menu.

- **Ctl+N:** New object. This command creates a new document in whatever application is currently running. This is the same functionality as pressing the New button at the bottom of the screen.

- **Ctl+Q:** Close window. Designed to work only on Microsoft Pocket PC applications, Ctl+Q will completely exit the application currently running. This is an extremely fast way to conserve memory on your device and has no equal for speed or handiness.

Cross-Reference

For more tips on how to use the keyboard, review the opening section of Chapter 3, "Input Methods."

Character Recognizer

Character Recognizer is a simple, single-letter recognition system that makes it extremely easy to write accurately without any training on the application and without significant change to the way you write. However, a simple examination of your own personal writing style can ease the transition of going from writing on paper to writing onscreen. If you usually write in block print (all uppercase letters), change the Character Recognizer to Uppercase mode (Start ⇨ Settings ⇨ Input ⇨ Options) and write as you normally do. Otherwise, the application's default of Lowercase mode should produce satisfactory results for most people's printed handwriting.

To enhance the accuracy of Character Recognizer when in Lowercase mode, follow the common principles for writing letters that you learned in grade school. For example, when in Lowercase mode (the Character Recognizer default), write the letter p with the stem beginning just below the dotted midline and ending considerably beneath the solid baseline, as shown in Figure 17.5. Notice how the letter never quite reaches the midline. Short letters (such as a, w, and o) should also follow this example and never reach the midline. Only letters that are tall even when lowercase (f, l, b, d, h, k, and t) should be written traversing the midline and these characters should never cross the baseline. Additionally, the letter "i" should be written with the stem beneath the midline and the dot above the midline. Uppercase mode does not require such painstaking precautions as all characters, by the very definition of uppercase, are written above the baseline and crossing the midline.

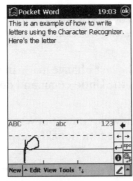

Figure 17.5 Writing correctly with Character Recognizer

Writing nonalphanumeric characters (such as parentheses or the @ symbol) can be done in two different ways. The easiest is to select the Symbols icon in the bottom-right corner of the Character Recognizer icon bar and then tap the symbol you want. The second — and much faster — way is to enter the symbol in the 123 section of the Character Recognizer input panel. Although most characters are fairly obvious to enter as they are normally written, some (such as the percentage and asterisk symbols) are totally unintuitive and require a somewhat steep learning curve to master.

Note

The quick reference appendix (Appendix E)in this book contains a complete list of all of the letters, numbers, and symbols that you can write in the Character Recognizer. It can be used as a practice guide or carried with the Pocket PC to act as a reference on the go.

Transcriber

Because of the incredible complexity behind handwriting recognition, there are many methods for improving Transcriber's accuracy. The first — and most obvious — method is to write neatly on the Pocket PC screen. Although you can write as quickly as you like, most people tend to write more neatly when they reduce their writing speed. Second, writing words much larger than normal also helps Transcriber to decipher your handwriting more accurately. Another way to accomplish this is to set the zoom level in the document to the highest possible setting. In Pocket Word, this can be accomplished by selecting View ⇨ Zoom ⇨ 300%. The Notes application, on the other hand, has the capability to permanently default to the highest possible magnification. Change the default zoom level for writing in the Input Options menu (Settings ⇨ Input ⇨ Options) to 300 percent and every new Note will default to maximum magnification when Writing mode is activated.

Tip

When writing at the top of the screen using Transcriber, avoid the temptation to rest your palm on the screen. Doing so can activate the touch screen and create an interruption in your writing.

As you write, Transcriber compares your handwriting to a built-in dictionary of 65,000 words. Although it will not correct your spelling automatically, the application prefers to return words that are in its dictionary when performing recognition. Therefore, if you repeatedly use unique terminology (such as medical terms) or have a name that is not common, you should add these words to Transcriber's dictionary. To accomplish this, write the word using Transcriber so that it is recognized with the correct spelling. Highlight the word by tapping it with the stylus and make the correction symbol by drawing a V from left to right with the two lines nearly overlapping each other. Figure 17.6 is an example of the pop-up window that appears with possible spelling alternatives and the Add to Dictionary feature. Select the option to add this word into Transcriber's dictionary. If the pop-up menu does not include the Add to Dictionary option as shown in the figure, the word you have selected already exists as an entry in the dictionary.

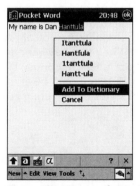

Figure 17.6 Transcriber's Add to Dictionary feature

Next, you can teach Transcriber your personal writing style using the Letter Shape Selector (launched by selecting Start ➪ Programs ➪ Letter Shapes Selector). Figure 17.7 shows the application learning how I write the letter a. It is important to observe that options are included for defining each technique of writing a single letter as Often, Rarely, or Never. This not only enhances Transcriber's accuracy, but it will also accelerate Transcriber's recognition engine as characters set to Never are eliminated from the list Transcriber reviews when trying to recognize your handwriting.

Figure 17.7 The Letter Shapes selector

As shown in Figure 17.7, often-used characters are untouched, rarely used characters receive one line through them, and characters that are never used are crossed out. Tap each character once to select it and a second time to view an animation of how the character is written according to Transcriber. The second tap may help you differentiate characters that appear to be similar. After you have watched the animation, select the radio button that best describes how often you write that character. Continue until all of the writing styles for that letter are complete, and then use the arrow buttons in the bottom-right corner of the screen to continue to the next letter. When you have completely customized all of the characters in the Letter Shapes Selector, choose File ➪ Save from the menu to store your settings. Your preferences can be erased and the system returned to the default mode of all styles by selecting File ➪ Use Original Settings.

Tip

If a second person (such as a family member or coworker) works on your Pocket PC extensively and uses Transcriber, you can set up a different profile for their handwriting style. Open the Letter Shapes Selector and select File ➪ Guest. Then have them customize the letter set using their personal writing style. Save their work (File ➪ Save) and you can quickly toggle between master and guest profiles when you switch off using the device.

Eliminating Transcribberish

There is a joke going around that if you misspell a word while using the Pocket PC, it must be because the handwriting recognition turned your perfect handwriting into *Transcribberish*. Transcribberish is when your handwriting is converted into a set of garbled, meaningless words. Or — even worse — when the words in your sentence are changed into different words that create a whole new meaning and you do not notice. Obviously, Transcribberish is something that should be avoided at all costs. And with a few simple tricks, you can keep Transcriber from making common mistakes.

Tip

If Transcriber is converting your handwriting to a set of question marks, check to that you do not have the Numeric Recognition mode activated. In the icon bar, glance at the black Recognition mode icon. If the icon has 12 displayed, it is in Numeric mode. Tap it once to return to Unrestricted mode, which is indicated by an icon with a lowercase letter a. If the icon bar is not activated, you can turn it on by selecting Start ⇨ Settings ⇨ Input ⇨ Options and activating the checkbox on the Show icon bar option.

Commas are notoriously difficult to enter using Transcriber. Because they closely mimic periods and are frequently mistaken for other characters, you have to learn to distinctively write punctuation and gestures for Transcriber to accurately recognize them. Although many users try to write a curved comma, Transcriber often recognizes this as a j or s. To avoid this problem, write a comma straight down, beginning at the baseline of the row of text. Figure 17.8 demonstrates how to properly write a comma for best recognition. Note how the comma begins where a period would normally be, then extends below the baseline.

Figure 17.8 Writing a comma correctly

Writing other characters on the same line as your punctuation greatly increases recognition accuracy. When entering any punctuation, make sure that you write each symbol as it would normally appear in relation to the other characters in the line. For example, a dash and an underline are only differentiated by where the line appears with respect to the characters alongside it. If, when compared to a word next to it, the line is at the middle or higher, it is a dash, but if it is lined up with the bottom of all of the characters in that row, it will be an underline.

Figure 17.9 is a chart of all of the symbols with a baseline and a midline. If a character in Figure 17.9 extends above the midline, it should be the same height as a capital letter. If a character extends below the baseline in the figure, it should be written so that the bottom of the symbol is lower than the line of text. Notice that the @ sign and the copyright and registered trademark symbols have two methods of creation: one with a single, continuous stylus stroke, and one with separate strokes for the character and the circle. If you prefer the two-stroke method, you should start the circle that surrounds the character at the three o'clock position and circle counterclockwise. When finished, the ends of the circle should meet. In addition, it is imperative that, when trying to write the registered trademark symbol, the letter R is capitalized and begins at the bottom-left leg. Finally, believe it or not, the smaller you write the registered trademark symbol, the more likely Transcriber is to recognize it.

Figure 17.9 Symbols for Transcriber

Gestures are an extremely tricky thing. Because the space gesture looks like an elongated letter L, Transcriber sometimes incorrectly assumes that you are writing letters when you meant to make a gesture. To eliminate this problem, write your gestures with short vertical strokes and long horizontal strokes. For example, when making a space, start at the far left side of the screen and draw a short down stroke, then a horizontal stroke that traverses the entire width of the screen. Using this technique, Transcriber should understand your intent with almost 100 percent accuracy.

Tip

Gestures must be performed one at a time. If you are writing text and wish to enter a gesture, lift the stylus off the screen, wait until the text is recognized, and then enter the gesture by itself.

First letter capitalization is sometimes a problem for Transcriber users who write too small. In almost every situation, you should write large when entering data into Transcriber. However, this limits the amount of information that you can write on the screen and is sometimes simply not practical. If you write small at all times, try overemphasizing the capital letters by making them abnormally larger than the other letters. Transcriber will be able to recognize these as distinctly different from all of your other characters and assume it is supposed to be capitalized.

Note

Transcriber will always capitalize the first letter after a period. To deactivate this feature, select Start ⇨ Settings ⇨ Input ⇨ Options and deselect the checkbox on the Capitalize the first letter of sentence feature.

The HP Jornada screen rotation modification

As a final tip for the true power user, a secret option exists that radically changes the Pocket PC interface in order to accommodate a more natural style of writing. If you do a lot of text entry and prefer additional horizontal space in order to write more on each line, you might want to consider rotating the device screen to work in Landscape mode. Figure 17.10 demonstrates the sensation of Landscape mode on the Pocket PC, demonstrating how the option is far more accommodating for longer words. Notice also how the Pocket PC application adjusts itself to fit on a much wider screen.

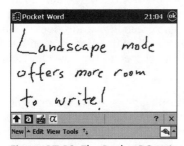

Figure 17.10 The Pocket PC in Landscape mode

Warning

This tip only works on the HP Jornada 540 Series Pocket PC, is very difficult to activate, and may produce unreliable results in applications other than Pocket Word. In addition, I strongly suggest that you deactivate the password protection feature (Start ⇨ Settings ⇨ HP Security) before activating this feature. Failure to do so may lock you out of your device permanently. In addition, you should select Start ⇨ Settings and make a mental note of where the System tab appears on your screen.

Because this is a hidden feature of the Pocket PC, activating the Landscape mode is a little tricky. To access it, perform the following five-step process:

1. Press the Action button (press straight down on the scrolling control) on your Pocket PC and tap and hold the clock display in the upper-right corner.

2. In a few seconds, a pop-up menu should appear with Run and Clock options. Select Run and in the resulting pop-up window enter **rotate r**.

3. The application will inform you that it is changing the display to Landscape mode. To finalize this change, you must soft reset your device.

4. When the system reboots, you will instantly recognize that all displays have now been rotated 90 degrees clockwise. Unfortunately, you will have to align the screen in order to make the stylus operate correctly. Select Start ⇨ Settings ⇨ System ⇨ Align screen by tapping the stylus where the Start menu appeared *before* the screen was rotated and using the scrolling controls to navigate down the Start menu to the settings option.

5. After the Settings window is open, select the System tab by again tapping where it would have appeared (at the bottom of the screen, near the application buttons) before the screen was rotated. Then use the scrolling controls to toggle to the Align screen icon and select it. Finally, tap around with the stylus to successfully find the Align screen button; targets will appear to correctly align the screen to the new Landscape mode.

Once the screen is properly aligned, all applications in the system will function rotated 90 degrees. In fact, this is a superior way to run many applications as Pocket Internet Explorer can render wider Web sites, Pocket Excel spreadsheets can display more columns at once, text is easier to review in the Reader application, long filenames can be read in File Explorer, and the Calendar's Week view is far less constricted. However, many other applications, including Media Player and most third-party applications, do not successfully operate in Landscape mode. Consequently, I consider this a temporary modification to make only when entering large amounts of data via Transcriber.

To return the device to the original Portrait mode, repeat the process: press the Action button and tap and hold the clock display in the upper-right corner. Then select Run from the pop-up menu. Enter **rotate r** in the Run window and reset the device. After you navigate to the Control Panel (now tapping where everything would have been in the Landscape mode) and realign the screen, your device will be restored to its original condition.

Create custom sound schemes

A compelling feature of the Pocket PC interface is how sound is used to provide user feedback, to deliver reminders, and to alert you to system changes. The Pocket PC has 14 different event sounds that you can customize to create your own sound scheme.

- **Asterisk:** An attention-grabbing sound, usually to signal you if a program has encountered a minor snag. For example, Pocket Internet Explorer will use this sound if it is not capable of locating a URL that you entered.

- **Critical stop:** An indication of a major malfunction halting the system or the current application, a critical stop sound most commonly occurs when attempting to launch an application that has a file missing.

- **Default sound:** The most frequently occurring sound on the Pocket PC. Used when Transcriber has successfully loaded and acts as the test sound that is played back when you are adjusting the volume on the Pocket PC.

- **Exclamation:** A sound that indicates substantial errors. Two of the most common examples of the exclamation sound are a program that experiences a fatal application error and the permanent delete confirmation window.

- **Infrared begin/end/interrupt:** These are the three melodies played when you start, complete, and inadvertently end an infrared transmission. These sounds are fun to customize, as they will always play when in the company of another Pocket PC user.

- **Menu pop-up:** This sound occurs when you activate any menu on the Pocket PC. This includes the Start menu, a program's Tools/Options menu, and any object's tap and hold menu.

- **Menu selection:** Related to menu pop-up, the menu selection sound activates when a start menu, program menu, or tap and hold menu item tapped.

- **Network begin/end/interrupt:** These three events indicate the starting, completion, and inadvertent termination of a network connection.

- **Question:** Triggered when an application launches a pop-up window with an inquiry, this sound is designed to draw your attention to a question. For example, when you make modifications to the system clock settings and press Ok, the system will ask whether you want to save changes.

▪ **Start up:** This sound, although it is deceivingly named, plays only when the Pocket PC is reset, not every time the system is turned on. I never customize this sound, as I infrequently reset the device.

To customize these sounds, open the Sounds & Reminders applet in Start ⇨ Settings ⇨ Sounds & Reminders ⇨ Sounds. Figure 17.11 shows the applet with the exclamation event sound being customized. As you can see, each event has its own row allowing you to select them and to individually modify each sound. To customize an event sound, highlight the event and select a new sound file from the Sound drop-down list, as shown in Figure 17.11. You can even press the Play button to the right of the drop-down list to preview the audio file.

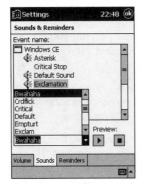

Figure 17.11 The Sounds & Reminders applet

Also, notice in the figure how Critical Stop is the only event without a speaker icon. This is because I have set the sound for this event to None, the very first selection on the pop-up list of sounds. This is a quick way to silence an individual event that you grow tired of; it can be easily reversed by picking a new sound for the event when you would like to activate it again.

In addition to just picking an alternate sound from the presented list, you can create or install your own sounds. Any recording that you make using the Voice Recorder application can be used by an event when it is copied to the Windows directory on the Pocket PC. Because the Pocket PC uses the popular .wav file format, you can download sounds from the Internet. One personal customization I always install is the sound of Arnold Schwarzenegger saying, "I'll be back!" to the exclamation event. It adds a comedic element to the crash of an application that makes me smile even if I just lost a document I had been working on for hours. Just use the Explore feature in ActiveSync on your desktop to open the \My Pocket PC\Windows\ directory and copy the .wav files into the folder. They will instantly be available on the drop-down menu.

Tip

Replacement sounds for menu pop-up and selection should be short, quick sounds because longer sounds will adversely affect how quickly the menu appears.

With a fully personalized sound scheme, your device is sure to grab the attention of even the most proficient Pocket PC user. To return the Pocket PC to its original sound scheme, highlight an event, and select the sound file with the abbreviated version of the event name. Repeat this process for each event. For example, the default sound associated with the exclamation event is named Exclam.

Ten Things Every User Should Change in the Control Panel

If you have read through the entire book thus far, you have learned that I have a certain disdain for the word *default*. The Pocket PC automatically makes assumptions about you how your device should be set up for daily use. Although many of the system defaults are designed to get you up and running quickly, your long-term satisfaction can be greatly improved by changing ten items in the Pocket PC's System Settings section. Each modification takes approximately 30 seconds and can significantly change the way you use your Pocket PC for the better.

Change the hardware buttons

Introduced in Chapter 1, the hardware buttons on your Pocket PC are the fastest way to launch an application. The Buttons applet (Start ➪ Settings ➪ Buttons) allows you to customize each button on the Pocket PC to launch any application you wish. Figure 17.12 shows the open Buttons applet with modified assignments for each button. As you can see, the window also lists each button with an icon, matching the actual images on the hardware buttons. This should be used to assist you in figuring out which button you are assigning an application to. In the example, notice that I changed the icon with a home on it to the Start menu (because I consider that the Pocket PC home), replaced the contacts application with AOL (my Internet software application for reaching contacts), and the calendar with the Today screen. Making clear associations between the icon graphics and the applications they load will help you to later remember where you assigned applications and help to make the assignments more effective.

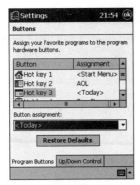

Figure 17.12 The Buttons applet

In addition, some Pocket PCs have extra button combinations that deliver more functionality. For example, if you scroll to the bottom of the list of buttons on the HP Jornada, you will find "Hot key 1 (hold)." This feature launches a different application (HP Settings, by default) if you press and hold the hardware button. This way, you can double the number of applications that can be launched from a single button. To reset all buttons to their factory default settings, push the Restore Defaults button.

Secure your device

No one would leave a few hundred dollars lying around on a desk completely unprotected, so why would you leave your Pocket PC alone without any protection? If you have not already done so, review Chapter 4 to learn how to password protect your system and how to set up the owner information. Also, be sure to set up the backup question and answer fail-safe system in case you forget the login password, and enable system logging to track every login attempt made on your device.

Power pack your New menu

By now, you have probably become accustomed to using the New menu whenever you want to create an item in any application in your Pocket PC. Although, in its present condition, this feature is adequate for standard use, you can power pack the New menu with a variety of new options. Select Start ⇨ Settings ⇨ Menus ⇨ New, and activate the Turn on New button menu checkbox. Ensure that all of the checkboxes in the list are also activated, and then press Ok to save your changes.

A tiny up arrow will appear to the right of the New button. Tapping this arrow will present a list of options that enable you to create new items for almost every application on your Pocket PC regardless of whether the program is currently running. Figure 17.13 shows the menu activated while in the Notes application.

Notice how, in addition to providing the list of new Notes options at the top of the pop-up menu, you now have the ability to create a new appointment, contact, e-mail, Excel workbook, task, and Word document from any application on the Pocket PC.

Figure 17.13 The New button menu

Tip

When you activate the New menu in Notes, Pocket Word, or Pocket Excel, you can easily select from among the many templates that are available to each application (Meeting notes, Memo, Phone Memo, To Do in Pocket Word, and the Vehicle Mileage Log in Pocket Excel).

Set your device information

When your device connects to the desktop, the network, or another Pocket PC via infrared, it transmits a name to identify itself to the machine it is communicating with. Other users will see this name, but it is set to the bland and uninformative Pocket_PC by default. To change this setting, select Start ➪ Settings ➪ System ➪ About ➪ Device ID. One suggestion is to change the device name field to your name and the device brand (I use DansJornada) and the description to a full text account of the device maker, brand, and model number. The next time you beam a file to someone else, they will see exactly whom it is coming from on their screen. In addition, it will be displayed in the ActiveSync window on your desktop every time you synchronize.

Note

Do not use spaces or any nonalphanumeric characters when entering your device name or description because some networks have difficulty processing them. Substitute an underscore (_) for spaces if you absolutely must.

Customize your Pocket PC notifications

Like the customized sound scheme that you created earlier in this chapter, you can customize the alarm sound and many other features of the appointment reminder in the Reminders applet (Start ➪ Settings ➪ Sounds & Reminders ➪ Reminders). Checkboxes for activating and deactivating the pop-up message, flashing light, and sound are available from this window, as well as the ability to adjust how long the reminder light flashes. The sound drop-down box enables you to select the audio file that you would like to play when the reminder appears on screen. Also like the customized sound scheme, this list is created from the .wav files in the Windows folder on your Pocket PC, so review the beginning of this chapter for ways to create custom sounds.

Tip

If you frequently keep your device in the docking cradle, or if you carry it in a protective case, set the device to repeat reminders so that you will be sure to hear them. Activate the Repeat sound feature (by default, it is off).

Get control over the volume and sounds

After you have customized your notifications, you will probably want to adjust the sound volume. The volume screen of the Sounds & Reminders applet (Start ➪ Settings ➪ Sounds & Reminders) enables you to control the volume of all the audio emanating from the speaker, as well as globally activating and deactivating system event sounds, program sounds, screen taps, and hardware buttons. The last two features are designed to provide audio feedback so that you know when you are making a selection with the stylus, or when you have depressed a hardware button. I prefer the sound at full volume and all sounds enabled except for Hardware buttons. Furthermore, I set Screen taps to Soft so that I don't disturb people around me when I am working on the device in a meeting or office environment.

Perform backups to secure your data

Although this feature is not available on all Pocket PCs, the HP Jornada ships with a built-in backup system that can copy PIM (Calendar, Contacts, and Tasks) data or the entire contents of the Pocket PC to internal memory or a CompactFlash card. The HP backup screen (shown in Figure 17.14) is available by selecting Start ➪ Settings ➪ System ➪ HP Backup ➪ Backup. Notice how the application provides estimations of time and memory requirements for both backup options.

Figure 17.14 HP backup

Before performing a backup, you can give the file a custom name, assign the folder in which it will be saved, and decide whether it will be copied to main memory or to a storage card. Because copying the data to main memory provides no protection from a complete system failure, it is highly advisable to acquire a memory card for backups. Data can be restored to the device by inserting the memory card in the Pocket PC and selecting Start ➪ Settings ➪ System ➪ HP Backup ➪ Restore and pressing the Restore all data or Restore PIM databases button. The application will display a list of backups made with the application that you can select from based on filename, folder, or time stamp.

Cross-Reference

For information on how to back up the Pocket PC to your desktop computer using ActiveSync, refer to Chapter 15, "ActiveSync: Desktop Connections for Maximum Speed and Security."

Set the Screen and Power settings to your personal preferences

The Pocket PC has a number of applets designed to maximize the readability of the screen and to adjust the timing of the automatic device shutoff. These can be quickly modified and should be set to your personal preferences when you are under the most common lighting conditions for your Pocket PC. This is because almost all of the screen and power settings designed for your Pocket PC have one setting. Thus, by adjusting it in your most common environment, the system will be set to provide the best screen settings for the environment in which it will be most frequently used. The individual applets are:

- Backlight: Start ➪ Settings ➪ System ➪ Backlight
- Contrast: Start ➪ Settings ➪ System ➪ Contrast

■ HP Settings: (HP Jornada users only) Start ⇨ HP Settings

■ Power: Start ⇨ Settings ⇨ System ⇨ Power

Cross-Reference

For information on how to set each of these applets to maximize battery power on the device, see Chapter 21, "Memory and Power Constraints."

Creating customized Backlight preferences for four different environments

If you own an HP Jornada Pocket PC, you have the luxury of being able to adjust contrast, brightness, and speaker volume in one location, and the ability save your modifications in four different environment slots. To begin, launch the HP settings applet (Start ⇨ HP Settings) and select one of the four environmental options on the left side of the screen. Figure 17.15 shows the HP settings applet with the Indoors environmental option activated.

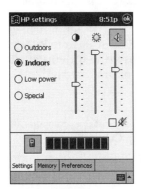

Figure 17.15 HP settings

After you have selected an environment option, adjust the three sliders to the optimal viewing conditions for that environment. When you are finished, move your Pocket PC to another location (for example, outdoors), change the environment option, and customize the device for optimal viewing by changing the settings. I recommend leaving the Low power option as the factory has set it, because you may want to activate it when you are trying to maximize battery life. The Special option should be used for an environment specific to your Pocket PC usage such as meetings, which would be indoor screen brightness but audio muted, or in the car, with maximum volume (to overpower the stereo) and outdoor brightness.

Tip

Tapping the speaker icon (shown in the upper-right corner of Figure 17.15) opens the Sounds & Reminders applet.

In addition to the all-encompassing screen control system, HP settings also has a number of unique system-management options on the Preferences tab. Checkboxes on this screen enable you to disable the Record button and HP hot keys so that the device is not turned on if the hardware buttons are accidentally pressed. Although I do not recommend disabling the Record button, because I find it an invaluable asset and because it is recessed, you may wish to disable the HP hotkeys if you have removed the HP Jornada's metal cover and do not want the buttons to turn on the device. The Tap screen to power on option enables you to activate the Pocket PC with a tap of the screen, rather than by using a hardware button.

Note

Some models of the HP Jornada 540 series have a Display mode drop-down box on the Preferences tab that displays options for 16-bit and 8-bit color; the device actually displays 12-bit color (4096 colors) when 16-bit color is selected. This is the maximum number of colors that the hardware supports and is the system default. When selected, 8-bit color works as stated, displaying 256 colors.

Schedule the Today screen appearance

The Today screen, an invaluable tool for managing a busy schedule, can be set to automatically appear when the device has remained idle for a certain number of hours. To change from the default setting of appearing every four hours, select Start ⇨ Settings ⇨ Today. The drop-down box at the bottom of the window provides 1-hour increments from 1 to 12 hours. I prefer to set my Today screen to appear after one hour of inactivity so that I can quickly refresh myself on what is yet to come in my day.

Get connected to a network

Many of the best features of the Pocket PC are better when the device is connected directly to the network. Using a CompactFlash Ethernet card (available from Socket Communications at `www.socketcom.com`) the Pocket PC can send and receive e-mail, connect to the Internet, and even synchronize with a desktop computer elsewhere on the network. Just obtain your network settings information from your company's system administrator and enter them at Start ⇨ Settings ⇨ Connections ⇨ Network.

Customize your Start menu applications

Nestled deeply within the system settings is a quick and easy way to customize the applications residing on the Start menu. If you press Start and look at the list of programs, you will probably see an application or two that you never use. You can customize this list by selecting Start ⇨ Settings ⇨ Menus and deselecting applications that you do not use regularly and by activating the checkboxes of applications that you use frequently. Press Ok to save your changes, and then press Start to see your new personalized applications menu. If you activate eight icons, the entire Start menu will move to the right to make more room for the applications, and if you select ten or more items, arrows will appear that allow you to scroll up and down the Start menu. I suggest installing no more than seven icons to keep the menu easy to navigate and all the icons in view at one time.

Note

You can only remove applications appearing on the Start menu between the Today application and the Programs icon. All other icons on this list are fixed system settings that cannot be deleted or moved.

Customize Your Start Menu and Startup Applications

If you liked the last tip in the "Ten Things Every User Should Change in the Control Panel," then you are going to love this section of the chapter. Although the Pocket PC provides the formerly discussed method for adding and removing items from the Start menu, with a little work, you can customize the entire Start menu to make it a breeze to navigate to all of your applications.

Menus made to order

First, practice with the menu you just edited. Because the Pocket PC has a tool for deleting and replacing the items on the Start menu, if you make a mistake and permanently delete an item, you do not have to worry, as it can be replaced by following the last tip in the previous section. To edit your Start menu, perform these steps:

1. Launch the Pocket PC File Explorer by selecting Start ⇨ Programs ⇨ File Explorer.

2. In the upper-left corner, tap the down arrow next to My documents and select My Device from the pop-up window that appears. You are now in the highest directory on your Pocket PC. For avid computer users this is equivalent to the C:\ (root) directory on your PC.

3. From this directory, open the Windows folder, and then open the Start Menu folder. You should now see a list of folders and icons similar to Figure 17.16. Although the icons may be different, it is important that the upper-left corner says Start Menu next to the down arrow, and that in this folder there is also a Programs directory. If these two elements do not match the example shown here, you should start all over again.

4. In the File Explorer command bar, select Edit ➪ New Folder. Name this folder Utilities.

5. Now, highlight several of the application icons in the list of files by dragging over them with your stylus. Do not highlight the Utilities folder you just made.

6. Tap and hold one of the highlighted files and select Cut from the pop-up list. The icons for all of the highlighted items will fade to indicate that you have cut these items.

7. Tap the Utilities folder to open it, and then select Edit ➪ Paste. All of the applications that you just cut should appear in the new folder.

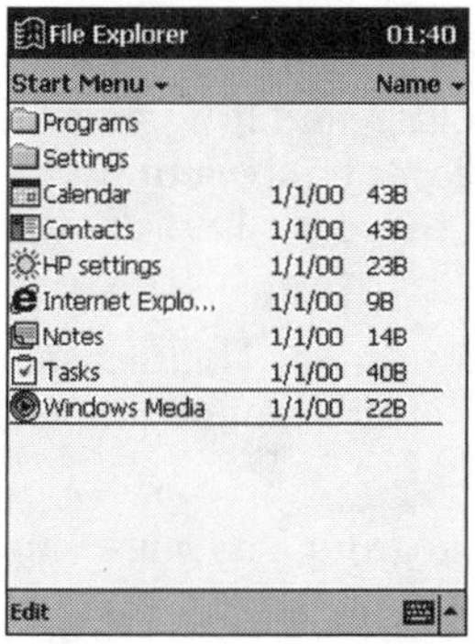

Figure 17.16 The Pocket PC Start Menu folder

In seven easy steps, you created your custom applications folder and made it available on the Start menu. To check your work, press the Start button. A folder named Utilities should appear below the Today icon. Tap the folder to open a window that lists all of the applications that you pasted into it, ready to launch with a touch of the stylus.

To remove the custom folder that you just created, repeat Steps 1 to 3, open the Utilities folder, and highlight all of the applications. Tap and hold a single application and choose cut from the list; then press the down arrow at the top-left side of the screen (next to Utilities) and select Start Menu. Select Edit ➪ Paste to return all of the icons to their original position on the Start menu; then tap and hold the Utilities folder and select delete to remove it.

In addition to creating folders on the Start menu and moving icons around, you can also rename all of the applications. While in the \Windows\Start Menu directory, tap and hold any of the icons and select Rename. Enter a new title for the application and press Enter to save your changes. Press Start and the new name for the application will be instantly displayed.

Spend some time using File Manager to customize your Start menu before continuing on to the next section. Should you accidentally delete a file, you can restore it by selecting Start ➪ Settings ➪ Menus and activating the checkbox next to the program.

Editing your Program folder

Now that you are comfortable with editing the Start menu, it is time to take on the real organizational chaos of the Start menu's programs folder. To begin, select Start ⇨ Programs. Chances are, you have rows and rows of application icons, some of which you use, some of which you do not ever want to see again. What is worse is that you probably have to scroll down the window just to find your favorite applications. You can clean up and tailor this menu to your needs by doing the following:

1. Launch the Pocket PC File Explorer by selecting Start ⇨ Programs ⇨ File Explorer.

2. In the upper-left corner, tap the down arrow next to My documents and select My Device from the pop-up window that appears.

3. Open the Windows folder, Start Menu folder, and Programs folder in succession. You are now in the File Explorer equivalent of the Programs folder you just saw moments ago. All of the icons here are the same ones cluttering up that essential folder.

4. Begin by identifying applications that are similar. Utilities, games, or communications tools are examples of sets of applications that you can group together.

5. Create individual folders named after the groups by selecting Edit ⇨ New Folder.

6. Move the applications into their folders using the same cut-and-paste technique described in the previous section. As you paste applications into their folders, feel free to rename them with more user-friendly names if you like.

7. Inside one of the folders, create a subfolder named Unused.

8. Cut and paste all of the applications that you never use into the folder named Unused. This will keep them out of the way, but still accessible, should you ever need them again.

9. Leave two or three of your most frequently used applications in the Programs directory, because these applications should be available at the top of the window, now that you have cleaned up the menu.

You have successfully created your own customized Programs menu. To view the fruits of your labor, select Start ⇨ Programs. You should have a nice, clean window, as shown in Figure 17.17. Notice how the one vital application is easily available without any scrolling or searching. If you have a menu system as easy and clear as this example, you will eliminate thousands of taps on the scroll bar over the course of your lifetime.

Figure 17.17 A customized Programs folder

Tip

Arrange the Programs folders in your Pocket PC just like the folders in the Start Menu of your desktop. They'll be much easier for you to locate because you use the same names on both!

Add your favorite Web sites to the Start menu

If you spend a lot of time surfing the Internet on your Pocket PC, you should place a few of your favorite places on the Start menu for quick and easy access. It is a simple process that is very similar to moving program icons around in the Start and Programs menu:

1. Launch File Explorer (Start ➪ Programs ➪ File Explorer) and navigate to \My Device\Windows\Favorites\.

2. The Favorites folder contains individual files for each Mobile Favorite that you download from your computer and every Web site that you have saved as a Favorite on your Pocket PC. Locate the Web site that you visit most often, tap and hold the filename and select copy from the pop-up menu.

3. Use File Explorer to navigate to \My Device\Windows\Start Menu\ and select Edit ➪ Paste from the File Explorer command bar.

When finished, you should have an icon similar to the one highlighted in Figure 17.18. Favorites can be distinguished from the Pocket Internet Explorer application because the favorites icon has a smaller e logo on top of a piece of paper. Selecting the icon launches Pocket Internet Explorer and loads the Web site in one easy step!

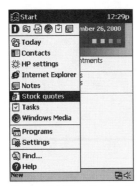

Figure 17.18 A Pocket Internet Explorer icon added to the Start menu

Note

Only Pocket Internet Explorer favorites can be added to your Start menu. AvantGo channels do not have a file that can be linked to.

Add any file to the Start menu

In the same way you can place Internet Explorer favorites on the Start menu, you can place almost any file (see the following tip for the exceptions) in the Start menu. To add a file to the Start menu, launch File Explorer and locate the document. Tap and hold the application, select cut or copy, and then use File Explorer to navigate to \My Device\Windows\Start Menu\ and select Edit ➪ Paste from the File Explorer command bar. After the document appears in the File Explorer window, you can press Start and the new icon will appear on the pop-up menu.

Tip

Files that are not associated with an application cannot be placed on the Start menu. A Windows icon preceding the filename usually means that a filename does not have an associated program. You can check whether the application has a related program by tapping on it in File Explorer. If it does not, File Explorer displays a pop-up window informing you that there is no application associated with the file.

Here are a few ideas for icons you might add to your Start menu:

■ A voice memo file in the Start menu will activate the pop-up Voice Recorder controls. This is a great way to remind yourself of a recurring task, because you will see it each time you open the Start menu or a convenient way to playback a recording of your children.

■ Copying a Pocket Excel spreadsheet or Pocket Word document will start the application and load the file automatically. Useful for frequent travelers with expense reports or reference documents in Word format.

■ Frequent travelers might also want to copy a Pocket Streets map to the Start menu which, when tapped, launches Pocket Streets and opens the map file.

■ Avid readers can place their favorite e-books on the Start menu to avoid the tedious process of loading Reader then selecting the book from the library. As you finish a book, you can remove it from the Start menu and add a new one. This will encourage you to read more often, as you will have to visually pass the icon to access any other programs.

■ Putting a Media Player playlist file in the Start menu will launch Media Player and start playing the first song on the list when the playlist file is tapped.

Cross-Reference

For information on how to create a playlist and how to locate the playlist file using File Explorer, refer to the "Create Customized Playlists" section of Chapter 12.

Rename items on your Start menu

After you begin customizing your Start menu, you may find that certain items (files you have copied or Mobile Favorites) are inappropriately named. After all, the Start menu can only display approximately 18 characters of a filename. If a filename is longer, it cuts off the end and appends three periods to the name. You can rename all of the programs in your Start menu as follows:

1. Open File Explorer (Start ➪ Programs ➪ File Explorer) and navigate to \My Device\Windows\Start Menu\.

2. Tap and hold the item that you wish you rename and select Rename.

3. File Explorer will highlight the name of the icon. To completely erase the name, enter new text immediately. Otherwise, tap anywhere on the selected filename to change to a cursor and use the backspace key to delete any unwanted text.

4. When you have finished entering in the new name, press the Return key on the keyboard, or perform a carriage return gesture in Character Recognizer or Transcriber. File Explorer will save the new filename and your Start menu will automatically be updated.

Make any menu your own

Many menus inside of the Pocket PC can be customized using the File Explorer methods you just mastered. Here are the file folders accessible via file explorer for all of the customizable menus around the Pocket PC:

- The Start menu (\Windows\Startup\Start Menu\): This is the Start menu that you edited at the beginning of this section. Icons placed here appear when you press the Start button.

- The Start menu (\Windows\Startup\Start Menu\Programs\): This is the Start menu's Program folder that you just customized in the last section of this chapter.

- The Startup menu (\Windows\Startup\): This is a list of applications that automatically load when the Pocket PC is reset. Although you should not create subfolders in this directory, you can copy application shortcuts into this folder so that the applications launch on system reset.

- Pocket Internet Explorer's Favorites (\Windows\Favorites\): This enables you to create subfolders in Pocket Internet Explorer's favorites, a feature previously unavailable in the application, but supported by the capability to designate a subfolder when adding favorites to Pocket Internet Explorer.

- The Settings ⇨ System tab menu (\Windows\Start Menu\Settings\): Oddly enough, you can add applications to the Pocket PC's settings window. A soft reset may be required to make the application icons appear.

Warning

Do not move the Mobile Favorites in \Windows\Favorites\; doing so will hinder ActiveSync from locating the files and prevent them from being correctly updated when you synchronize. However, favorites that are not synchronized from the desktop can easily be moved to whatever folder you desire.

Summary

You now understand the concepts behind the Pocket PC input methods and are able to confidently personalize your Pocket PC to work the way you do. Moreover, if you have read straight through this book, at this point you have gone from Pocket PC novice to Windows Powered expert!

Because of your new status as an expert user, the next chapter changes the focus from mastering the built-in software to adding new software to your device to meet your personal and professional needs.

CHAPTER 18

Killer Apps for the Pocket PC

IN THIS CHAPTER
- Information management
- Utilities
- Entertainment
- Internet applications
- Freeware
- How to trade software with other Pocket PC users
- HP exclusive software applications

Without a doubt, the Pocket PC has the most robust set of software applications available on a handheld device, including a complete set of Personal Information Management (PIM) programs, a pocket version of the Microsoft Office suite, and "edutainment" applications such as Reader and Media Player. But who could not want more? The very point of owning a Pocket PC is the compelling vision that every man, woman, and child could have every technological need accounted for in the palm of his or her hand. As a result, countless software developers have heeded the call to develop solutions for the Pocket PC. And, although an entire book could be written on the software available for the platform, this chapter is dedicated to the best programs on the market today.

Third-party Applications — What Are They and Where Do I Get Them?

Because companies not affiliated with the Pocket PC hardware or software manufacturers create them, these software programs are dubbed *third-party applications*. Third-party apps are modern day treasures, hidden on the Internet where only an avid Web surfer or dedicated Pocket PC user can find them. The software companies that develop third-party apps can be industry giants such as Symantec Corporation or McAfee, or they can be the kid next door, developing innovative software in his parent's garage. So although some software for your Pocket PC might be easy to locate, some of the most innovative (and least expensive) software applications are harder to find.

Cross-Reference

Appendix A offers an entire list of Web sites that index software that's available for the Pocket PC.

To begin, you need a desktop computer with an ActiveSync connection to your desktop PC. Although you can surf to software developer Web sites using the Pocket PC, most applications include an installation program that must be downloaded and installed from the desktop. Although many users complain that this excludes the Pocket PC from being a stand-alone device, installing applications from the desktop provides a number of ancillary benefits that are explained in Chapter 15.

Note

If the software you are about to download does not include an installation application, you will need to know which processor your Pocket PC uses in order to download the correct version. To find out, go to Start ➪ Settings ➪ System tab ➪ About and make a note of the Processor type (The HP Jornada 540 series uses the SH3 processor). Then download the file for your device's processor and copy it directly to your Pocket PC \Windows\Start Menu\Programs\ folder using ActiveSync.

Almost every application covered in this chapter has an evaluation version available for download. An evaluation version of an application is one that *times out* (stops working) after a preset number of days or a specific number of times that you launch the application. This is a great way for you to try before you buy and helps keep you from spending money on applications that you may never use.

Information Management

The built-in applications on the Pocket PC are remarkable for their ability to store contact information, notes, tasks, and files. But today's information-centric world requires a person to be equipped with volumes of other information; ordinary people carry around far more than just a rolodex, to-do lists, and yellow sticky notes. To combat the information overload, eWallet and Image Expert CE are available for the Pocket PC.

eWallet — keep personal information stored securely

The finest application deserves first mention in this chapter: eWallet puts the *killer* in the phrase "killer app." Designed by Ilium Software (www.iliumsoft.com), this application is the ultimate solution for storing and managing information. With templates for bank account, credit card, health insurance, and 25 other types of information, this application provides the fastest and easiest way to quickly organize your critical data. Figure 18.1 presents fictitious credit card data entered into the eWallet application. Take a look at the Show PIN button that conceals the secret code from prying eyes until you push the button, and also look at the area for notes at the bottom of the screen, which enables you to add comments for which the template may not have included specific fields.

Figure 18.1 eWallet by Ilium Software

In addition to the financial templates, eWallet contains useful forms for storing network and Web site passwords, automobile registration information, and even serial numbers for valuable possessions. This way, if your car, wallet, or personal property is ever stolen, you can quickly deliver serial numbers to the police and call your credit card companies from the list in eWallet. My favorite template is for voicemail — this template provides a form for entering the cryptic commands for my company's voicemail system, reminding me which button forwards a message and which one deletes it.

Tip

By default, eWallet uses a tree-menu navigation system. If you prefer to use an icon-based system (similar to the Pocket PC's program menu) to display your eWallet information, select View ➪ Icon View while in the eWallet tree menu.

With all of this personal information in one location, you should probably be concerned about the security of the data stored by eWallet. Well, rest assured, the information is password protected, so would-be thieves will not be able to access the information on your device. Furthermore, eWallet uses 128.bit encryption, so hackers attempting to access your information will have so much difficulty cracking the code that they would be better off trying to break into a bank. eWallet is available from the Ilium Web site for $29.95 and — if your company's voicemail system is like mine — it is worth every penny.

Image Expert CE — carry around pictures of your family and pets

As with health insurance cards, many people carry family photographs with them everywhere they go. And with the advent of digital cameras and photo developing companies that offer scanning services, photo albums have gone high-tech. Image Expert CE brings you out of the dark ages by enabling you to display and edit photos on your Pocket PC. Files can be copied from the desktop computer, received via infrared from another Pocket PC, and even downloaded directly from the camera using a CF card or a serial link. Figure 18.2 shows a number of pictures downloaded to the application. You may immediately notice that instead of searching by filenames, Image Expert CE provides a thumbnail of each photo. Once the images are in the Pocket PC you can add voice, ink, and typed annotations and then put them all together in an animate slide show.

The slide show feature of Image Expert CE enables you to combine all of the annotations with the photo to create a multimedia presentation. When activated, the screen clears, then changes to landscape mode, and then a remote control appears that enables you to run the show. Voice annotations are played when the annotated picture appears, and text and ink notes can be customized to display according to your personal preferences. The slides can be automatically forwarded on a preset timer or you can manually advance them by pressing the appropriate button on the remote control.

Figure 18.2 Image Expert CE Browse mode

Tip

If you are good with HTML (Hypertext Markup Language), you can create your own slide show that can be displayed in Pocket Internet Explorer. Just create a Web page that links to each photo and then download the pictures and the Web page to a subdirectory of your device's My Documents folder.

Image Expert CE is provided on the accessories CD.ROM that came with the HP Jornada Pocket PC; however, a new version has been released and Jornada owners can download it for free. For more information, visit the "products & services" section of the Jornada Web site (www.hp.com/jornada/). Owners of other Pocket PCs can obtain the application for $39.95 from www.sierraimaging.com.

Utilities

Utilities are the power tools of the computing world. Although some of them help you work more efficiently, others let you customize your Pocket PC like a hot rod. In this section, you have both options. For the accountant in you, bTask adds to your everyday efficiency. For the rebel in you, the Today screen customization section will make you the envy of every Pocket PC owner. Well, don't just stand there — read on!

bTask — switch and close applications quickly

The Jornada ships with the HP Task Switcher installed on the device. Although the application enables you to switch between and close running applications, the icon for the Task Switcher is only available on the HP Home Menu. An excellent upgrade from the Task Switcher is bTask, shown activated in Figure 18.3. As you can see, bTask is available in any application. The demure "b" icon shown in the bottom-left of the screen shot is all that is visible until the icon is tapped and the menu is activated. In addition to providing the task-switching functionality, bTask shows you how much memory each application is currently consuming. And, the program offers three different solutions for application shutdown: Close Active, Close All, and Close All but Active.

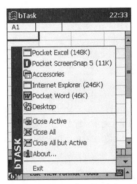

Figure 18.3 The bTask application

A hidden gem in the bTask application is the About screen, which displays the free memory, IP address, hostname, and battery power status of the Pocket PC. bTask is available in the bUseful Utilities Pak from bSQUARE Corporation (http://www.bSQUARE.com/) for $59.95. Although the price may seem expensive for one application, the suite includes nine other utilities including Backup, Benchmark, Automated Scheduling, Memory Clearing, and PKzip Compression File Management applications.

Customize your Today screen

As you can probably tell by now, the Today screen is my favorite feature of the Pocket PC. I use the feature constantly to manage my schedule and help control the chaos that occurs throughout the day. As a result, I am constantly trying to customize and fit as much information into the Today screen as I possibly can. Thankfully, some third-party developers have helped quite a bit.

Developer One, a software company responsible for creating some of the most innovative applications for the Windows Powered platform, has created a Web page that provides free tips on how to customize your Pocket PC. Figure 18.4 shows an excerpt of this Web page that instructs you on how to create a customized Today screen graphic. Visit www.developerone.com/pocketpc/tips/ for ready-made replacement graphics for the Today screen, and then complete instructions on how to customize the owner information screen that appears when you power up your device.

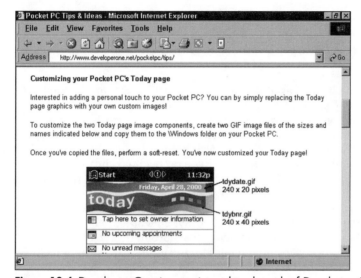

Figure 18.4 Developer One is a registered trademark of Developer One, Inc.

Developer One Today screen plug-ins

In addition to the free customization tips, Developer One has also created a trio of plug-ins for the Today screen that should not be overlooked. Even a casual glance at Figure 18.5 will expose the plug-ins from Developer One that inject a load of new functionality into the Today screen. From top to bottom, the plug-ins are called TaskView Today, TaskPro Today, and PointStart.

TaskView Today packs a super-powered task manager into the Today screen. With it, you can see all of your to-do items without opening the tasks application and you can customize the sort order by status, priority, subject, or start/due date. Custom colors can be selected to highlight past due, due, future, undated, and completed tasks. All tasks can be displayed or you can filter the application to display only tasks fitting certain criteria. The application even has the ability to hide all private tasks — so nosey people won't see that you have to remember to buy flowers for Mom.

Figure 18.5 Three Developer One Today screen plug-ins

The second plug-in, TaskPro Today, adds a system resources monitor to the Pocket PC Today screen. This program gives you real-time visual updates of your memory conditions for storage, program, and memory cards. Additionally, the program offers a quick shortcut to the Pocket PC's memory and running application control panel settings. TaskPro Today also has user-selectable pop-up warnings to notify you when memory is low if you are preoccupied in another application.

Last on the list, PointStart is a customized application bar that enables you designate up to seven programs that you can launch by tapping their icons on the Today screen. You can set up your personal PointStart bar by simply assigning an application to a space from 1 to 7. If you clear an item from the middle of the PointStart bar, the program icons will automatically join together so that there are no empty spaces on the bar and the entire row automatically justifies to the right side of the screen.

Each of the Developer One applications have free 14.day evaluation versions and registration of PointStart and TaskPro Today are an economical $9.95 each. TaskView Today is reasonably priced at $19.95. For more information, visit www.developerone.com.

Stellarmetrics plug-ins

Not to be outdone by Developer One, Stellarmetrics has created a number of customized plug-ins to modify the Today screen. Two of their most impressive applications are Today's the Day and TTime, shown in Figure 18.6. Designed to add a little zest to the Today screen title graphic, Today's the Day provides a custom graphic header for each day of the week. The header automatically changes at midnight and their Web site includes cool themed headers from movies such as The Matrix and the James Bond flicks. TTime, on the other hand, provides informative frivol and includes eight clocks that can be displayed on the Today screen. Choose from several different analog, digital, or world clocks, as is depicted in the example. Today's the Day is free, although a $5 donation is requested; TTime has an easy-on-the-pocket $10 registration fee.

Figure 18.6 Stellarmetrics Today's the Day and TTime

Entertainment

Now that you have worked so hard to become a Pocket PC expert, it is time to put your feet up on the couch and relax for a moment. The Pocket PC comes with Solitaire, a card game that — although addictive — gets old fast. Replace that tired standby with a slew of these new strategy, action, and classic games, and you will never have a dull moment if your Pocket PC is nearby.

Bubblets — a legal addiction

Ask Pocket PC users about an addictive game made exclusively for the Pocket PC and *Bubblets* might be the first words from their mouth. Each round begins with a screen full of bubbles. You can burst adjacent bubbles if their colors match and the more bubbles you burst at one time, the more points you obtain (two points for two bubbles, six for three, 12 for four, 20 for five, and so on). Figure 18.7 shows a player making a rather favorable burst. Four different styles of game play offer unique challenges, and you can boast about your high scores on the developer's Web site by entering a secret code that the Bubblets application generates. Available from www.oopdreams.com, a 15.day demo of the game is available to get you hooked. Once the trial period is over, I am confident you will return to register the game for $15.

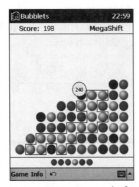

Figure 18.7 A round of Bubblets mid-game

Microsoft Entertainment Pack — get games galore

Naturally, Microsoft has an advantage in this category because they have produced the games for three generations of past Windows Powered devices. As a result, they deliver their popular Entertainment Pack for the Pocket PC platform. The 10.game set includes the following:

▪ **Blackjack:** This casino standard offers playing by the rules of Atlantic City, Las Vegas, Reno, or with your own custom playing conventions. The game also provides hints on strategy and card counting.

▪ **Chess:** The age-old game of wise men everywhere, chess can be played against a friend, against the computer, or even by pitting the computer against itself. The computer opponent has eight skill levels and the game can give you hints if you find yourself frustrated by losing to a computer.

▪ **Cinco:** One of my favorite games of the entire set, Cinco envisions a word and you have to try and guess it. The application tells you if any of the letters in the word you guessed are correct and if they are in the right place. This game supports two-player play, so you can beam the five-letter word to another Pocket PC and compete against your fellow wordsmith.

▪ **FreeCell:** Microsoft's "other" solitaire card game, FreeCell is the game of getting all the cards of the same suit to their home cells in order. Only four FreeCell spots will accept any card in the deck. After that, you had better make progress.

▪ **Hearts:** A card game where you play against three other players and try to stick everyone else with the hearts and the Queen of Spades. Or you can *shoot the moon* by collecting all of the hearts and the Queen of Spades, and the other three players lose the round. This game is infrared-enabled, so you can play against a friend and two computer-generated opponents.

- **Minesweeper:** Microsoft's classic desktop game perfectly transformed to the Pocket PC interface. Tap squares to reveal empty spaces, or mines that detonate and end the game. Each of the three levels is timed and the game records the name and score of the player with the fastest round.

- **Reversi:** The ancient Chinese tile game called Othello in the board-game version. The objective is to surround your opponent's tiles until the board is full. It is designed for one-player games against the computer or two player infrared games against another Pocket PC.

- **Sink the Ships:** Another knockoff, Sink the Ships brings Battleship into the electronic age. Plant your ships on the grid and then try to sink your opponent before they sink you. This game is an absolute must to play via infrared because nothing is as satisfying as hearing the explosion when you breech an opponent's ship and getting to watch the expression on their face.

- **Space Defense:** Shown in Figure 18.8, this game requires a fast stylus to protect your bases from incoming laser fire. The three levels of play include beginner, intermediate, and deathwish. If that's not enough, high scorers can proudly document their feats by saving their names and scores in the application.

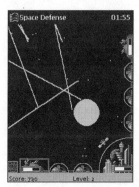

Figure 18.8 Space Defense

- **Taipei:** The classic game of eliminating tiles by finding their equal. The only real feature on this game is that any one who beats it receives a corny fortune.

Tip

In Blackjack, if you select Game ➪ Change Player, you start a new bankroll for the incoming player and will save your winnings in a hidden account. Select Game ➪ Change Player and reenter your name to retrieve your stash and return to play.

Each game is available for $9.95 each or you can purchase the entire 10.game Entertainment Pack for $34.95. The package deal is a steal even if you only play the infrared games against your friends.

ZIOGolf — killer sports simulation

Even if you have never picked up a golf club in your life, you will appreciate ZIOGolf for its incredible realism and addictive nature. The first sports-simulation game designed for Windows Powered devices, ZIOGolf delivers 18 holes of three-dimensional golf for up to four players. As with popular desktop golf games, you use the swing meter, shown on the bottom-right of Figure 18.9, to control the power and the accuracy of every shot. And, while playing a round of golf, you encounter high winds and trees that prevent a perfect shot, or land in the rough, or in sand traps that steal a par score.

Figure 18.9 The fourth hole in ZIOGolf

Once you master the course that comes with ZIOGolf, the company has a handful of other famous courses from around the world that you can install on your Pocket PC. Each course offers unique golfing challenges and localized scenery that matches the famous locales. The application is available for $34.95 and additional courses are $14.95 each from www.ziosoft.com. A three-hole demo version is available on the company's Web site and on the CD.ROM that comes with the HP Jornada Pocket PC.

Internet Applications

Because the Pocket PC has built-in Internet connectivity, the device has created a market for third-party software companies to develop applications that use the Internet as a conduit for messaging and transferring information. As a result, many Internet applications are available for the Pocket PC, ranging from chat programs to HTML editors and File Transfer Protocol (FTP) programs.

Cross-Reference

All of the applications listed here are compatible with the wireless communications options discussed in Chapter 16. So whether you connect to the Internet via a cell phone, wire line modem, or wireless modem, you can rest assured that these applications will work flawlessly.

Messaging applications

Online chat is a hot topic in any computer platform, but the Pocket PC will bring Instant Messaging into the 21st Century with the advent of wireless communications. Imagine receiving an instant message from a family member while you're shopping in the supermarket because they just opened the refrigerator and you are out of milk. And imagine the power of being able to get updated sales numbers from a coworker during an executive staff meeting. Truly, the options for wireless communications are only limited by your imagination.

And apparently all of the major messaging software developers have already discovered the importance of delivering chat applications to the Pocket PC. AOL, Yahoo!, and MSN have ported their instant messaging applications to the handheld platform.

America Online Instant Messenger

Reportedly hosting the largest population of online messaging, America Online (AOL) could be credited with pioneering the online chatting revolution. Now, their popular AOL Instant Messenger (or AIM, for short) is available on the Pocket PC. The robust software client, available for free at www.aol.com/aim/ downloads your buddy list from the AOL server and instantly displays the status of each of your conversation partners. As with the desktop version of the software, AIM for Pocket PC includes customized font size, type and treatment, as well as a drop down list of 16 smiley icons to liven up your messages. The application even includes the popular "save password" and "auto-login" features that enable you to quickly activate the AIM client without tedious stylus taps. Privacy features enable you to designate permissions for users to locate you on the service, and you can personalize an "away" message to inform your buddies that you are unable to chat.

In addition to the communications features, the AIM for Pocket PC client offers news headlines and stock quotes by launching Pocket Internet Explorer. You can personalize these to include business news, sports, entertainment headlines, and ticker symbols, as well as monitors of the major exchanges. News and stock information is cached on the device for a preset time that you can set yourself. Figure 18.10 shows the main screen of AIM, which includes buttons for the chatting, news, and stock-quotes features of the application.

Figure 18.10 AIM for Pocket PC

Yahoo! Messenger

Almost a mirror image of AOL's Instant Messenger, the Yahoo! chat client enables you to exchange messages with users of the Yahoo! Messenger and offers a few improvements over AOL AIM. Yahoo! Messenger for Pocket PC adds the local weather to the nonchat-related news and information available and displays it — as well as news, stock prices and sports scores — in the Messenger application. This is somewhat more intuitive than AOL's method of launching a Web browser session while a chat could be going on. Yahoo! Messenger is available for free at messenger.yahoo.com.

Note

A copy of Yahoo! Messenger is available on the HP Jornada CD-ROM that came with your Pocket PC.

MSN Messenger Service (bSQUARE Messenger)

The third and final text chat application is developed by the talented bSQUARE Corporation. bSQUARE Messenger enables you to communicate with users of the desktop MSN Messenger Service. As with the other programs, Messenger automatically downloads your list of contacts from the MSN Messenger server upon log in and enables you to change your status to "offline" in case you are otherwise occupied.

Although Messenger does not include the news and information features as the other two chat clients do, the application does include an excellent security feature from the desktop MSN Messenger program. Whenever another user adds you to their contact list, you will receive a notification; this enables you to block messages from bothersome users and control who can monitor your online status. bSQUARE is the only company to charge for their chat application, although $9.95 is a small price to pay if you are loyal to the MSN messenger service. The a free trial version of the software and a full retail version is available at www.bsquare.com.

bInTouch

The last messaging application is a world apart from the three programs
we have just covered and could be considered the equivalent of upgrading your
Pocket PC to a Star Trek communicator. From the makers of bSQUARE Messenger
comes bInTouch, a voice communication client that enables you to use your
Pocket PC like a walkie-talkie. Designed for use over high-speed Internet connections or corporate networks, bInTouch uses Voice Over Internet Protocol (VOIP)
communications technology to deliver real-time audio communication between
Pocket PC users.

Figure 18.11 shows the main screen of the bInTouch application. As you can
see, the Push to Talk button is featured prominently on the application window.
This is because the massive amounts of data that are transferred during voice
communications enables only one user to talk at a time. Because it is so frequently used, the Push to Talk and Mute features can be mapped to hardware
buttons on the Pocket PC. You can make bInTouch calls by looking up a user
on the bInTouch directory server or by entering an IP address. Users with high-
speed Internet access or a wireless corporate network can obtain bInTouch from
www.bsquare.com for $49.95.

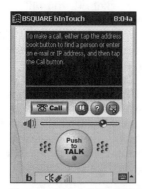

Figure 18.11 bSQUARE bInTouch

Internet utilities

Although the Pocket PC comes with a Web browser and a fully functional
e-mail client, some Internet power users might find themselves craving more
connectivity. A number of applications have been developed by third-party
software companies to provide a complete suite of Internet utilities for the
Web-savvy worker.

H-bomb

While it might sound like a program that you would not want to willingly install on your Pocket PC, H-Bomb is actually an HTML editor. These days everyone has a Web site, so why shouldn't you be able to update the Web site from your Pocket PC? Featuring almost all of the tags in the HTML 3.2 specification including tables and form elements, H-Bomb enables you to create Web pages using simple menu-driven commands. Once you have completed your page, you can preview it in Pocket Internet Explorer by selecting File ➪ View In Pocket IE.

H-Bomb costs a mere $14.95 and is available from www.aeonigmasoft.com. Also available is a shareware version, which offers complete HTML development functionality but does not enable you to cut, copy, paste, or save your work.

Tip

Remember, Pocket Outlook can receive HTML files via e-mail and open them with Pocket Internet Explorer. So if you frequently receive HTML documents and want an inexpensive and convenient way to edit them, H-Bomb is for you.

Scotty FTP

Once you have developed the HTML pages on your Pocket PC, you will have to upload them to the server. Most Web-hosting companies enable you to send files to the server via FTP. Although many desktop applications support FTP, the Pocket PC only has one: ScottyFTP by Ruksun Software Technologies. Designed to mimic desktop applications, ScottyFTP offers a three-pane application window to display files on your Pocket PC, files on the remote server, and transfer logs. The graphical navigation system enables you to travel through the file directories in a manner similar to the Pocket PC File Explorer application.

ScottyFTP can access the Windows CE dial-up system to automatically connect to your ISP and retains server profiles including login information for fast access to FTP servers. The application even includes proxy support for establishing FTP connections through corporate firewalls. Available from www.ruksun.com, ScottyFTP is $29.95.

InkSpot

Hardcore Internet junkies rely on the Usenet newsgroups (a public discussion area similar to a message board) to talk about hobbies, work, or research. And, because most of the Usenet users need their newsgroup fix as much as a e-mail junkies needtheir e-mail, InkSpot was created. Designed to download an unlimited number of messages, the application enables you to search for articles containing a word or phrase in the subject or body and it can be set to filter messages by sender or subject.

InkSpot can download message headers to give you a preview of the articles on the newsgroup — and save memory on your Pocket PC — or grab the entire group for offline reading. Responses can be written offline as well and are uploaded upon the next connection. Ink Spot features the ability to customize fonts, signature, and display settings. Available from www.dejavusoftware.com, InkSpot is $25.

Video via the Internet

On the desktop, video is just beginning to become a reality as bandwidth nears reasonable levels for full screen viewing. But the Pocket PC has an advantage: Because the screen is significantly smaller, video files played on the Pocket PC do not need as much detail. This means that file sizes are much smaller and that they transfer faster to the Pocket PC. Two companies have recognized this competitive advantage and have created video players for the Pocket PC.

MpegTV LLC, a company dedicated to the development of platform-independent video streaming and playback has created PocketTV. Designed around MPEG.1 video, an open format for streaming video, PocketTV can play .mpg files on the device or it can stream video downloaded from the Internet. Figure 18.12 shows PocketTV in action. The video picture automatically fits to the width of the screen. Notice that a display bar indicates time and video frames/kbps per second in real time.

Figure 18.12 PocketTV

The video files are so compressed that the company reports that an hour-long audio and video program can fit on one 64MB memory card with room to spare. The application includes a slew of professional features including 3 levels of audio quality, mono or stereo sound, dynamic picture resizing, and looping playback. PocketTV is free for noncommercial use and available for download from www.mpegtv.com.

Tip

If you install Pocket TV, activate the Fast Video feature (Tools ⇨ Options ⇨ Fast Video) to make the video run more smoothly on the Pocket PC.

ActiveSky (available for free at www.activesky.com) is a competing product using proprietary .sky video files. Despite the proprietary format, the company has many content providers delivering customized video for the Pocket PC. Undergoundfilm.com, Atom Films, and 10 other video media Web sites offer hundreds of original video titles.

Freeware

The best things in life are free, or so the saying goes. Just as there are third-party software developers looking to make a buck by programming Pocket PC applications, there are also developers who throw caution into the wind and offer their wares for absolutely nothing. These programs are dubbed *freeware* because they are available at no cost and can usually be freely exchanged with other Pocket PC users.

Warning

Another adage, You get what you pay for, should be remembered when downloading freeware applications. Because they are not commercial applications, they normally do not undergo rigorous testing for bugs or system compatibility.

Pocket Millionaire

If you cannot get enough of that popular TV program "Who Wants to be a Millionaire" or if you have ever wanted to try your own luck at winning a fortune based on your wits alone, Pocket Millionaire is for you. As you can see in Figure 18.13, the screens on Pocket Millionaire are closely modeled after the quiz show. The four icons at the bottom of the screen represent the lifelines and they disappear as you use them. As you play, music increases the drama of higher dollar values and crowds cheer when you answer a question correctly. The application even asks "Is that your final answer?" before accepting each response.

Figure 18.13 Pocket Millionaire

The Pocket Millionaire program comes with approximately 75 questions based on the Pocket PC platform. Additional question sets can be downloaded and users can create their own questions, making the application perfect as a study guide for school. Pocket Millionaire, information on how to create custom questions, and the complete source code for the application are available at pocketgamer.org/pm/.

Pocket Shortcut

Pocket Shortcut is a simple application that creates an icon in either the Start menu or the Programs menu if the installation application failed to do so. This is an extremely helpful application when you download a piece of freeware that does not have an install program. Simply copy the freeware to \My Device\ Program Files\[freeware name]\ and then enter the location into Pocket Shortcut. The application instantly creates a shortcut wherever you specify. Use \Windows\Start Menu\ to add the icon to your start menu and \Windows\ Start Menu\Programs\ to add it to your Programs menu. Pocket Shortcut is available from www.aeonigmasoft.com.

Cross-Reference

For complete information on how to customize your Programs menu and Start Menu, review the "Menus Made to Order" section of Chapter 17.

Tipster

From Ilium Software, the company that created eWallet, comes Tipster, a simple program designed to calculate the appropriate tip for any kind of service. Enter the total from your bill and Tipster automatically calculates the tip. You can adjust the percentage with Up and Down arrows or by clicking the Tip, Small Tip, or Big Tip buttons. And, if you have dinner companions, enter the number in your party and Tipster automatically divides the tip equally among the group. Available for download from www.iliumsoft.com.

How To Trade Software with Other Pocket PC Users

Naturally, once you begin using freeware you will become addicted to obtaining every free piece of software available for your Pocket PC. After all, if it is free, it is worth trying, right? Well, not always. Freeware is often buggy and sometimes does not work as well as it might seem to. Without a doubt, the best way to find freeware is to get recommendations from friends and coworkers who have been using it. Perhaps they'll even let you test it out while it is installed on their device. Once you are convinced it is a great application, you may want to install it. However copying software from another Pocket PC is not as easy as it sounds.

Warning

While the following process enables you to copy all software applications, you should avoid the temptation to copy retail software from friends and coworkers. Remember, software piracy robs the developer of royalty money and it is illegal. Besides, Pocket PC software is typically far less expensive than the desktop equivalent, so register it yourself and make a developer happy.

Naturally, the easiest way to transfer an application to another Pocket PC is to install it from a computer. If the software has previously been installed from the desktop, you can install it in five quick steps:

1. Dock the device with the desktop.
2. When prompted to create a partnership, select No.
3. In the ActiveSync window, select Tools ⇨ Add/Remove programs.
4. Locate the program in the list on the pop-up window and click the application's checkbox.
5. Press Ok and the software will be installed on the Pocket PC.

If the second Pocket PC uses a different docking cradle or if you would like to trade freeware at a coffee shop or another remote location, you can transfer applications using infrared, but it takes some preparation, as detailed in the following list:

1. Find out what processor the destination Pocket PC is using (see the Note at the beginning of this chapter).
2. On your desktop, locate the installation directory for the program you want to send to your friend (usually C:\program files\microsoft activesync\ [application name])
3. Find the file with the processor type in the file name and a .cab extension (for example: `game_mips.cab`).
4. Dock your Pocket PC to the computer and press the Explore button in the ActiveSync window to open the device's My Documents folder.
5. Copy the .cab file into the device's My Documents folder by dragging it and dropping it.
6. Now transfer the file to your friend's Pocket PC by activating File Explorer (Start ⇨ Programs ⇨ File Explorer) on your device, tapping and holding the file name, and selecting "Send via Infrared. . ."
7. On the destination device, select Infrared receive (choose Start ⇨ Programs ⇨ Infrared receive) and then open File Explorer and tap on the program name. The application should automatically install itself, create an icon in the Programs menu, and delete the .cab file.

Note

Notice that, in the final step, the installation file that you have worked so hard to locate and copy automatically deleted itself after the installation was completed. If you receive a freeware application that you would like to share with other friends, copy the .cab file before you install it on your own device.

HP Exclusive Software Applications

The HP Jornada line of Pocket PCs includes a number of exclusive applications that reside in ROM. This means that the applications are already built-in to your Pocket PC and you don't need to install them. Created by Hewlett-Packard (HP) in order to fill gaps in specific areas of Pocket PC functionality, the five applications are HP Settings, HP Backup, HP Security, Task Switcher, HP Game Buttons, and HP Home Menu.

HP Settings (Start ⇨ HP Settings) provides one location where you can manage your screen settings, program your hardware buttons ,and monitor storage, program, and CompactFlash card memory. HP Backup (Start ⇨ Settings ⇨ System tab ⇨ HP Backup) copies the entire system or just your PIM databases to internal, or *random access*, memory (RAM) or a CompactFlash card. HP Security (Start ⇨ Settings ⇨ HP Security) is a replacement for the standard Pocket PC password application and includes the following enhancements: the ability to delay activation of the password screen for up to two hours, a secondary reminder password (which asks you a question and then grants you access to the Pocket PC if you correctly answer it), and the ability to log all attempted entries to the Pocket PC.

Cross-Reference

For more information on HP Settings, HP Backup, and HP Security, review Chapter 4, "Care and Maintenance of your Pocket PC."

Another HP innovation that adds increased functionality to the Pocket PC is the HP Task Switcher. Designed to automatically load every time the Pocket PC is reset, this application should always appear as an icon at the bottom of the Today screen. If the icon, which looks like two boxes surrounded by arrows, does not appear on the Today screen you can load the application by selecting Start ⇨ Programs ⇨ HP Applications ⇨ HP Task Switcher. Return to the Today screen and tap the icon to activate the Task Switcher menu. All applications that are currently running can be instantly activated or closed by a tap of the stylus. To close the Task Switcher application, tap the icon and select Close Window ⇨ HP Task Switcher. The HP Task Switcher is also prominently displayed at the bottom of the HP Home Menu, which can be activated by pushing the Home button program key on your Jornada.

A second icon that appears infrequently in the Today screen is the HP Game Buttons program. Designed to appear only when a game is launched on the Pocket PC, the application enables you to map the hardware buttons on the HP Jornada to commands in a game. For example, the Action button can provide up and down commands in Pac Man, and the HP Home Menu and Contacts application buttons instruct the program to move left and right. Up to six profiles can be created, providing a different set of commands for each game. To create a profile, tap the Program icon and select Settings. On the pop-up window, notice the commands for left, right, up, down, and start game, and three different shoot commands. Highlight any command with the stylus and then press the hardware button you wish to assign to this task. Remember that depressing the Action button, moving it up, and moving it down can be assigned three separate commands. To delete a mapped command, tap and hold the command name and select Unmap this action. When you have satisfactorily programmed your Pocket PC controls, select Ok and return to the game. To deactivate the application and remove the icon from the Today screen, tap the icon and select Disable Mapping, and then tap the icon again and select Exit.

Note

To manually activate the HP Game Buttons application, run File Explorer on your HP Jornada and open \Windows\Home Menu\HP Game Buttons. If you wish to create a permanent shortcut to this application, copy the HP Game Buttons file to the \Windows\Start Menu\Programs\ folder.

Perhaps the best application developed by HP for the Pocket PC is the HP Home Menu, which you can get to by selecting Start ⇨ Programs ⇨ HP Applications ⇨ HP Home Menu. Designed as a Start Menu alternative, the HP Home Menu actually performs a far more impressive task. Figure 18.14 shows the main screen of the HP Home Menu. There are 21 buttons across the two screens, providing easy access to launching applications. Tap and hold any button to delete, rename, or customize it with shortcuts to your favorite applications. However, take a look at the bottom of the figure and you will notice four icons. These are the true gems of the HP Home Menu, offering (from left to right) shortcuts to the Pocket PC Power Settings applet, the Memory applet, the HP Settings application, and the HP Task Switcher. The Battery icon on the left side even provides a visual indicator of the amount of power remaining.

Figure 18.14 The HP Home Menu

Summary

This chapter is only the foundation for obtaining and installing third-party applications. By now you have surely acquired a preference for specific applications and probably want to know more. As previously mentioned, Appendix B offers a comprehensive list of Web sites offering software listings along with the third-party developers mentioned in this chapter.

Once you have satisfied your need for software, you may be interested in adding more features and functionality to your device. Chapter 19 explores the world of Pocket PC hardware accessories, which improve battery life, increase memory, and enhance the natural good looks of your Pocket PC.

Pocket PC Accessories

IN THIS CHAPTER
- Type faster
- Get connected
- Increase your power
- Add more memory
- Find your way
- Enhance the good looks of your Pocket PC
- Add Extras

Although third-party applications are a great way to power up the interior of your Pocket PC, hardware accessories spice up the exterior of your device. With the right accessories you can type faster, get connected, increase the power, add more memory, find your way, and enhance the good looks of your Pocket PC.

Typing Faster

The Stowaway Portable Keyboard deserves a chapter all to itself. Designed exclusively for the HP Jornada line of Pocket PCs, this little beauty is an external keyboard that does more than meets the eye. Figure 19.1 shows the keyboard connected to the Pocket PC. As you can see, the Pocket PC plugs into the keyboard and rests at a slight angle, to provide a pleasant screen perspective when working at a desk on an airplane. The HP Jornada power cord (not included with the keyboard) plugs into the back and charges your HP Jornada while it is docked in the keyboard.

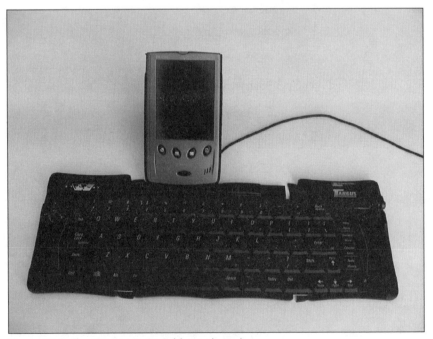

Figure 19.1 The Stowaway Portable Keyboard

But what really makes the keyboard a must-have item is its amazing portability. When you are finished typing, retract the docking station, slide two levers to move the keys and the keyboard folds up—accordion style—into a package just slightly larger than the Pocket PC (3.6"×5.1"×8"). With a weight of just 8.2 ounces, the Stowaway is a breeze to drop in a travel bag, purse, or briefcase without sacrificing any storage space or feeling as though you are lugging around a laptop.

Once you start using it, you might forget you are working on a Pocket PC. The system is a full-size keyboard (with laptop-size 19mm keys), and provides special shortcut keys for the Start menu, Today screen, Inbox, Notes, Contacts, Pocket Word, Calendar, Pocket Excel, Tasks, and Pocket Money. The Stowaway also ships with a software driver (to get the Pocket PC to recognize keyboard input) and an application that enables you to customize special key combinations. Holding the Function key and pressing another key initiates Clear Screen, Help, Power Down, Contrast, and Brightness commands. In addition, you can set 26 custom key combinations to insert blocks of text (such as your e-mail signature or name and address) and stamp the open document with the current date and time. The Stowaway Portable Keyboard was designed and manufactured by Think Outside Incorporated and is available from Targus (www.targus.com).

If you are looking for a nonfoldable keyboard, or if you own another brand of Pocket PC, you can purchase the KeySync CE by iBIZ Technology Corporation (www.ibizcorp.com). To be compatible with all Pocket PCs, the Pocket PC must be placed in a serial cradle or attached to a serial cable and then connected to the KeySync CE keyboard. Pictured in Figure 19.2, the KeySync CE, in comparison with the Stowaway, has smaller keys (16 mm) than the Stowaway and does not fold up. The KeySync uses three AAA batteries so as not to drain power from the Pocket PC and has six programmable text macro keys and ten application launch keys.

Figure 19.2 The KeySync CE

A third option available for all Windows Powered device users is KeyMate Deluxe, by Micro Foundry (www.microfoundry.com). Designed to work with standard PS/2 computer keyboards, KeyMate Deluxe is a small black box that connects to the Pocket PC using infrared or serial communications. Included software runs on the device to enable customization of repeat and delay rates, as well as auto Num Lock and 12 user programmable hot keys.

Getting Connected

Connecting to the Internet has been a recurring theme throughout this handbook. Just as there are countless activities that you can do on the Internet, there are also countless ways in which you can connect to the Internet. For connecting to the Internet via a regular phone line, Pretec (www.pretec.com) makes the Compact Modem 56K. Designed to operate at the same speed as desktop computer modems, the Compact Modem 56K plugs into the CompactFlash slot of the Pocket PC and has a matchbox-sized protrusion for plugging in a standard telephone cord.

Note

Owners of the Casio E115/125, Compact Aero 1550, and Compact iPAQ with CF expansion slot can also use the Xircom (www.xircom.com) CompactCard Modem. It is a 56K modem that requires a Type II CompactFlash slot (The HP Jornada has a Type I slot).

If you have access to a corporate Local Area Network (LAN) at work, Socket Communications' Low Power Ethernet Card inserts into the CompactFlash port of the Pocket PC. Because the HP Jornada already has drivers for the Socket Ethernet card, the device is plug-and-play for network connectivity. Socket offers a hardware and software bundle called the Ethernet PocketPak, which includes the Low Power Ethernet Card and an evaluation version of bSQUARE's bInTouch voice over IP communication software (discussed in Chapter 18). When connected to an Internet-enabled LAN, you can use the entire set of Internet software applications discussed in Chapter 18, plus surf with Pocket Internet Explorer at network speed.

Cross-Reference

For information on the Psion Travel Modem and wireless Internet connectivity accessories, refer to the "Going Wireless" section of Chapter 16.

After you have mastered the connection to the Internet, you might want to reexamine your connection to the desktop. Regardless of whether you use USB or serial to connect to your desktop, if you are currently synchronizing with a cable, upgrade to a synchronization cradle. This way, you can communicate with the desktop and recharge your Pocket PC batteries just by dropping it in to the cradle. Because the Pocket PC will not power off when connected to the desktop, this also prevents the system from losing power and accidentally erasing data when left unattended but connected to the desktop via a cable. Manufacturers of every model of Pocket PC have accessory cradles available for universal serial bus (USB) and serial connections.

Increasing Your Power

If you synchronize at work and at home you will need a second AC adapter to avoid depleting your device's power supply while connected to a PC. If so, check to whether your Pocket PC has a travel version of the AC adapter available. Travel adapters are generally smaller than the power cords that come with your Pocket PC and international travel adapters often automatically convert foreign voltages to the required 110-volt power that is used in the United States.

Cross-Reference

The HP Jornada ships with an international travel adapter. For more information on the HP Jornada travel modem, skip ahead to Chapter 23.

For road warriors that find themselves with little need for a second AC power adapter there is an automobile DC adapter for every line of Pocket PC. Plugging into the car's cigarette lighter socket, the DC adapter will charge your Pocket PC while driving. And, for travelers who find themselves without AC or DC power, Hewlett-Packard has developed the Power Pack for the Jornada Pocket PC. Shown in Figure 19.3, the Power Pack is charged using the HP power cord or docking it in the synchronization cradle. It can be carried around until the Pocket PC becomes low on power. When needed, the power cord at the top of the illustration extends to plug into the HP Jornada and to recharge the internal battery for up to four hours of additional use. If the Power Pack is connected to the HP Jornada full-time, it reportedly adds as much as seven hours additional battery life. This is a great way to keep your Pocket PC running when you are traveling on international flights or out in the wilderness.

Figure 19.3 The Jornada Power Pack

Adding More Memory

If you have read this far in the book, it is almost certain that you have experienced low memory problems because of all the use you have gotten out of your Pocket PC and the third-party software that you have installed. A number of different manufacturers make memory cards for the Pocket PC. Some of the more popular manufacturers are Kingston (www.kingston.com), Sandisk, and Simple Technology (www.simpletech.com). Kingston Technology has compiled a complete software bundle on their media card specifically for the Pocket PC. The package includes a 32MB CompactFlash card containing the ActiveSky Media Player, short films by AtomFilms, Eveo, and CinemaElectric, Bubblets, (the additive game mentioned in Chapter 18), and an Audible.com sample featuring comedy clips from Dennis Miller, Scott Adams, John Pinette, and Dave Berry. Visit www.kingston.com for more information. In addition, each company has Type I CompactFlash cards (which work in the HP Jornada) with a maximum storage capacity of up to 128MB.

Tip

The Jornada also works with Type I CompactFlash memory cards used in digital cameras. Because some digital cameras come with a CF card, you might already have a free way to expand your memory. Plus, you can pop the card into your Pocket PC after you have taken pictures to preview them using Pocket Internet Explorer.

Other Pocket PCs (such as the Compaq iPAQ and Casio E-1xx series) support Type II CompactFlash cards. The Type II format includes high-capacity memory cards, such as Simple Technology's 512MB card, and the IBM Microdrive, which is available in models offering 340MB to 1GB of storage.

Cross-Reference

For information on how to automatically save documents to the memory card instead of main memory, read the "Advanced Memory Management" section of Chapter 21.

Finding Your Way

A Global Positioning System (GPS, for short) is a piece of electronic hardware that defines your location on earth by tracking the position of orbiting satellites. Accurate to within meters, GPS quickly became paired with software mapping applications to provide directions and location finding. Moreover, in just the last few years, hardware manufacturers have begun developing GPS systems and software for Windows Powered devices.

Pocket CoPilot, from TravRoute (`www.travroute.com/`) is a GPS system and software application bundle that plugs into the Pocket PC and delivers door-to-door directions anywhere in the United States. The application installs to main memory, but enables map data (which can vary from several to 100MB) to be stored on a memory card. Once launched, the application contacts the GPS system, locates your position, and awaits a destination address. When entered, the program quickly calculates the fastest route to the address and begins plotting your course. Figure 19.4 is an example of the Drive screen that displays a course map and text descriptions for the next turn you must make. Note how the application displays the distance to the next turn (labeled Just ahead in the figure) and the total distance to your destination. In addition to the visual directions, Pocket CoPilot provides audio cues such as left turn ahead. This enables you to keep your eyes on the road and focus on driving. If you miss a turn off, or try to take a shortcut against the application's suggested route, Pocket CoPilot instantly recalculates the directions to your destination.

Figure 19.4 Pocket CoPilot

Other screens on Pocket CoPilot include a full-screen map display, a satellite data screen, and an itinerary screen that displays turn-by-turn directions with distance information. Pocket CoPilot supports trips with multiple destinations, enabling you to customize the order of the stops and providing icons to quickly enter work and home addresses. Every destination entered into Pocket CoPilot is saved as a favorite that can be later recalled with a tap of a button.

Tip

The Pocket CoPilot ships with a cigarette charger divider that plugs directly into the car's cigarette lighter port and provides two receptacles for DC adapters. This is provides a great way to recharge your Pocket PC and cellular phone simultaneously when the GPS system is not in use.

Because of the popularity of GPS systems, several software and hardware manufacturers have Pocket PC solutions. The Pocket PC Navigator is a competing GPS software application from Pharos GPS (www.pharosgps.com). The system uses a full-screen graphical map and provides voice prompts to deliver turn information. Pocket PC Navigator is available with the iGPS-180 Global Positioning System hardware, which includes a special harness that connects the Pocket PC to the GPS system and plugs into the cigarette lighter to power both devices. And for devices with a CompactFlash slot, Pretec (www.pretec.com) has developed CompactGPS, a GPS system in CompactFlash card format, and the NextCell PocketSpider Modem (discussed in Chapter 16), which has GPS capability included as an additional option.

Enhancing the Pocket PC's Good Looks

You will be the envy of all your friends when they see you with your Pocket PC. Chances are, however, that your friends will quickly jump on the bandwagon and buy a Pocket PC for themselves. With a few simple accessories, you can make them jealous of your stylish device and make the Pocket PC much easier to identify if you frequently hand it off to other people.

By far, the coolest accessory you can add to your HP Jornada is a color cover. With eight different hues divided into @play (boisterous and fun) and @work (subtle and professional) Hewlett-Packard lets you shed the HP Jornada's conservative gray skin and show your true colors (Figure 19.5). There are four colors in @play: yell-o, burnt orange, electric lime, and surf blue; and four colors in @work: passion red, french beige, classic navy, and deep plum. These covers are available from www.hpshopping.com. With a simple snap-on method of attachment, you can easily change covers to match your outfits. Each cover comes with a new (black) stylus.

Figure 19.5 Color covers

If you want to go the more conservative route, every Pocket PC manufacturer makes a customized carrying case. I always recommend that users purchase a carrying case made by the hardware manufacturer rather than a generic PDA case because the hardware manufacturer's cases usually include openings for the device controls and the case fits better (keeping the profile much smaller). The HP Executive Leather Case is a perfect example of this, with a leather cover that lowers over the Jornada similar to the original metal lid, while still providing access to the Voice Recorder button even when closed. The snap that fastens the case has an attractive Jornada logo emblazed on it and the top of the leather cover includes a stylus holder.

Extras

Let's be honest. Everyone loses a stylus once or twice in a lifetime. In fact, I could probably fill an entire room full of styli if everyone returned the ones I have dropped between car seats, on airplanes, or loaned to friends who have never returned them. Thankfully, every company that makes a Pocket PC sells a replacement stylus set. The stylus replacements come in multipacks and, while many people give some styli away or share a package, I recommend keeping them all for yourself.

 Tip

Instead of using your finger when you misplace a stylus, turn your finger over and tap the screen with the top of your fingernail. With practice, you will be able to hit the keys on the soft keyboard and even use Character Recognizer or Transcriber to enter text. Moreover, using your fingernail will keep the screen clear of oil, perspiration, and dirt from your hands.

Another option is to purchase a high-end stylus. Although they do not fit in the Pocket PC's stylus holder, these alternatives to the built-in stylus are usually larger in size and have a better ergonomic fit for your hand. This will prevent hand cramping and reduce the amount of pressure required to grip the stylus to hold it securely. The A.T. Cross Company (www.cross-pcg.com), long-time makers of writing instruments, manufactures the DigitalWriter Duo, a two-sided pen/stylus combination that delivers their high quality ink pen on one end and a plastic tipped stylus opposite end. The company also offers DigitalWriter Duo Morph, a pen/stylus combination with an adjustable soft grip pad on the ink pen end. The DigitalWriter Duo is available in black, blue, and burgundy, and the DigitalWriter Duo Morph is available in electric blue, mars red, quicksilver, and Sherwood green.

Another alternative that is sure to grab attention is the Fingertip Stylus by Concept Kitchen (www.conceptkitchen.com). Designed to slip over your index finger, the metal appliance provides an accurate method of launching programs by tapping them with your finger. It even provides a faster method of single-character input (using Character Recognizer) with practice. Because the tip is metal, I strongly recommend using a screen protector with this product. The company also offers a PDA stylus with a desktop stand and PenCap, a four-pack of product that fits over disposable pens to transform them into a stylus. This is the most economical solution for users (such as me) who lose a stylus at regular intervals.

If you spend a lot of time in your car traveling for work or pleasure or decide to purchase a GPS system for your Pocket PC, it makes sense to invest in an automotive cradle for your Pocket PC. The automotive cradle will not recharge your Pocket PC and does not enable you to synchronize to a laptop in your car, but it does provide a simple way to hold your Pocket PC in the automobile that keeps it off the passenger seat or car floor. Figure 19.6 shows the HP Jornada in a Universal Cup Holder Kit by Arkon Resources Incorporated (www.arkon.com). Notice how the mounting kit makes use of the automobile's cup holder so that no permanent installation materials, such as screws or adhesives, are necessary.

Figure 19.6 The Arkon Universal Cup Holder Kit

Warning

Obviously, using a Pocket PC is extremely distracting and should not be attempted by the driver while the vehicle is in motion. Furthermore, having a Pocket PC mounted in view of the driver may be illegal because many locales prohibit video screens in the driver's area of the vehicle. Check your local vehicle laws and let the passenger manage the controls of the Pocket PC when the vehicle is in motion. Additionally, do not forget to remove your device from the vehicle on hot days. The Pocket PC is not designed to withstand high temperatures and may sustain permanent damage if left in an automobile on a hot summer day.

Summary

Now that you've completed this chapter, you now know that there are many accessory options available for your Pocket PC. As a rule of thumb, if you can imagine a need for a handheld computing solution, someone has already figured out how to attach it to your Pocket PC. And with new Pocket PC accessories arriving on a continual basis, your device can evolve to continually meet your changing needs.

Now that you have supercharged your Pocket PC with all of the perfect accessories to fit your needs, it is time for the educational portion of the handbook. The next chapter focuses on e-books, the electronic form of publishing.

Advanced E-book Tutorial

IN THIS CHAPTER
- E-book formats
- Alternate e-book applications
- Making e-books

Just as the Internet has revolutionized the way that we communicate in our daily lives, e-books are changing the way we access educational, entertainment, and reference materials. Now, in an electronic device far smaller than a paperback book, we can carry the equivalent of an entire shelf of paperback and hardback books. By adding a high-capacity memory card, volumes of information can be stored and carried with you in a device that you already rely on. Moreover, the versatility of the e-book and the availability of new titles online make owning a virtual library easy and cost effective.

Cross-Reference

For an introduction to using Pocket Reader and e-books on your Pocket PC, review the second half of Chapter 12.

Although Pocket Reader is built-in to the Pocket PC, which should be the ultimate competitive advantage, there are competing e-book formats and programs both for the Pocket PC and as stand-alone e-book hardware accessories. This chapter explores the different e-book formats, introduces e-book reader application alternatives for the Pocket PC, and shows you how to create an e-book.

E-book Formats

Regardless of all the hype, an e-book is a just another document format, plain and simple. Just like files created in Microsoft Word, e-book files are created in a program that applies certain tags that tell the e-book reader to change the font size or to bold the text. These tags, along with information such as book title, author, and description, are all stored in metadata. Similar to Hypertext Markup Language (HTML) tags used in Web pages, metadata provides a common platform for communicating information. Each reader application uses slightly different meta tags, some of which include copyright protection.

The DOC format

Probably the most popular and prominent e-book format on the Internet, DOC (lesser known by its official title: the AportisDoc file format) is the e-book format owned by Aportis Technologies. The DOC format includes compression technology that decreases the size of e-books and offers broad cross-platform reader support. Countless extensions of the DOC format (like DOC PDB) exist, but they are all based on the DOC specifications for e-book compilation.

Tip

A great online resource for downloading DOC format e-books is the Memoware Web site (www.memoware.com).

HTML format

An HTML format e-book uses the same tags as Web pages use on the Internet. This format enables you to open an e-book on any platform with a Web browser. Text formatting and embedded graphics are supported in HTML e-books.

Microsoft Reader (LIT format)

This is Microsoft's proprietary e-book format readable by Pocket Reader and the desktop version of Reader that supports embedded graphics and audio. Streaming video is reportedly in the works for a future version of Reader.

OEB Publication Structure

A newly developing format is the Open E-book Publication Structure. This free format is developing into an industry standard but has not yet gained wide acceptance, and none of the Pocket PC applications support this format. For more information, visit www.openebook.org.

Portable Document Format

Adobe's Portable Document Format (PDF) and e-book technology is a natural union because of the popularity of Adobe Acrobat. Acrobat, a desktop plug-in for Netscape Navigator and Microsoft Internet Explorer enables people to view PDF files in their browser while maintaining the design and layout integrity of the original document. PDF files are generally larger than any other e-book format because of their focus on layout over compression. PDF files can be viewed on the Pocket PC using Ansyr PDF Viewer, which is available at www.ansyr.com.

Rich Text Format

A common file format used in word processing applications, Rich Text Format (RTF) is an enhanced version of the plain text file. The enhancements enable e-books to be formatted with textual design elements but no graphical elements.

Text file

The TXT file format is a plain ASCII text file that can be created in Windows Notepad on the desktop. TXT e-books contain no formatting or graphics. Sometimes the reader application automatically spices up a text file e-book to make it more presentable.

Proprietary reader formats

Glassbook, Rocketbook, and SoftBook are all proprietary formats designed for viewing only on specific reader software and hardware products. Glassbook is a downloadable desktop software application from Glassbook Incorporated (www. glassbook.com), while Rocketbook and Softbook formats work only on stand-alone e-book hardware devices licensed by Gemstar (www.e-book-gemstar. com). These proprietary formats are not supported by any third-party software for the Pocket PC.

Alternate E-book Applications

Now that you have seen how many different formats there are, you might be wondering how you can access these e-books on your Pocket PC. The Microsoft Reader for the Pocket PC application only supports the MS Reader e-book format. Later in this chapter, you will learn how to create e-books in the Reader format. However, because e-books cannot be converted from one format to another, you may want to consider installing a second e-book reader application in order to take advantage of the plethora of electronic texts available in the DOC and other formats.

In my opinion, the best third-party e-book reader application is MobiPocket designed by the French firm Mobipocket.com SA. MobiPocket is a multiplatform PDA e-book reader that is available for free at www.mobipocket.com. The application boasts a number of features that belong on a full-cost retail application including full-screen mode (by pressing the Action button), infrared e-book transfer for noncopyrighted texts, four levels of text magnification, and the capability to customize the text and background using 48 different colors. Bookmarks, Dictionary, and Find features are also built into the software application.

Figure 20.1 shows MobiPocket with an e-book open. The application bar at the top of the screen offers access to the MobiPocket menu, table of contents, bookmarks, font size, and page navigation. This bar can be removed by depressing the Action button to activate full-screen mode, which will squeeze two more lines of text onscreen (using the normal font size). Note the bar at the bottom of the page, showing your progress through the e-book. Tapping anywhere on the right or left side of the e-book page turns to the next or previous page of text, respectively.

The company created the XDOC PRC file format, an extension to the DOC PRC format. This means that MobiPocket uses the compression system of DOC but has its own copyright protection for MobiPocket-purchased texts. In addition to the MobiPocket e-books, the application can read DOC, HTML DOC, HTML, and TXT e-books. In addition, the company is a member of the Open E-book Forum (OEB), so support for any OEB formats should be expected in MobiPocket.

MobiPocket also includes a desktop application that seamlessly integrates with ActiveSync. The Web Companion application downloads news updates from the Internet and compiles it into a book that is automatically downloaded to the Pocket PC for your later perusal. This feature is what sets MobiPocket apart from all other e-book readers and makes a freeware application that is really worth owning. As a grand finale, every e-book downloaded is registered in My Mobipocket Personal Virtual Library, the online portion of the MobiPocket service. This library gives you access to any e-book that you have purchased through the service, even if you delete it from your desktop and Pocket PC.

Figure 20.1 MobiPocket

The second — and quite popular — application is Peanut Reader from peanutpress.com, Inc., a division of netLibrary. In addition to novels, peanut-press.com includes nonfiction books, newspapers, magazines, and reference guides, as well as out-of-print works from popular authors. Their e-book format is based on the DOC PBD format that also uses compression techniques to keep the book sizes small. Figure 20.2 shows a sample e-book loaded into Peanut Reader. The background is black and the text white because inverse mode has been activated. The six icons at the bottom of the screen represent (from left to right) chapter index, bookmark index, inverse screen toggle, book information, annotation index, and a back button for hypertext books. The down-turned page corner at the upper-right of the e-book indicates that this page has been bookmarked.

Figure 20.2 Peanut Reader

Peanut Reader includes a number of great nuances, including the capability to designate any font from the Pocket PC as the book typestyle and the ability to tap anywhere on the bottom half of the screen to advance to the next page. Annotations can be exported from the e-book, and e-books can be deleted from within the application. Although Peanut Reader is not as feature rich as MobiPocket, it deserves a chance because of all of the great content available from `www.peanutpress.com`.

Other third-party software developers have created somewhat less capable e-book reader applications. ThumbsUpSoft (`www.thumbsupsoft.com`) publishes an e-book reader application called StarBuck, a no-frills reader application that displays ASCII text, HTML, bReady, and Pilot PRC/PDB documents. Oopdreams Software Inc., (`www.oopdreams.com`) offers *peekabook*, a simple e-book application that reads DOCs and textbooks. Handheldmed Incorporated offers a free e-book reader to open and read all of their PocketClinician Library medical reference books.

Making E-books

Because the Pocket PC ships with Pocket Reader, the rest of this chapter focuses on creating an e-book for the Reader (LIT) format. There are two applications for creating a LIT format e-book: the Microsoft Reader add-in for Microsoft Word and ReaderWorks. The Microsoft Reader add-in for Microsoft Word enables you to create an e-book in just minutes with no technical knowledge. ReaderWorks, an application developed by OverDrive Incorporated, creates more complex e-books with cover art, a table of contents, and copyright capabilities.

Microsoft Reader add-in for Microsoft Word

Designed for the home user, the Microsoft Reader add-in for Microsoft Word (available for free download at `www.microsoft.com/reader/info/selfpublish.htm`) enables you to convert a Word document to a Reader file in three easy steps. To perform this process, complete the following steps:

1. Create a document with text and graphics in Microsoft Word.

2. Click on the Reader icon in the Microsoft Word toolbar.

3. Enter the e-book title, author, and filename information when the pop-up window appears, and then select whether you wish to save the file on your reading device (Pocket PC) or the computer. If you select the reading device option, the application will create a My Library subfolder in your Pocket PC's synchronized documents folder and build the e-book in it. The next time you synchronize, the e-book will be copied to your device.

Because the Microsoft Reader add-in for Microsoft Word is free, many of the advanced e-book features are not available. For example, the images on the cover and library thumbnail always appear as a Microsoft Word icon.

Overdrive ReaderWorks

If you want to become a professional e-book publisher, or just look like one, you will need ReaderWorks from OverDrive Incorporated. Using the application takes considerably more preparation, a general working knowledge of HTML and the capability to create graphical images, but it is worth the effort. An e-book published in ReaderWorks looks like a professionally created electronic volume that you can share with pride.

Overdrive offers two versions of the ReaderWorks software on their Web site (www.overdrive.com). ReaderWorks Standard and ReaderWorks Publisher. The standard version is a free download from their Web site that enables you to create e-books quickly and easily with the ReaderWorks wizards and interface. The program is fully functional and will never expire, but does not enable you to customize the cover art cover art, insert marketing metadata into your e-book, or create pages for copyright and About this title, or designate the Begin Reading page. These advanced features are available in ReaderWorks Publisher for $149.

Requirements to create a complete e-book text in ReaderWorks

Before you publish your first work, you will need to organize your materials like all great authors. ReaderWorks has a very specific set of requirements for assembling the content. Following is a shopping list for what you will need to begin:

- **Text content**: The manuscript in either HTML or plain text (txt) format. ReaderWorks will accept content that has been developed in a word processing program and saved as HTML. If you want to include graphics, perform any text formatting, or control the look and feel of your e-book, you should use HTML.

- **Desktop Reader Cover Page Art** (ReaderWorks Publisher only): This image is displayed while the desktop version of Reader loads the book into memory. The dimensions for this graphic should be 510×680 pixels. Acceptable file formats are .jpg, .gif, and .png.

- **Desktop Reader Spine Art for Title Page** (ReaderWorks Publisher only): This image will appear on the cover page of the e-book on the desktop version of Reader. The dimensions for this graphic should be 108×680 pixels. Acceptable file formats are .jpg, .gif, and .png.

- **Desktop Reader Library Thumbnail Art** (ReaderWorks Publisher only): This image will appear when the book is displayed in the Reader Library on the desktop computer. The dimensions for this graphic should be 99×132 pixels. Acceptable file formats are .jpg, .gif, and .png.

- **Pocket Reader Cover Page Art** (ReaderWorks Publisher only): This image will appear on the cover page of the e-book on the Pocket PC version of Reader. The dimensions for this graphic should be 90×45 pixels. Acceptable file formats are .jpg, .gif, and .png.

■ **Pocket Reader Library Thumbnail Art** (ReaderWorks Publisher only): This image will appear when the book is displayed in the Reader Library on the Pocket PC. The dimensions for this graphic should be 480×240 pixels. Acceptable file formats are .jpg, .gif, and .png.

Note

Graphics are not required to make an e-book. If you do not have images for some or all of the art items, ReaderWorks Publisher will insert a ReaderWorks logo in its place.

Creating an e-book

Because ReaderWorks requires all of the e-book content to be in the same directory, create a working directory on your desktop computer's hard drive where you can assemble all of these items. Put all of the items mentioned earlier in this working folder and then launch ReaderWorks. When open, you will notice that the program is divided into five sections: source files, properties, table of contents, cover page, and marketing data.

Figure 20.3 shows the source files panel of the ReaderWorks application. In this section, you compile all of the actual text content for your book. Notice that the files are arranged in order. If you have a manuscript that is broken up into multiple parts (such as chapters or acts) you can insert them, one at a time, into ReaderWorks, and then order them as they should appear in the e-book. Raw graphic files can also be inserted as source files — they will appear in the book between chapters.

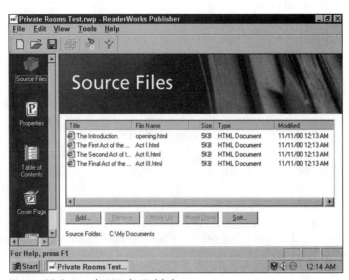

Figure 20.3 ReaderWorks Publisher

After you have imported all of your source files, switch to the Properties section. This workspace enables you to designate the title, author, subject, description, publisher, contributor, date, type, format, identifier, source, language, relation, coverage, and rights. Note that an e-book can have multiple authors, subjects, contributors, and identifiers. When the e-book is built, this information is inserted into the document metadata to protect your e-book.

The third section, Table of Contents, is where you can create a hyperlinked index for your e-book. ReaderWorks offers two options. First, you can create your own table of contents using HTML and simply load it in this window. If you do not have a table of contents, the alternate option is to use the ReaderWorks Table of Contents Wizard. The wizard automatically creates the index from the separated files or from the HTML headings in your source files. The wizard offers four styles of design for your table of contents: classic, distinct, fancy, or formal.

Cover Page, an option available only to users who purchase ReaderWorks Publisher, enables you to insert the cover and library art specified in the previous section of this chapter. In addition, it enables you to identify which page readers should jump to when they press the begin reading link on the e-book cover. It also enables you to create pages for copyright, as well as and About This title links.

The final section, Marketing Data, is for designating marketing and merchandising data for your e-book. Because the metadata marketing standards were not completed in time for the release of ReaderWorks v1.0, this section is not currently active. When the standards are released, registered users will be able to upgrade ReaderWorks Publisher to activate the Marketing Data section with support for industry standard data formats. Published authors can convert an e-book from an existing print title with an ISBN by using the online Extensible Markup Language (XML) file-creation utility at www.readerworks.com. This XML file will enable you to submit your e-book title to bn.com for their Microsoft Reader e-bookstore.

After you have finished filling out all of the above sections in ReaderWorks, you are ready to publish your first book. Select File ➪ Build e-book and ReaderWorks prompts you for the name and location to create the LIT file. Once entered, the application compiles all of your source files and imports the graphics into the system. Depending on the size of your e-book, the build process may take a few minutes but once it has completed, you will have a professionally designed e-book. Figure 20.4 shows three e-books that I created using ReaderWorks Standard (My Family Vacation), ReaderWorks Publisher (Private Rooms), and the Microsoft Reader add-in for Microsoft Word (The Great American Novel). Instantly, you can see the difference between Private Rooms and the e-books created using the free applications because of the customized thumbnail image.

Figure 20.4 Homemade e-books in Pocket Reader

Tips for designing an e-book for optimal viewing on Pocket PCs

Because e-books are being read on the Pocket PC, you have a controlled environment as far as screen settings and software capabilities. Conversely, there are a few things you need to watch out for in order to hone the design of an e-book for optimal viewing on a Pocket PC.

Text layout

- Use the heading (H1 or Heading 1) and formatting features in the HTML editor or Microsoft Word to arrange text.

- Never use multiple spaces to align or indent text because the text will be in a different location on the Pocket PC screen and moves again if the user resizes the text.

- ClearType, the Microsoft technology that greatly improves the readability of your e-book, only works when you use these fonts: Berling Antiqua, Frutiger Linotype, and Lucida Sans Typewriter.

- Do not use tables in your e-book documents because they are not supported on Pocket Reader.

- Remove the following frequently used word processing items from your documents, because they are not supported by the Microsoft Reader format: form elements, headers, and footers.

- Pocket Reader does not recognize these common HTML tags: background, background color, border, font, height, img align, img border, li type, link type, ol type, listing, menu, plaintext, Q, span, table, vertical align, and width.

Graphics

- When creating graphics for cover and library art, make sure they are sized using the dimensions listed in the "Requirements to Create a Complete E-book Text in ReaderWorks" section of this chapter. Otherwise, ReaderWorks will resize the images for you and they may become disproportional.

- When using the Microsoft Reader add-in for Microsoft Word, only Joint Experts Photographic Group (JPEG) graphics are supported by Pocket Reader, so make sure all of your images are converted to .jpg before importing them into ReaderWorks.

- Remember, the Pocket PC screen is only 240 pixels wide and 320 pixels tall. Images included in the e-book manuscript should be resized to under 200×250 pixels to accommodate the Start menu and controls at the top of the screen, and the margins on either side of the e-book.

- The Pocket PC screen on the HP Jornada is 107 dpi. To make your graphics appear crisp, ensure that image resolutions are set to 103 dpi.

- When creating a book with ReaderWorks, all images that are referred to in the HTML manuscript files must be included in your working directory. In other words, if you place a graphic in your manuscript, you need to copy that image file into the same working directory where the HTML resides before you select Build e-book from the ReaderWorks menu.

E-book ideas

Obviously, the options for creating electronic books is only limited by your creativity and the amount of content you can gather. Here are a few ideas for starting out:

- Publish your company's corporate guidelines, bylaws, and policies electronically.

- Create a family album full of pictures, or create an album for a special vacation, using text to describe the photos or tell a memorable story.

- For each project you work on, create a personalized virtual whiteboard where people can annotate your concepts and return the comments to you.

Cross-Reference

Chapter 12 describes the method for sending and receiving e-book annotations between Pocket PCs.

- Write your life story and publish it on the Internet.

- Create a set of Frequently Asked Questions (FAQs) about your company's products or services and distribute it to your sales and marketing organizations or directly to your clients.

- Make a children's story with your kids' names as characters in the book. Read it to them or, better yet, have them read it to you.

- Create a Points of Interest guide of your hometown, or your favorite vacation spots. Share the guide with your friends and family, or post it on the Internet.

- Create a reference of technical terms used in your industry for quick reference when you are in a meeting or on the road.

- Assemble your family tree and then publish it in an e-book for all your relatives.

- Write the great American novel.

Remember that LIT format e-books are also compatible with the desktop version of Microsoft Reader. This means that friends, family, and coworkers who do not own a Pocket PC can view the e-books that you create. The desktop version of Reader is available for free download at www.microsoft.com/reader/.

Summary

With the completion of this chapter, you should have a very clear picture of the benefits of the e-book, an understanding of the various e-book formats, and the ease with which you can create an e-book at home. Although e-book readers may seem like an attractive alternative to a Pocket PC, the $200 to $700 devices do not offer the flexibility or convenience already built into the Pocket PC platform. In addition to the competitive advantages of integrated organizer functions, third-party software expandability, and hardware accessories, this chapter covered how the Pocket PC supports open e-book formats and offers a variety of tools for creating your own e-books.

Now that you have downloaded your favorite novels on e-book and created your own albums and stories, your Pocket PC is probably very low on memory. Chapter 21 discusses the tricks for maximizing memory and battery life on your Pocket PC, so that you will never run out of power while you are sharing your newly authored e-book with friends and family.

Pocket PC Challenges

Memory and Power Constraints

IN THIS CHAPTER
- How memory works on a Pocket PC
- Learning advanced file management
- Using a memory card
- How power works on a Pocket PC

I have always said that "anything worthwhile requires a little extra effort," and the Pocket PC proves this rule by possessing a few inherent challenges which most users experience but few know how to overcome. Studying this section and spending just 15 minutes every month on upkeep will make the difference between a Pocket PC that performs like a Ferrari Testerosa and a system that chugs along slower than your father's beat up 1976 Cadillac.

Just as everything in life requires food and water, everything in your Pocket PC requires memory and power. They are the necessities for the good health and good performance of your Pocket PC. This chapter introduces you to the secret techniques of memory and power management. Afterward, we will explore the real-world challenge of working with the countless number of Palm Pilot devices.

Understanding Your Pocket PC's Memory

If you have owned your Pocket PC for at least a month, you have undoubtedly experienced an occasional sluggish response when you run an application or possibly even had the Pocket PC freeze completely while performing a task. The common cause behind slow performance and system lock ups is constraints on the Pocket PC's memory. Memory is the workspace on the device and once you understand how it works, you can easily control it to prevent system sluggishness and lock ups. Some third-party software applications also contain bugs that cause the system to slow down or freeze.

As with all computers, the Pocket PC uses memory to store data and perform calculations. There are two types of memory: read-only memory (ROM) and random access memory (RAM). ROM contains all of the built-in applications and the Pocket PC operating system. Because ROM memory is *read-only*, it cannot be erased or overwritten even if your Pocket PC loses power or is corrupted. This protects all of the applications that come with your device and has the added benefit of freeing up valuable RAM memory. RAM is used to store all of the applications and information that you install on the device and is used to perform tasks such as running programs. On the Pocket PC, the segment of RAM that stores applications and information is called storage memory and the segment that performs tasks is called program memory. Creating a well-proportioned balance of storage RAM and program RAM is the key to a fast and stable Pocket PC.

The Control Panel Memory applet

Microsoft has developed the Control Panel Memory applet to enable you to monitor and adjust the amount of RAM allocated to storage and program memory. Select Start Menu ⇨ Settings ⇨ System tab ⇨ Memory to open the Memory applet. Figure 21.1 shows the main screen of the Memory applet. Notice the shaded area on the bar, which delivers a quick visual indication of the amount of free RAM. The slider enables you to change the memory allocation.

Note

Before you continue to the next section, write down the amount of program memory that you have in use. When you complete the next section, return to the Control Panel Memory applet and see how much memory you were able to free.

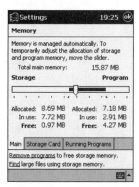

Figure 21.1 The main screen of the Control Panel Memory applet

Cleaning up Program Memory

Because program memory is used by the Pocket PC to perform tasks such as running programs and making calculations, it is also primarily responsible for the sluggish performance and system lock ups. This is the memory that must be managed vigilantly. In the Memory applet, the easy way to increase program memory is simply to move the slider further to the left. However, although this allocates more RAM to program memory, it reduces the amount of storage memory available on your Pocket PC. Although changing the memory allocation is a quick solution, I consider this the last option a user should explore because it reduces the space available to save files on your device and does not actually clean up the program memory area.

Tip

Under extremely low memory situations, remove the CompactFlash card from your device. You will instantly free as much as 10k of program memory.

Instead of changing the memory allocation, select the Running Programs tab on the memory applet. Figure 21.2 shows the screen after Running Programs has been selected. The list is the applications that are currently running and therefore occupying program memory. You can regain more program memory by shutting down any applications that you are not currently using. To shut down an application, highlight the application name and press the Stop button. The Stop All button closes down all of the applications simultaneously.

Warning

Using the Stop feature immediately shuts down the application you have selected. If a document is open in the application, any information that is new or changed will be lost. You can ensure that you will not lose any data by highlighting an application and pressing Activate. Make sure that all open documents are closed and then return to the Control Panel Memory applet and shut down the application.

Figure 21.2 The Running Programs tab of the Control Panel Memory applet

Once you have shut down all of the open applications on your device, you can safely clear out the residual memory left by the applications by performing a soft reset on your Pocket PC. Simply use the tip of the stylus to press the recessed Reset button on the back of the device. The Pocket PC screen will blank out and then display a startup logo. This is very similar to rebooting your desktop computer and restarts the device with a cleansed program memory area.

Following these steps once a month should keep the Pocket PC's program memory free and clear. Just remember that the operating system always uses some program memory any time the device is turned on. However, if you still have over 2 megabytes of program memory occupied right after you reset the device, there might be applications loading in your Startup menu.

Cross-Reference

See the "Customize Your Start Menu and Startup Applications" section of Chapter 17 for complete information on how to prevent applications from automatically loading when you reset the device.

Advanced File Management

While storage memory should never be neglected, program memory maintenance can be performed much more infrequently, or even on an as-needed basis. In fact, the Pocket PC will attempt to equally distribute memory by converting program memory to storage memory when the system becomes depleted. And, because this memory does not cause lock ups or have residual effects, maintaining the storage memory is a much easier task.

Begin by deleting all of the unwanted data files from your device. You can preview each document in its native application and then delete it by simply holding the stylus down on the filename and selecting Delete from the pop-up menu. Figure 21.3 shows the Delete feature being used in Pocket Word. The Pocket PC confirms your delete request so you do not accidentally remove a document when you were trying to perform other file management tasks.

Figure 21.3 Deleting a file directly from the Pocket Word application

If all of the files on your device are essential or if you have removed all of the excess files but still need more storage memory, your second option is to remove applications. The Control Panel Remove Programs applet will enable you to delete all of the files related with a specific program from your Pocket PC. Select Start Menu ➪ Settings ➪ System tab ➪ Remove Programs to open the applet. Figure 21.4 shows the Remove Programs applet populated with the list of installed applications as well as the "Total storage memory available" gauge, so that you can monitor exactly how much free space you are creating each time you remove a program.

Tip

If you would like to see exactly how much storage memory each application occupies on your Pocket PC, connect the device to your desktop and select Tools ➪ Add/Remove Programs in ActiveSync. ActiveSync displays the same list as the Pocket PC Remove Programs applet, but includes the actual amount of memory that installed programs are occupying.

Figure 21.4 The Control Panel Remove Programs applet

Eliminating unnecessary files incorporated in the Pocket PC

When you first start your Pocket PC, the device already has more than half a megabyte of information occupying storage memory. While most of this data is configuration information that the Pocket PC needs in order to function properly, you can safely remove a few files from your device in order to regain some of the precious memory.

Warning

The following instructions will permanently delete information from your device. Once deleted, the only way to retrieve this information is to perform a hard reset on your Pocket PC. If you are concerned about the information you are about to lose, open ActiveSync on your desktop and copy each of the files onto your desktop before performing a file deletion on the device.

To begin, launch File Explorer (Start ➪ Programs ➪ File Explorer). Navigate to the following folders and then tap and hold the folder name. Select Delete from the pop-up menu and answer Yes when asked to confirm your deletion command. As the deletion process proceeds, File Explorer may warn you that some files are read-only. Press the Yes button to confirm that you still want to delete it.

Cross-Reference

For complete information on how to employ the File Explorer application to navigate around your Pocket PC's file folders, refer to the "Using File Explorer" section of Chapter 17.

■ **\My Documents\Templates** — This folder is actually a set of redundant template files. The original files are read-only (meaning that they cannot be deleted) and reside in the \My Device\Windows\ directory. (Amount of free memory restored: 15.91 KB.)

■ **\Windows\Demo** — This folder contains the HP Jornada Pocket PC feature demonstration. It can be viewed by launching the HP home menu (Start ➪ Programs ➪ HP Applications ➪ HP home menu). Once you have seen it, the demo will probably be of little use to you, compared to the amount of memory it occupies. (Amount of free memory restored: 122 KB.)

When you have deleted these folders, you will have cleared more than one-quarter of the half a megabyte (137.91 KB total) of memory that was previously taken. If you are still desperately in need of some extra memory, you can delete these files to regain nominal memory:

■ **\My Documents\Welcome to Windows Media** — The default music file that is played by Windows Media Player. (Amount of free memory restored: 0.24 KB.)

■ **Files inside of \Windows\Help** — Every piece of software you install on your device includes a Help file. Selecting Start ➪ Help loads the help file while the program is being used. If you have installed a large number third-party applications, these files may be occupying a significant amount of memory. Delete the largest files or the files for programs that you are sure you will never need help using. (Amount of free memory restored: approximately 1 KB for each file deleted.) You can always reinstall the third-party application if you need to access the Help file.

Using a Memory Card

You can increase the amount of available memory on every Pocket PC by adding a memory card accessory. The HP Jornada, for example, supports the popular CompactFlash memory standard, which is available wherever laptop computer accessories are sold. When inserted into the device, the memory card is instantly recognized and available to the Pocket PC using File Explorer (Check the Pocket PC hardware manufacturer's Web site for a complete list of memory cards compatible with your Pocket PC).

Warning

When you insert a memory card into your device, the Pocket PC may ask you if you would like to format it. Occasionally, it may present you with this option even though you have already stored data on that card. If you are certain that you have already stored data on the card, remove it immediately from the device. Selecting Yes will reformat the card and erase all of your data; selecting No will not enable you to access the information on the memory card. Reset the device (by pressing the stylus into the recessed hole in the back of the device) and reinsert the memory card.

While memory cards can store hundreds of megabytes of information, it is important to note that it can only be used as storage memory and not the more precious program memory. Moving documents onto the memory card will enable you to allocate more RAM the program memory, but this must be accomplished by manually adjusting the slider as discussed in the beginning of this section.

Setting up a memory card

Before you can begin storing documents on your memory card, you must set up the card to work properly with the Pocket PC file system. To do so, insert your memory card into the slot on your Pocket PC and perform the following instructions:

1. Open File Explorer by selecting Start ➪ Programs ➪ File Explorer.

2. Tap the drop-down arrow in the upper-left corner of File Explorer and select the My Device folder.

3. You should see a Storage Card folder in the File Explorer window if the Pocket PC has recognized the memory card. If a Storage Card folder does not appear on the list, remove and reinsert the memory card into the slot. Take great care to ensure that you have firmly seated the card all the way into the slot.

4. Tap the Storage Card folder and select Edit ➪ New Folder from the File Explorer command bar.

5. Enter **My Documents** as the name of the folder and press Enter, or perform a carriage return gesture in Character Recognizer or Transcriber. When you have completed these steps, the Pocket PC recognizes the memory card as a location where documents can be saved. While working in a Pocket Word document or Pocket Excel spreadsheet, select Tools ➪ Save Document As (for Pocket Word) or Tools ➪ Save Workbook As (for Pocket Excel) and then change the location field to Storage Card. In the Notes application, you can move a file that has already been saved by opening the Note, selecting Tools ➪ Rename\Move and changing the file's location field to Storage Card.

Note

A gray memory card superimposed over the standard Document icon will visually indicate which files have been saved to a memory card.

If you plan to have a memory card permanently installed in your device, you need to instruct the Pocket PC to take full advantage of it. In the options menu of Pocket Excel, Pocket Word, and Notes, select Save to: Storage Card in order to have all of the documents created in these applications saved on to the memory card. Next, open the Pocket PC Inbox application, select Options ➪ Storage tab, and enable "Store attachments on storage card." These quick steps will ensure that you do not consume main memory with large files.

As with main memory, the Control Panel Memory applet enables you to monitor the room on your memory card. Select Start Menu ➪ Settings ➪Memory ➪ Storage Card tab to display a graphical representation of the free memory on the CompactFlash card.

Installing applications onto a memory card

If you want to conserve the most memory possible, you should install all of your third-party applications directly onto a memory card. Although the applications will only run when the memory card is inserted into the device, this conserves all of the RAM on the Pocket PC for program memory. To install an application onto a memory card, perform the following steps:

Note

Some applications cannot be installed on a memory card. If you install an application and then it does not launch from the Programs menu, or works erratically, uninstall the application by choosing Start ➪ Settings ➪ System tab ➪ Remove Programs, and then reinstall it into main memory.

1. Insert the storage card into your Pocket PC and dock the device with your desktop computer.

2. Wait until the synchronization process is complete and then double-click the third-party application's installation file.

3. Depending on the set-up process for the particular application you are installing, the program presents a number of on-screen questions on your desktop computer. When the question "Install [program name] to using the default application installation directory?" appears, press No.

4. The Select Destination Media window appears with the default set to Main memory. Change the option to Storage Card, as shown in Figure 21-5. Note that ActiveSync is unable to ensure that you have enough free memory on your storage card. If you need to check the amount of available memory on the storage card, select Start ➪ Settings ➪ System tab ➪ Memory ➪ Storage Card tab on your Pocket PC. Compare the amount of free memory listed on the Storage Card screen to the amount required by the application on the Select Destination Media window on your desktop.

5. Press the OK button on your desktop computer and ActiveSync will install the third-party application to the storage card. When the installation is complete, the application will be available from the Pocket PC Start menu.

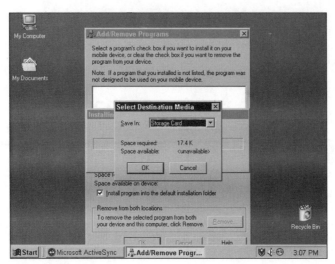

Figure 21.5 Selecting the Storage Card installation option

If you have already installed the application in main memory but you wish to move it into storage card memory, or if you are installing an application using ActiveSync's Add/Remove programs feature, the installation procedure is entirely different:

1. Remove the program (if you are trying to move it to a memory card) by selecting Start ⇨ Settings ⇨ System tab ⇨ Remove Programs, highlighting the application, and pressing the Remove button.

2. Insert the memory card into your device and dock the device with your desktop computer.

3. When the synchronization process is complete, select Tools ⇨ Add/Remove Programs from the ActiveSync window on your desktop computer.

4. When the Add/Remove Programs window appears, scroll down the list of applications and activate the checkbox of any programs that you wish to install.

5. Deselect the Install program into the default installation folder option as shown in Figure 21.6. The "Space available on device" item shown in Figure 21.6 is reading of the free main memory so, again, you will have to check the free memory on the storage card by selecting Start ⇨ Settings ⇨ System tab ⇨ Memory ⇨ Storage Card tab on your Pocket PC and comparing the free memory to the "Space required for selected programs" option displayed on your desktop.

6. Press the OK button on the Add/Remove Programs window and ActiveSync prompts you for an installation location with the Select Destination Media window. Change the option to Storage Card, as shown in Figure 21.5 of our previous example, and then press Ok to immediately begin installing the applications you have selected to your Pocket PC's storage card.

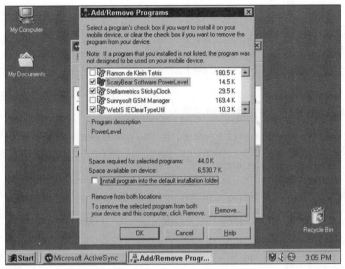

Figure 21.6 The Add/Remove Programs screen

Note

Applications installed to a memory card are set up in subdirectories directly beneath the Storage Card folder. This is different from applications installed in main memory that, generally, install in a subdirectory of Program Files. This is important to remember when searching for applications that you have installed using File Explorer.

How Power Works in a Pocket PC

Supplying a constant stream of energy to the Pocket PC is a requirement for healthy computing. The lithium ion battery on the HP Jornada will supplies approximately four to five hours of full-time use when set at the out-of-the-box defaults. With a little work, you can squeeze 25–75 percent more power from your Pocket PC, and that means a lot when you are on a plane or traveling thousands of miles away from your power cable.

Warning

The HP Jornada is designed with a backup battery supply that stores all of the data on the Pocket PC for up to five days. Because of this feature, all of the tips described in this section have been tested and are safe to attempt with the HP Jornada. Devices that use a separate backup battery (the Compaq Aero and the entire line of Casio devices) will be safe as long as the back up battery is new. The Compaq iPAQ should not, under any circumstances, be drained of power because its backup battery is 20 percent of the Jornada's and has not been tested under these conditions.

Not to overstate the obvious, but *always* keep your Pocket PC fully charged. The lithium ion battery uses technology that does not retain memory like older technology batteries did. This means that you can start recharging the HP Jornada when it is only partially discharged, without worrying about causing strain on the battery or deteriorating its effectiveness.

Low-power warnings

Should the battery power in your Pocket PC dip to dangerous levels, the Pocket PC has two levels of low power warnings. The first advises you to save and close all files that are open on a memory card. When you receive this warning, you should immediately do as you are instructed. Should your device lose power while memory card documents are open, you may lose or permanently corrupt your files. The second warning (shown in Figure 21.7) indicates a critical power-depleted situation in which the unit will power down within moments.

Figure 21.7 The level 2 critical low power warning

Tip

If the second level low power warning appears but you desperately need to get some information from the device, such as a phone number, ignore the warning and use the Start menu. You'll have almost 10 seconds to get it before the device powers off. Remember to ignore the warning window because if you press the Ok button, the system instantly turns off and will not regain power until you attach the device to an external power source.

The Control Panel Power applet

As you would expect, the first step to conserving battery power is to adjust the Pocket PC's built-in Power settings. Select Start ➪ Settings ➪ System Tab ➪ Power to access the Control Panel Power applet. Figure 21.8 shows the Power applet when the battery is fully charged. Notice that the Power applet displays the type of battery (lithium ion) and the amount of power remaining, and also provides a link to the backlight settings. If battery conservation is your utmost concern, I recommend setting the "On battery power: Turn off device if not used for" field to its lowest possible setting. This obviously will not work if you spend a lot of time reading an e-mail or e-books, but will certainly give you more bang for your energy buck. This setting need not be adjusted because your Pocket PC will be using an external power source that won't affect battery life.

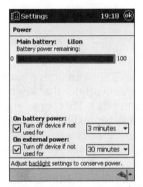

Figure 21.8 The Control Panel Power applet

Adjusting the screen settings

Once you have set the Power Off feature, the next step is to adjust the screen settings. The brightness of the screen is directly related to the amount of power that the Pocket PC consumes during operation: therefore, a dimmer screen will result in better battery performance. Select Start ➪ HP Settings to access the HP screen adjustments. Figure 21.9 shows the HP settings panel with the Low power option selected. Although this choice will enable you to squeeze the longest battery life from your device, the screen becomes unreadable under most conditions. I suggest finding a happy medium between the Indoors and Low power settings. The Jornada automatically saves this setting under the Special option, so you can switch back and forth as your environment dictates.

Cross-Reference

The HP settings feature can save four different screen-setting configurations. For complete information on how to customize the Outdoors, Indoors, Low power, and Special options, review the "Creating customized backlight preferences for four different environments" section of Chapter 17.

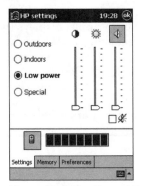

Figure 21.9 The Control Panel HP settings applet

In addition to the standard screen settings, devices with an active backlight (such as the HP Jornada) have a separate Control Panel applet that enables the Pocket PC to dim the screen when the device is not in use. This is the equivalent of the Energy Star feature that conserves power on your desktop by turning off your monitor when not in use. To access this Control Panel Backlight applet, select Start ⇨ Settings ⇨ System Tab ⇨ Backlight. Figure 21.10 reveals the meager Control Panel Backlight applet containing only two options. I strongly recommend activating the backlight dim feature and setting the time field to the lowest possible delay, as is shown in the example. This will ensure that the screen dims whenever you are not using it.

Figure 21.10 The Control Panel Backlight applet

HP Jornada Users Only: a Special Power-saving Tip!

If you own a Jornada and have already read through nineteen chapters of this book, you deserve a tip that is intended exclusively for your wonderful device. The HP Jornada Pocket PC has a special power-saving feature designed to benefit users who listen to MP3s or audio books. If you press and hold the alert light button on the top of the Jornada, it turns off the screen but keeps the system running. The alert light flashes to remind you that the system is on, but the display is not activated. Tap the alert light button again to bring the screen to life. This is extremely useful if your Jornada is busy performing calculations that do not require you to watch the screen or if you are playing MP3s.

Third-party applications to power-up your Pocket PC

By now, you should have a very clear understanding of how critical power conservation is on the Pocket PC. Without battery power, the Pocket PC can lose all of the data that it stores. Two applications offer relief for the power-conscious Pocket PC user. The applications are called PowerTap and PowerLevel, and they are priced reasonably.

Ilium Software's PowerTap

HP Jornada users are very fortunate. We have a Pocket PC that has excellent product design and places the Power button in the front of the device, where it is easy to locate. Other Pocket PC users are not as fortunate because their devices' Power buttons are hidden on the side of the device, or at the top, where a lid or leather case can interfere with access to the button. Of course, with all Pocket PCs, including the HP Jornada, the Power button is not easy to employ if you are holding a stylus. The solution to all of these problems is PowerTap from Ilium Software.

The application is incredibly simple, but very well designed. Once installed, the PowerTap application icon appears in the Start menu, as shown in Figure 21.11. Tapping the icon turns off the Pocket PC. This obviously enables you to turn off your device with the stylus or even with the scrolling controls. Moreover, if you use an external keyboard, you can configure a key to run PowerTap, which enables you to turn your off Pocket PC right from your keyboard.Best of all, the application is available free of charge from Ilium Software's Web site (www.iliumsoft.com). Users with Power buttons that are placed in inconvenient positions can even map another hardware button to the PowerTap application.

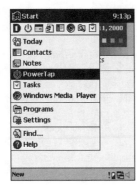

Figure 21.11 Ilium Software's PowerTap

Shortly after I took this screenshot, I renamed the PowerTap icon to zShut Down so that it moved to the bottom of the list and made more sense to users that borrow my Pocket PC. Other Pocket PC owners that have taken note of the feature make comments such as "Hey, shut down, just like on my desktop!"

Cross-Reference

For step-by-step instructions on how to rename the icons in your Start menu, refer to the "Customize your Start Menu and Startup Applications" section of Chapter 17.

ScaryBear Software's PowerLevel

As you may have noticed from reading earlier parts of this chapter, checking the battery level in your Pocket PC (Start ➪ Settings ➪ System tab ➪ Power) is a lengthy task. To solve the problem, a small third-party development company named ScaryBear Software has created a power meter for your Today screen called PowerLevel.

PowerLevel, shown in Figure 21.12, has a status bar to indicate the amount of power remaining as well as a percentage display of the exact amount of power left. As battery life becomes depleted, PowerLevel displays text warnings of Low or Critical, as displayed in Figure 21.12. Once the Pocket PC is connected to a power source, PowerLevel indicates that the system is recharging and informs you when the battery is fully charged.

Note

This product will not work on Pocket PCs with MIPs processors (such as the Casio line of Pocket PCs) because, according to the company, those products do not use the Pocket PC's standard method of communicating the amount of battery power remaining.

Figure 21.12 PowerLevel by ScaryBear Software

A free fourteen-day trial version of the software is available for download at www.scarybearsoftware.com, and the full version of PowerLevel is $9.95. The registered version of PowerLevel also adds an option to launch the Pocket PC Power applet when you tap the PowerLevel icon.

Summary

Using the techniques you have learned in this chapter, you should be able to proactively resolve any memory and power problems. The preventative maintenance concepts introduced in this section will help your Pocket PC live a long and trouble-free existence.

In Chapter 21, you will learn how to work with the vast number of Palm Pilot users who shudder at the sight of a Pocket PC.

The "All My Friends Use a Palm Pilot!" Constraint

IN THIS CHAPTER • Make them jealous of your Pocket PC

• Beam contacts, appointments, and more to a Palm

• Getting any other personal digital assistant into your Pocket PC

With millions of Palm personal digital assistants (PDAs) in the workplace, I would be surprised if you have not already encountered many Palm users. Most of them look on the Pocket PC as an inferior imitation of their device of choice. But if you are skillful enough to bend their ear for a second, you might be able to convince them otherwise, and maybe even make them a little jealous. If jealousy isn't your thing, the second section of this chapter focuses on making the two devices play well together using infrared communication to quickly beam information to the Palm without any additional software! Finally, we close this chapter by discussing the techniques for transferring large amounts of data from a Palm, or any other PDA, to your Pocket PC.

Note

The information in this chapter also can be used to communicate with or confront users of the Handspring Visor. The Visor is another PDA that uses the Palm OS and has a proprietary accessory slot. This means that the infrared communications (covered in the "Beam Contacts, Appointments, and More to a Palm" section) will work and you can humble them because your Pocket PC uses an open-architecture slot (Compact Flash on the HP Jornada) that is compatible with laptops and digital cameras.

Make Them Jealous of Your Pocket PC

I'll be honest with you. Nothing makes me feel better than knowing that I hold in my hand the most powerful PDA available. I bring the device into meetings just to watch the waves of envy wash over my coworkers' faces. You should, too; it is a power rush and an ego boost. The Pocket PC is the most effective and adaptable handheld computer on the market today, and it's your job to let everyone know it.

When a Palm user starts to scuffle with you (and believe me, they will) about how their device is so much better, glance over at what they are holding. Chances are, its screen is black and white. Even if it is a color screen, it still pales in comparison to the Windows Powered device you are holding. The Pocket PC has thousands of colors, versus the Palm's miniscule 256 colors, and more than three times the pixel resolution, which means that photos and Web pages display more vibrantly and clearly than on the Palm. However, the display is not the only multimedia feature with which to trample the Palm. After you get started, be sure to "accidentally" activate the MP3 player, an audio book, or the Voice Recorder. Audio features on the Palm are nonexistent without third-party utilities, so the fact that yours came free bundled with the device might just incite a riot.

If the Palm user thinks those features are fluff, open up Pocket Word or Excel and explain that you can receive file attachments in the Inbox and just double-click to open them. While you have Word open, activate Transcriber and show them what handwriting recognition can do. Finish by displaying the full-featured Web browser and the full-fledged money management program, and by demonstrating Pocket PC's capability to connect to the Internet with built-in Transmission Control Protocol/Internet Protocol (TCP/IP).

If all that does not make them jealous, it is probably Jeff Hawkins, the inventor of the Palm, to whom you are talking. I suggest that you smile and change the subject to how your device is compatible with the Palm.

Beam Contacts, Appointments, and More to a Palm

If your motto is *can't we all just get along?* you'll be happy to know that the answer is yes. A program called Peacemaker enables the Pocket PC to transmit and receive data via infrared light with the Palm, among other PDAs. Using infrared communications means that no cables are required and that the devices communicate at an extremely high speed.

Note

The HP Jornada series Pocket PC ships with the standard version of Peacemaker already installed on the device ROM. If you own another Pocket PC, you can download the application for free from the Conduits Web site at `www.conduits.com`.

Sending contacts to a Palm

Peacemaker Standard edition enables you to transfer contacts from your Pocket PC to a Palm. Figure 22.1 shows the Contacts application with the Peacemaker menu active. Simply tap and hold the contact that you wish to transfer and press (Beam Selected). If your contact has more than one address, you will have to select which address you would like to send over infrared, as the Palm address book can only store one address per person. After that selection is made, Peacemaker will search for a Palm device to send the contact to. In less than a second, it should recognize and transmit the contact.

Figure 22.1 Peacemaker Standard contact exchange

Tip

If you frequently exchange your contact information with Palm users, select Tools ➪ ((Card Exchange)) in Pocket Outlook. It remembers your contact information and automatically sends it to the Palm with just one click.

Sending appointments and other files

If you find yourself surrounded by Palm users, you may want to upgrade to Peacemaker Professional. For just $14.95, you can transfer tasks, appointments, and files to the Palm. It works in exactly the same manner as Peacemaker Standard, but it also includes a spiffy interface for multiple file transfer. Figure 22.2 reveals the multifile transfer interface which also acts as a ready-to-receive indicator.

Figure 22.2 Peacemaker Professional multiple file exchange window

Getting data from a Palm (or any other PDA) into your Pocket PC

Should you win over a Palm user, or if you have owned a Palm in the past, you will probably want to retrieve all of the contacts, appointments, birthdays, and other data for use on your Pocket PC. If using Peacemaker to beam bundles of information to your Pocket PC does not sound like fun to you, you can use your desktop computer and the synchronization cradles to copy the data to your Pocket PC. To do so, complete the following steps:

1. Connect your Palm to the desktop computer and install the Palm Desktop and PocketMirror synchronization software that came with the device. When asked what application you wish to synchronize with, select Outlook from the menu.

After the software installation, perform a synchronization by pressing the Palm Hot Sync button. Open Outlook to confirm that your data was successfully transferred from the Palm.

2. Disconnect the Palm synchronization cradle from the PC and uninstall the Palm Desktop and PocketMirror synchronization software. Connect your Pocket PC cradle to the desktop computer and, if necessary, install the Microsoft ActiveSync software on your desktop. After the software installs, the Pocket PC automatically synchronizes with Outlook and copies the data to the device. That is all there is to it.

Getting data from other PDAs

If you have another brand of PDA, the procedure is basically the same steps as outlined above. Consult your old PDA's manual or support staff for information on how to synchronize with Microsoft Outlook, and then follow the steps in the preceding section for connecting and removing devices from the desktop. Believe me, if you already have entered the data into one device, there isn't any sense in entering it again!

Summary

In this chapter, you have learned the tricks that you need to compete with and communicate with the Palm. Although using these tricks may seem to be an insignificant achievement, doing so will show that you have the pride and joy in the Pocket PC that makes our small but vigorous group a formidable competitor to the Palm masses.

Chapter 23 gives you a behind the scenes look at the technology inside the Pocket PC as you begin the final section of this handbook: Technology and Tomorrow.

Technology and Tomorrow

Inside The Pocket PC

IN THIS CHAPTER • The Pocket PC hardware

• Special Jornada hardware enhancements

The Pocket PC is a marvel of modern technology. The same computing power that crowded your desktop a few years ago is now able to slip into a coat pocket, and at a fraction of the cost. Moreover, the Pocket PC's capabilities outperform every other handheld device on the market thanks, in part, to the hardware manufacturers' ingenious design and the initial specifications provided by Microsoft as a foundation for building a Windows Powered device.

The Pocket PC Hardware

The Pocket PC uses many of the same hardware components common to desktop computers. Much of the technology, in fact, was developed for the laptop computer industry and then enhanced for the handheld space. Battery life and miniaturization are key factors in designing components for all portable computing products, but become make-or-break features when selecting parts for the Pocket PC.

The processor

The heart of the Pocket PC is the central processing unit (CPU). As with desktop computers, this component is the engine on which the Windows Powered operating system runs. However, the Windows Powered operating system and all its applications must be rebuilt for every processor they run on, as opposed to the desktop version of Windows, which can run any software product regardless of the CPU inside the computer. Because the operating system is designed to work in embedded systems (such as Coke machines and refrigerators), automobile stereo systems, and other handheld computer platforms such as the Handheld PC, a countless number of Windows Powered supported processors exist. Currently, the Pocket PC uses the technology of three different processors: SH3, MIPS, and StrongARM.

The entire HP Jornada 540 line of Pocket PCs uses the Hitachi SH3 processor. Designed by Hitachi Semiconductor and running at 133 megahertz, the SH3 is a 32-bit reduced instruction set computing (RISC) processor. Hitachi uses the processor in the Windows Powered devices they manufacture in other form-factors, such as the Handheld PC Professional.

The Casio line of Pocket PCs and the Compaq Aero 1550 use the millions of instructions per second (MIPS) processor. Developed by MIPS Technologies Incorporated, these processors use the RISC processing technology and have played an instrumental role in the development of Windows Powered devices. The company calls their processor platform "the premier architecture for Windows CE" and boasts that there are more than 40 Windows Powered products running on MIPS processors.

The last processor, designed in a joint effort between Advanced RISC Machines Limited and Digital Equipment Corporation, is the StrongARM. Created specifically to spawn fast processors that conserve power, the 32-bit RISC system is employed on the iPAQ 3650, which runs at 206 megahertz. The HP Jornada 720 (a Handheld PC Professional product) uses the StrongARM processor.

Note

Because the StrongARM was introduced as a processor in more modern Windows Powered devices, the software development community was not equipped with the tools for StrongARM development. It is for this reason that some third-party applications do not support the StrongARM chip.

The battery

Although the Pocket PCs use a variety of CPUs, almost all of them use the same battery technology. *Lithium Ion* (Li-Ion), as its name implies, is a battery composed of ions of the element Lithium. The Li-Ion rechargeable battery is superior to Nickel Cadmium (NiCad) and Nickel Metal Hydride (NiMH) because it does not have a memory. This means that the amount of battery power will not diminish if the battery is recharged before being completely discharged. Li-Ion batteries are also extremely lightweight, which adds to the portability of the Pocket PC product.

The Casio Computer Corporation has equipped its rugged line of Pocket PCs with a super-slim Lithium Polymer battery. Available in small and medium sizes, the thin film ceramic design allows for a thinner profile and, reportedly, better battery life. In order to reduce costs, the large capacity battery is Lithium Ion technology.

The HP Jornada 540 series and the Compaq iPAQ 3650 reserve a small portion of the Li-Ion battery for backup power. Once the battery has been drained down to the reserve power level, the device powers off automatically to protect all of the data stored in RAM. Other Pocket PC devices use a small, disposable watch battery for backup power.

Cross-Reference

For information on conserving battery power on the Pocket PC, refer to Chapter 21 "Memory and Power Constraints."

The screen

Obviously, the biggest drain on the Pocket PC battery is the screen. With built-in backlighting and touch-screen technologies, the screen is also the most expensive component of the Pocket PC. The screen resolution on the Pocket PC is superior to the desktop monitor because of a higher dpi (dots per inch) measurement. This measurement describes the number of pixels (or dots) that fit into a square inch of real estate on the screen. The more dots that fit into that space, the finer the detail. This enables the programs to create a clearer, crisper picture and text that is easier to read at small sizes. The HP Jornada screen has 107 dpi versus the 72 dpi of desktop computer screens.

The HP Jornada uses a color super-twist nematic (CSTN) screen. Developed by Sharp Electronics Corporation, CSTN screens are based on liquid crystal display (LCD) technology. The display is passive matrix, because the LCD passively controls the display by either blocking or enabling light to come through the screen. The CSTN screen is cheaper than a thin film transistor (TFT), which is the other model of Pocket PC screen, making the device less expensive.

TFT technology is employed on the Casio line of Pocket PCs. More expensive because it is active matrix technology, TFT is most commonly used on flat panel displays. *Active matrix* refers to the fact that a transistor manages when the light appears, rather than just enabling it to pass through, as it does on passive matrix screens. The Compaq iPAQ uses *reflective* TFT (RTFT), which reflects the natural light that passes through the screen back to the user's eyes. This enhances the readability under low-light conditions and makes the screen completely viewable in broad daylight.

Special Jornada Hardware Enhancements

As with all aspects of the Pocket PC, Hewlett-Packard has introduced some unique elements into the hardware design specifications of the HP Jornada. With a combination of brilliant technological innovation and intelligent industrial design, the Jornada owners have a host of new features that seamlessly meld together to create the perfect handheld platform.

Compared to the screen on other Pocket PCs, the Jornada CSTN screen is rotated 90 degrees before being installed. Tilting it on its axis creates a screen with vertical lines (as opposed to horizontal lines). According to Microsoft, vertical screen alignment is the optimal environment for the Microsoft ClearType technology, which enhances the viewability of text in the Pocket Reader application.

The second, and more obvious, advantage that the Jornada offers is the metal case. Designed to protect the Pocket PC and resist scratches, this case envelops the entire device. Even the flip-top cover on the device offers a metal exterior casing that protects the screen and a plastic interior that provides a soft contact point for the rest of the device.

And finally, for the frequent traveler, HP has supercharged the customary travel charger. Where most manufacturers would include a standard, bulky (but inexpensive) AC power cord, Hewlett-Packard includes a lightweight and compact AC travel charging system. The two-piece unit breaks down into the Jornada charging cord and a universal wall plug. This plug is commonly used by audio and video electronics, which means that you could potentially travel with only one wall plug and carry adapters for your Pocket PC, laptop, cell phone, and any other electronics. And, the AC adapter supports electricity ranging from 100-240 volts and 50-60Hz. This means that using the charger in another country is as simple as buying a plug adapter. The heavy and expensive power converter is not required.

Summary

After reading this chapter, you should have a clear understanding of the technology inside the Pocket PC. As you have read, the Pocket PC takes the very best of the desktop computing technology and adds finishing touches to perfect it for the handheld platform. This enables us to carry cutting edge technology with us in a pocket-sized form factor.

The next chapter of this handbook covers the other Windows Powered devices that share the same operating system as the Pocket PC. Although some of the devices are very similar to the Pocket PC in style and design, you might be surprised by how many devices run the Windows Powered OS.

Other Devices That Use the Windows Powered OS

IN THIS CHAPTER • The Handheld PC

• The Stinger cellular phone

• The AutoPC

• Internet appliances

• Embedded systems

While the focus of this book has been the Pocket PC platform, I would be remiss in my duties if I did not briefly cover the other devices that run the Windows Powered platform. Many of the Windows Powered systems interact with the Pocket PC via infrared or over networks, and it is comforting to know that — unlike other PDA platforms — the success of the Pocket PC is bolstered by the achievements of the entire platform. Three distinct products categories — the Handheld PC, Stinger cellular phone, and Auto PC — make up a majority of the Windows Powered product line, but broad categories, such as Internet appliances and embedded systems, offer vast opportunities for future development.

The Handheld PC

The Handheld PC (or HPC) was the first Windows Powered device available to the public. Formerly known as a device running the Windows CE operating system, the Handheld PC now belongs to the family of Windows Powered products, and is in its fourth generation of hardware designs. One of the most popular Handheld PCs is the HP Jornada 720, shown in Figure 24.1. As you can see from the photograph, the Handheld PC differentiates itself from the Pocket PC because of its larger form factor. The device is designed to bridge the gap between information-viewing devices, such as the Pocket PC, and information-creation devices, such as a laptop computer. This makes the Handheld PC a mid-level data-editing device that enables you to work with information using the slightly larger screen and the compact QWERTY keyboard.

Although the Handheld PC has third-party solutions for handwriting recognition, neither Transcriber nor Character Recognizer is included with the Handheld PC operating system. Conversely, the applications unavailable on the Pocket PC, yet standard on the newest line of Handheld PC products, are Terminal Server Client, Pocket Access, and InkWriter. The Terminal Server client enables you to connect to a Microsoft Windows 2000 Terminal Server via a LAN or a dialup connection to run full-function desktop applications on your Handheld PC. Pocket Access is a slimmed-down version of the Microsoft Access database application on the desktop. It enables you to use ActiveSync to gather a dataset from an Access database and synchronize it to your Handheld PC. Changes made on either database are automatically synchronized the next time the Handheld PC is docked. InkWriter is the Handheld PC equivalent of NoteTaker on the Pocket PC, as it enables you to mix handwritten notes, drawings, and typed text in the same document.

While the Pocket PC interface has been considerably modified to work better in the palm of your hand, the Handheld PC interface closely imitates the experience of the Microsoft Windows desktop operating system. This is because the applications on the Handheld PC are designed to mimic the features and functionality of the desktop and, when in terminal server mode, it might be confusing for users to switch between a Start button at the top of the screen and the bottom. The location of the Start button and the ability to close programs by clicking an X in the upper corner are two of the biggest differences between the Handheld PC and the Pocket PC versions of the OS.

Figure 24.1 The HP Jornada 720 Handheld PC

In addition to the clamshell-style folding design that is similar to the HP Jornada 720 design, the Handheld PC is available in a slate form that looks like a large tablet and a folding design that enables you to convert the Handheld PC to a laptop, slate, or easel form. Hitachi's ePlate (www.hitachi.com/eplate/) is an example of the slate design, while MainStreet Networks' Clio (www.clio.com) is an example of the folding design. An even larger version, called the Handheld PC Professional, was announced in late 1998 to compete directly against the laptop market. These products looked and performed like real laptop computers, but they ran the Windows Powered operating system, keeping their price low and the speed and performance high. One such product is the HP Jornada 820 Handheld PC Professional, a nearly laptop-sized device with a touchpad for cursor control instead of a touch-sensitive screen.

Cross-Reference

For a complete product timeline and a description of all of the Hewlett-Packard Windows Powered products, refer to Appendix D "Hewlett-Packard Handheld Computing Milestones"

The Stinger Cellular Phone

A product that merges the PDA and the cellular telephone has been under development at Microsoft since 1998. Codenamed Stinger, the project is a joint effort with telecommunications companies and hardware vendors to provide a Windows Powered mobile phone. Although Microsoft believes in the PDA market and continues to support the desktop PC platform, the company has consistently remarked that smart phones (cellular telephones with screens to access the Internet) will eclipse even desktops as the primary method of Internet connectivity in coming years.

Indeed, cellular phone hardware manufacturers agree with Microsoft, as every company has announced plans for developing a smart phone. Samsung Electronics is one of the hardware manufacturers that has sided with Microsoft and will reportedly have a Stinger cellular phone on the market in 2001. According to Microsoft, there are five key points for developing their cellular telephone platform — it must:

■ Be a great phone

■ Offer remote control for communications management

■ Be up and running in five minutes without support

■ Offer over-the-air device management

■ Offer personal information manager (PIM) and e-mail synchronization

But the important point is that the Stinger cell phone merges the handheld computer and the mobile phone, offering a combination of voice and data communications in a package that fits in the palm of your hand. Figure 24.2 is a photograph of the Stinger phone prototype. Although the interface does not match the Pocket PC exactly, there are many similarities. The current display shown on the Stinger screen is similar to the Pocket PC Today screen, offering a customizable location for, date, time, appointments, and Caller ID information. The Programs item in the bottom-right corner of the phone display is the equivalent of the Start menu, offering a scrollable menu of applications.

The software installed on the Stinger cell phone is very similar to the applications on the Pocket PC. Naturally, the Contacts application plays a major role in replacing the standard phonebook with a powerful address book application that can quickly dial phone numbers. In addition, the rest of the Pocket Outlook suite (Calendar, Contacts, In-box, Notes, and Tasks), and Pocket Internet Explorer supporting Hypertext Markup Language (HTML), Extensible Markup Language (XML), and Wireless Application Protocol (WAP) are standard applications on the Stinger phone.

Figure 24.2 The prototype Stinger phone

Note

Pocket Internet Explorer on the Pocket PC does not support WAP (Wireless Application Protocol), which uses Wireless Markup Language (WML) to compose documents instead of HTML. For a WAP-compatible Pocket PC browser, download the free HP Jornada WAP Browser from the Hewlett-Packard Web site www.hp.com/jornada/.

Like all Windows Powered companions, the Stinger phone can be synchronized with your desktop. This way, you will never have to worry about updating your mobile phone address book with the latest contact information. Microsoft reports that the Windows Powered operating system running on the Stinger phone was modified to use less memory and to increase battery life.

The AutoPC

The AutoPC is a Windows-powered device for your automobile. Designed to replace the car stereo, it uses voice recognition to perform all of the standard features of a car radio plus provide navigation, information, communication, and entertainment. The standard Clarion AutoPC 310c consists of an AM/FM radio and one-disk CD player. The CD player doubles as a CD-ROM reader that can install applications. The system has 16MB of RAM, a CompactFlash slot, a USB port, an infrared port, and an eight-color LCD display on a detachable (antitheft) control panel.

The basic applications included in the AutoPC are Voice Memo (similar to the Pocket PC Voice Recorder feature) and Address Book. A package called the Nav310c includes an eight-channel GPS system, a CD-ROM of maps of your local area, and InfoGation's Odyssey Navigation software for driving directions based on input from your built-in address book, or the GPS receiver. Other Clarion accessories include a six-CD changer, a cellular phone kit that enables you to verbally control dialing and speakerphone functions on your mobile phone, and a data receiver to obtain news and weather reports, real-time traffic information, and e-mail messages through your AutoPC. However, some incredible third-party hardware accessories make the AutoPC a truly functional system.

Note

The AutoPC navigation system can be given a destination address by simply sending a contact from your Pocket PC via infrared.

InfoGation (www.infogation.com) has developed Odyssey 2000, a dynamic navigation system and step-by-step direction application that provides integrated real-time traffic and alerts for the AutoPC. Odyssey 2000 is an upgrade of the Odyssey software included in the Nav310c. In addition to the new real-time traffic features, the application enables you to select destinations by scrolling around on the map, from a list of places you previously visited or pick points-of-interest (such as restaurants or hotels), from the application's database.

Vetronix (www.vetronix.com) manufactures two accessories for the AutoPC, Carport and VIP. CarPort is an advanced logging and data analysis application that enables you to track mileage for expense reports, reminds you when vehicle maintenance is due, records the speed and RPMs when the car is borrowed by your children or parking attendants, and audibly reminds you when you exceed a speed limit which you set. In addition, Carport features direct inputs and outputs that plug into your device to set a passcode-protected starter kill feature, operate door locks, power trunk and dome lights from your AutoPC, and diagnose the Check engine light when it is activated. The company's VIP (Vehicle Internet Port) product enables you to send and receive e-mail on the road, and to receive wireless Internet pages. Both e-mail and Web pages are read aloud using the AutoPC's built-in speech synthesis feature.

A small third-party development community has even sprung up to create custom applications for the AutoPC. Mobile Visions Software (www. mobilevisionssoftware.com) has created a number of applications including Speed Trap, an application that uses the GPS system to determine your speed of travel and to warn you when you exceed the speed limit; Mobile Combat, a game to release road rage stress by combating imaginary opponents; and a slideshow viewer application. As with the Pocket PC, third-party applications add variety and entertainment to an otherwise all-business application.

The second-generation version of the AutoPC (the Clarion 320DV) includes improved speech recognition and support for a secondary screen to play DVD movies. A special accessory designed specifically for the 320DV is InfoGation's AccuRoute, an application that displays two-dimensional and three-dimensional maps on the secondary display. Information on the complete line of AutoPC products and accessories is available at www.autopc.com.

Internet Appliances

Everyone has a friend or relative that is not on the Web. Whether it is a cost-conscious decision to avoid expensive computer hardware or a fear of computers that keeps your friends and family offline, a Windows-powered product might solve the problem. Internet appliances are products designed at a lower cost and in different form factors to give anyone access to Web surfing and e-mail. Two such products are the MSN Companion and the Smilephone.

Cross-Reference

For information on how Internet appliances will communicate with the Pocket PC and other Windows Powered devices, refer to the "CoolTown and other e-services" section of Chapter 25.

The MSN Companion

For users that want a computer for Web surfing and e-mail, but do not want to put out the cash for the latest and greatest system, the second best thing is Compaq Computer Corporation's MSN Companion. As Figure 24.3 shows, the MSN Companion is designed to look like a desktop computer, but the Windows-powered operating system makes the device available at a fraction of the cost of a desktop PC. The device has 32MB of RAM, a 56 Kbps modem, and a large 800×600 10.1-inch flat panel color display. Because MSN Companion uses the Windows-powered operating system, it turns on instantly, instead of having a boot-up process, and when powered down, the screen becomes a digital photo frame, displaying pictures like a screen saver.

Figure 24.3 The MSN Companion

The system has four USB Ports and two RJ11 phone jacks as well as a stereo earphone or speaker output plug. The system also accepts Type I/II MMC (MultiMedia Card) memory for updates. The included wireless keyboard has a touchpad for cursor control, and a USB mouse is available as an additional accessory. A flashing light illuminates when your have new e-mail messages, and ten hardware buttons on the device launch your e-mail, news, shopping, Internet chat, and more. Compaq makes a few different models of the MSN Companion, with varying features and functionality. With an extended ISP service contract through MSN, certain models are available for less than $200, or even for free. Visit the Compaq Web site (`www.compaq.com`) for more information on pricing and current rebate offers.

The Smilephone

Developed by IPM and bSQUARE, the Smilephone is an interactive screen phone that features Web browsing and e-mail access in addition to the features of a standard voice telephone. The device, shown in Figure 24.4, has a 7.5-inch touch screen LCD screen that displays full VGA (640×480 pixels), and has a 33.6 Kbps modem and an alphanumeric keyboard. Accessory ports include an MMC memory card slot and a parallel interface for connection to a printer. The Smilephone also includes a Smart Card reader that can enable or disable Internet access, e-mail, and international calls, or even set a maximum duration for nonemergency calls. Other options include one-touch Internet log on and the ability to talk on the phone while Web surfing on another line. Connection to ISDN/ADSL lines and LAN networking are planned as future options. For more information on the Smilephone and a list of authorized distributors, visit www.smilephone.com.

Figure 24.4 The Windows-powered Smilephone

Embedded Systems

Embedded systems are devices that you would never guess have been infused with the Windows-powered operating system. A Coke machine, refrigerator, or any device with a 32-bit processor has the potential to be a Windows-powered device. The real-time processing (meaning a superfast response time) and modular capability (the capability to add and remove components) of the operating system make the difference for many of the companies that develop Windows-powered embedded system products.

One of the coolest Windows Powered products is the iRAD-S Internet stereo system from AudioRamp (www.audioramp.com). Although it is designed to work with regular CDs and deliver regular AM/FM broadcasts, the iRAD-S uses the Windows-powered OS and Media Player to play MP3 CDs. In addition, the iRAD-S connects to the Internet via phone line or Ethernet to play streaming audio music and thousands of Web radio stations that broadcast in Windows Media Audio, the format that the Windows-powered Media Player uses. Because the iRAD-S connects directly to the Internet, the company has created a customized music portal called MyAudioRamp, which presents you with the music and artists it believes you will prefer. The advantage that the culmination of all of these technologies in one stereo system provides is that the iRAD-S enables you to collect and manage your personal music library from AM/FM broadcasts, online music sites, CD, or Internet streaming broadcasts, and to play them from a single touch point. Music can also be moved from the iRAD-S to the PC and back.

Two noncommercial applications of the Windows Powered operating system include the Spotter and the TruckPC. The Spotter, developed by Sports Guide Incorporated (www.spotter-tm.com) is a golf course guide, attached to the golf cart rented from the pro shop. With a 12-inch, daylight-viewable screen and a built-in GPS system, the Spotter shows golfers an overhead view of the current hole and the remaining yardage to the pin. The built-in software also includes a scorecard, so that individual rounds can be tallied electronically and tournaments can be scored with updates sent back to the clubhouse over a wireless network. Other optional wireless communication features include the capability to send messages to one or all golf carts, ordering food from the menu before arriving back at the clubhouse and an emergency button to indicate medical problems or equipment failure.

The TruckPC, by DriverTech Incorporated (www.truckpc.com) is a route-planning system designed for mounting inside delivery and shipping trucks. With four COM ports, a GPS connection, keyboard port, mouse port, and two CompactFlash slots, the TruckPC is the most customizable Windows-powered device available. Included software directs the driver on a stop-by-stop route, reporting progress status back to the main office, enables sending and receiving of e-mail, and has Internet browser capability.

Cross-Reference

For information on GPS mapping and navigation solutions available for the Pocket PC, refer to the "Finding Your Way" section of Chapter 19.

Although an entire book could be written on the number of embedded systems that run on the Windows Powered operating system, it might interest you to know that gas pumps, highway signs, cash registers, and electric company automation systems are run on the same operating system as your Pocket PC. With this "invisible pervasiveness" of the Windows Powered operating system, you can be sure that the platform will always be a major focus for the Microsoft development team and the hardware manufacturers.

Note

If you ever visit the Experience Music Project (EMP) in Seattle, Washington, be sure to use the electronic Museum Experience Guide. The MEG, a Windows-powered embedded system device, enables you to point to exhibits that interest you to learn more about it through the device's interactive audio capabilities. Narrative stories, associated music clips, and more are played through the MEG.

Summary

You now have a better understanding of the role that Windows Powered products play in the PDA, cellular phone, automotive, Internet appliance, and embedded systems arenas. If you are not in awe of the sheer number of products that Windows Powered devices encompass, you should be impressed by the thoroughness of how each product solves a problem using complex and innovative combinations of software and hardware.

If the current line of products did not amaze you, the final chapter of this handbook focuses on the future of the Pocket PC platform and Windows Powered devices. See where the platform is going and what possibilities lie ahead.

The Future of the Pocket PC

IN THIS CHAPTER
- Smaller, faster, and more powerful
- Communications integration
- More expandability
- Embedded systems

Because of its CompactFlash expandability and the popularity of the platform with hardware accessory developers, the Pocket PC is a handheld hotbed for expandability and growth in the years ahead. Moreover, as the Pocket PC product becomes more advanced, so will the software and accessories that are available from the hardware manufacturers.

Smaller, Faster, and More Powerful

Naturally, *Moore's Law* is applicable to the Pocket PC. Essentially, Moore's Law says that the amount of information that can be stored on a 1-inch square chip will double every year (although it has recently been modified to doubling every 18 months). This means that the computer circuitry inside the Pocket PC will decrease 50 percent in size in the next 18 months. However, as we discussed in Chapter 23, the Pocket PC is mainly composed of the battery and the display screen. These two critical elements of the Pocket PC provide great challenges to shrinking the size of the device.

In fact, the screen may be the single most important argument for having such a large device. Many users have told me that the large, clear screen is a primary reason for purchasing the Pocket PC instead of other devices. Applications such as the e-book reader are designed to take advantage of the larger screen area to display larger amounts of text on a single page. One device, called the eCase, solves the problem in a unique and innovative way. Shown in Figure 25.1, the eCase contains a one-inch screen that is used by placing the entire device up to the eye of the user. According to the company, this method is the equivalent of looking at a 19-inch computer monitor at a distance of 30 inches. The system is controlled by a touchpad and includes four application hardware buttons and a voice recorder microphone. Although the eCase is primarily designed for viewing documents, the soft input panel includes the Pocket PC pop-up keyboard. The system is designed to use voice recognition for input.

While the eCase is an extreme example of how Windows Powered Pocket PCs could appear in unique and tiny shapes in our future, history shows us that devices have been reduced in size from the larger, clamshell-sized form factor to a unit that can easily slip into a pocket. As consumer acceptance of a smaller screen grows and the battery technology improves, it is a certainty that you will see devices that can fit — sight unseen — into the palm of your hand, and perhaps even smaller.

Integrating Communication

If there will be a single hot topic in the next few years for the Pocket PC, it will be wireless communication. Because the Pocket PC is designed as such a powerful communications system with Inbox and the Pocket Internet Explorer, it is almost assured that the next line of Windows Powered devices will have built-in wireless communications. And, like the add-on solutions already available today, Pocket PC hardware vendors will partner with the communications carriers to provide complete wireless bundles.

Figure 25.1 The eCase by Inviso/Venturecom

Cross-Reference

For a complete list of add-on wireless solutions for the Pocket PC, review the "Going Wireless" section of Chapter 16.

These Web-ready devices can be sold online from the carriers, or even in stores, with only a credit card needed for activation. Internet service providers such as MSN or AOL could easily retrofit their existing Pocket PC applications for use over the wireless services and provide discounted packages for users that sign long-term contracts for Internet access. In fact, because they could purchase the Pocket PC in such high quantities, the units could be given away free if they were reconfigured to run only on the Internet service provider (ISP) that provides the system.

CoolTown and other e-services

With the advent of true wireless technology, mobile e-services will also arise. Development has already begun on location-specific information services that provide traffic, entertainment, and even advertising, based on your location. One service that is already under development is a chat client that identifies your location via the cellular network of your wireless modem and then sends you an instant message with a coupon for products and services in your immediate area.

Hewlett-Packard is already developing its own line of e-services. Carly Fiorina, president and CEO of HP, has been promoting the CoolTown technology, an imaginary town where anything with a chip works together. Created as a research project of HP's Internet & Mobile Systems Lab, CoolTown is based on what HP calls the do-it-for-me model — information is customized to your personal needs and habits, and is then provided to you. Traffic reports, for example, are only delivered for routes that you normally take; stock quotes are given for companies that you have invested in. HP has already promised that the dream will become a reality with products expected to arrive in the marketplace in 2001.

As a primer, an early version of CoolTown's client software for the Jornada Pocket PC has been released to the public. The software is limited to e-squirt capabilities, enabling the HP Jornada Pocket PC to receive a graphic-rich Web experience by interacting with Web-connected appliances via infrared communication. The application, shown in Figure 25.2, looks like a Web browser when copied and loaded onto the Pocket PC. Similarly, all content is transferred as Hypertext Markup Language (HTML)-formatted documents. These documents can be received while connected directly to the Internet. Beacon mode, indicated by the red icon shown in the upper-left corner of the figure, indicates that the Jornada is ready to communicate with other e-squirt–enabled devices. The software, and more information on CoolTown, is available from the CoolTown Web site at `cooltown.hp.com`.

Figure 25.2 The Pocket PC CoolTown client

The desktop version of the software, called the E-Squirt Viewer, runs on any Windows 98, 2000, or Millennium PC with an infrared port. It can receive content sent via the e-squirt beacon and can automatically create hardcopies of the content through any printer connected to the PC. As the E-Squirt technology progresses, the software will be capable of printing directly to printers and of sending information to other Web devices. In addition, CoolTown technology will also be adapted to support Bluetooth wireless technology as Bluetooth is launched in the coming months.

Bluetooth

A major new technology in our immediate future is the Bluetooth communications technology. Like infrared technology, Bluetooth enables devices to communicate when they are in close proximity with each other. This technology, using radio frequency (RF), is superior to infrared because it does not require direct line of sight. This means that instead of pointing the infrared port on your Pocket PC at the infrared port on a cellular phone, a phone that is stored on your belt or in your briefcase can connect to the Pocket PC you hold in the palm of your hand. Likewise, the Pocket PC will be able to synchronize with the PC every time you approach your desktop computer. More information on the technical aspects of Bluetooth technology is available at the Bluetooth Special Interest Group Web site (www.bluetooth.com).

Socket Communications (www.socketcom.com) has developed a Bluetooth CompactFlash card for the Pocket PC that can transmit data to devices within a 30-foot radius. The company has also played a large role in furthering Bluetooth development by creating a Bluetooth evaluation program and partnering with ZIO Software to launch some of the first Bluetooth-enabled games. ZIOGolf, the flagship product of ZIO, is a golfing game that enables Bluetooth-enabled Pocket PC users to play a round of golf together.

Cross-Reference

For more information on ZIOGolf, see Chapter 18.

Future drivers and Bluetooth peripherals will add wireless printing capabilities as well as LAN access whenever you approach a Bluetooth network zone. Because the technology works with laptop and desktop computers, a vast number of Bluetooth solutions are sure to appear in the coming months. Imagine a fax machine that can download documents for faxing when you pass by, or that have the capability to download MP3 music from friends' servers when you visit their homes.

Note

A new buzzword becoming popular with the advent of Bluetooth technology is Personal Area Network (PAN). A PAN is a group of products that are united by your presence, as Bluetooth technology links devices via radio frequency when you bring one product within close proximity of another.

Fusion of technology

One device that merges all of the previously discussed technologies is the PC ePhone. Figure 25.3 shows the ePhone with a Bluetooth-based handset pen. The ePhone is a Windows Powered device with a built-in cellular phone that can run on Code Division Multiple Access (CDMA) or Global System for Mobile communications (GSM) phone networks. The larger ePhone device can be held up to your face like a normal cellular telephone or you can use the tiny pen-shaped instrument as a phone handset to dial and speak into. Bluetooth technology enables the handset to communicate with the PC ePhone. As for PDA performance, the device has a 206 MHz processor, 16MB of RAM, a CompactFlash slot, and a 640×480 screen. The obvious advantage of a device such as the PC ePhone is that users have the ability to use the superslim handset module for normal phone conversation, with the added advantage of a full-featured PDA for Web surfing, e-mail, and document review. For more information on the PC ePhone, visit www.pc-ephone.com.

As more devices are released into the marketplace, cross-communication between the various hardware solutions will make the Pocket PC more powerful and provide a level of interoperability amongst all Windows Powered products. A real-world example of cross-communication of Windows Powered devices is the AutoPC and any Windows Powered PDA. The AutoPC, a car stereo with communications and GPS features, has the capability to receive a contact's information beamed from a Pocket PC. When the AutoPC receives the contact, it extracts the address, plots a route using the built-in mapping system and an optional Global Positioning system (GPS) receiver, and guides the driver to the contact's location.

Cross-Reference

For more information on the AutoPC, see Chapter 24.

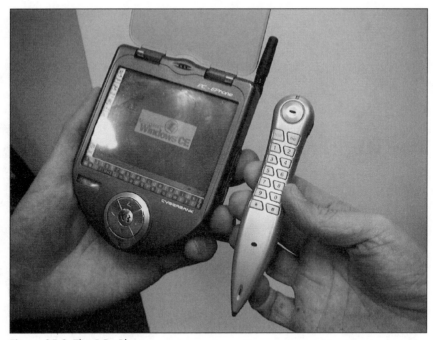

Figure 25.3 The PC ePhone

More Expandability

The HP Jornada Pocket PC has one very important feature that enables it to be instantly compatible with an infinite number of peripherals and accessories: the CompactFlash (CF) slot. Designed as an open-architecture input port, the CF slot enables any developer to create a hardware accessory that is instantly compatible with the Pocket PC. This has been a major boon for the Pocket PC, because accessories such as the Socket Digital Phone Card, many landline modems, and countless memory cards were in development even before the launch of the Pocket PC. At launch, the platform had a number of accessories available for immediate purchase.

But the future holds even more exciting expandability options for the Pocket PC. Pretec Electronics Corporation (www.pretec.com), the creators of the CompactModem and CompactLAN communications cards, have been developing a number of innovative accessories specifically designed for the Pocket PC. Pretec's latest product is the CompactGPS card, a CF peripheral that has all the components of a Global Positioning System in a unit that only protrudes a few inches from the top of your Pocket PC. A second product, which is still under development at Pretec and expected to arrive in the first half of 2001, is the CompactFM radio card shown in Figure 25.4. As you can see, the device is modeled after a CF modem and designed to slip into the CompactFlash slot to provide FM radio capabilities without adding excessive size or weight to the Pocket PC.

Figure 25.4 The Pretec CompactFM radio card

Naturally, with all of the personalized content and private information stored in the Pocket PC, security is going to be a growing issue in the coming years. One company has created the BioHub, a CompactFlash fingerprint identification system. Shown in Figure 25.5, the BioHub is inserted into the Pocket PC and provides a plate for placing your finger on the card for recognition. Although the company only provides the hardware, third-party software developers are expected to create software to provide power-up fingerprint ID security and biometric (fingerprint) network login security.

Embedded Systems

The Windows Powered operating system is becoming established as an operating system for many household components. As the appearance of Windows Powered devices in the home grows, the opportunity to communicate information and use the Pocket PC as a control unit for heating, cooling, and appliance management increases. But the Pocket PC could easily become much more.

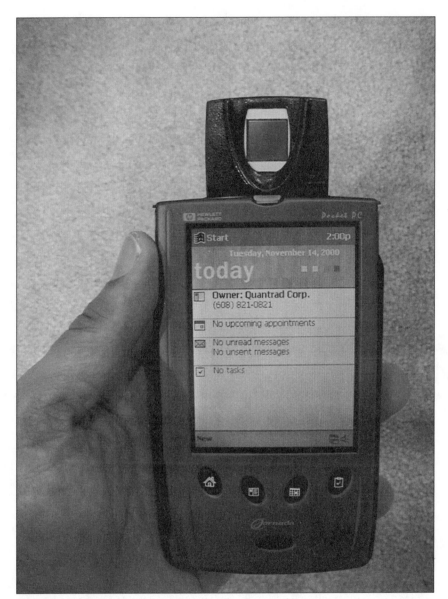

Figure 25.5 The BioHub fingerprint identification card

Microsoft's X box is a TV-connected home entertainment system like the Sony Playstation 2 or Sega Dreamcast (which is a Windows Powered device). Due out at the end of 2001, the system will use Microsoft software technology and be supported by third-party software developers. Almost a year before its launch,

Microsoft has already been talking about creating a handheld Windows Powered companion for the system. This device could hold high scores from the X box, which can be transferred to other systems, play games on its own, and provide all of the current functionality of the Pocket PC in one system.

Like computer gaming, home networking has always been a hot topic for the technically inclined. And with the explosive popularity of MP3 music and instant messaging, more and more people are wiring their homes for Internet traffic via wireless network. In addition to music and instant messaging, systems equipped with a wireless network card can share a single Internet connection, files, and printers. This means that your Pocket PC can access most of the resources of your desktop home computer without wires. Two emerging home networking technologies currently support Windows Powered devices. These technologies are HomeRF and a wireless network technology simply named 802.11.

The HomeRF Networking Group is an organization dedicated to creating an entire line of home networking products that work together. They believe that networking a home using wireless technology is less expensive and far more convenient than creating a complete wire-line network. Companies such as Intel, Compaq, and Motorola have developed servers, computers, and peripherals that communicate using the HomeRF network. The Proxim HomeRF CompactFlash card and all HomeRF products use a "relaxed" version of the 802.11 specification to keep the cost of their products low.

Warning

The HomeRF CompactFlash module announced in late 2000, was a Type II CF card. This will not work in the HP Jornada. Visit www.proxim.com to learn whether a Type I card has been manufactured by the company or visit www.homerf.org to search for other companies manufacturing a Pocket PC-compatible CompactFlash card.

Proxim, a leader in Pocket PC peripheral development has created a CompactFlash card that is compatible with the HomeRF network. The card has Pocket PC drivers and uses 40 percent less power than previous wireless networking cards, making it perfect for a battery-constrained device such as the Pocket PC. The Proxim HomeRF CompactFlash card is currently being distributed through e-service providers such as TouchPak (www.touchpak.com). These companies will create a service that sends data and marketing information to your device dependent on your locale.

Figure 25.6 shows a sample news and information panel from TouchPak. Note the advertising in the bottom-left corner of the screen. The benefit to this technology is that it is based on a local network, so information can be routed to you based on your position (within just a few feet). As interest and support in the TouchPak service grows, you could expect to enter a sports arena and receive complete player statistics in your TouchPak browser, or walk down the Fiction aisle at a library and receive a list of books based on their popularity. Conversely, the TouchPak service will have the capability to link you to sports merchandising companies based on your team preference and suggest books at online resellers based on your browsing preferences. TouchPak is very similar to the CoolTown e-service discussed earlier except that it would not be considered a PAN, because the Pocket PC is the only hardware product involved.

Figure 25.6 Sample TouchPak screen

The protocol 802.11 is another home networking protocol that enables computing devices to talk to each other. It is named after the Institute of Electrical and Electronics Engineers (IEEE) committee responsible for developing it. It is a previously developed and stricter version of the HomeRF standard, because it was used in corporations and home networking. Although only Personal Computer Memory Card International Association (PCMCIA) cards were available for Windows Powered devices in the year 2000, the future is sure to bring a CompactFlash format 802.11 card for the Pocket PC.

Note

Both HomeRF and 802.11 operate in the 2.4 GHz radio frequency band. This band is an unlicensed frequency, which enables any company to create a product that operates in this range. In addition, in the year 2000, an FCC ruling granted companies the right to develop advanced frequency-hopping communications systems in the 2.4 GHz band, paving the way for low-cost wireless networking systems with advanced functionality.

Summary

Although Pocket PCs are unlikely to replace the desktop computer, they are quickly finding their way into the home and workplace by providing greater power and functionality in a smaller package. As the technologic needs of the mobile population increases, the Windows Powered operating system will play an increasingly important part in solving the problems of the mobile workforce and the technologically advanced home user. This problem-solving factor, combined with our need to constantly be informed and entertained, will bring the Pocket PC into the limelight as awareness of the Pocket PC platform continues to grow.

As this is the last chapter in the handbook, you have reached the end of the formal guidance on how to use the Pocket PC. Now you are fully equipped to handle any task using your Pocket PC.

Should you have trouble with your Pocket PC, you can take on even the most formidable technical challenges by exploring Appendix A, which includes a list of Frequently Asked Questions and troubleshooting information. Appendix B features a list of Web sites that you can surf to in order to learn more about the platform and locate software and accessories available for the Pocket PC. Appendix C includes the technical specifications of the HP Jornada line of Pocket PCs and Appendix D includes a list of handheld milestones achieved by the Hewlett-Packard Company. Finally, Appendix E provides a quick reference that will help you get started working with a stylus.

FAQ and Troubleshooting

IN THIS APPENDIX
- Operating system troubleshooting
- Pocket PC application troubleshooting
- Resetting your device
- Hardware vendor technical support contact information

The material in this appendix is designed to help you diagnose and solve problems that occur on your Pocket PC. As with the rest of this book, the problem solving strategies involved in this section can be applied to any brand of Pocket PC. I suggest you read this section even if you are not currently experiencing problems, so that you can quickly identify issues in their early stages. In addition, you might discover a nuisance you have been experiencing for which you did not know there was a resolution.

The multipart solutions shown are designed to provide the quickest remedy for complex problems that could have many different causes. If a multiple-step resolution listed here solves a problem but the problem returns again later, make an effort to uncover the cause by performing each step individually and checking to see if the issue has been resolved.

Operating System Troubleshooting

This section applies specifically to global features and functions of the Pocket PC's Windows Powered operating system. Listings include power up, general use, desktop synchronization, and infrared communications troubleshooting.

Power up troubleshooting

My Pocket PC does not turn on when I press the power button.

If the device has removable batteries, ensure that they are correctly installed in the device and that the battery door is closed and locked. Connect to external power such as the AC adapter or DC charger and ensure that the battery charging indicator is illuminated. Remove any accessories from the device's memory slot and perform a soft reset. If the system does not respond, you may have to perform a hard reset.

The device is reporting that the backup battery power is low.

For every device in the entire Casio Pocket PC line and the Compaq Aero 1550, replace the disposable backup battery. Be sure to completely charge the main battery and power down the Pocket PC before removing the backup battery for replacement. If the backup battery still occurs after replacement, check to ensure that you have installed the battery properly.

My Pocket PC turns off without any warning.

First, make certain that the device is fully charged by checking the power level on Start ➪ Settings ➪ System tab ➪ Power. Next, review the settings at the bottom of the Power applet to ensure that the device is automatically powering down to conserve power.

I forgot my password and cannot access data on my Pocket PC.

Unless you set a backup password on your Pocket PC (available only on the HP Jornada), you will have to perform a hard reset, which erases all data on the device.

General use issues

The Pocket PC runs slowly or locks up frequently.

Perform a soft reset to clear out the device's program memory. (For more information on enhancing system performance, review Chapter 21.)

The screen is difficult to read

Ensure that the device is turned on. If you are in a setting with bright lighting, move to a darker location then adjust the screen settings at Start ⇨ HP Settings (or Start ⇨ Settings ⇨ System tab ⇨ Backlight). If the text is difficult to read because of the small font size, follow the instructions in the "Make Pocket Outlook data easier on your eyes" section of Chapter 9.

The screen gets darker after a short interval.

The auto-dim feature is turned on by default on the HP Jornada. To deactivate it, select Start ⇨ Settings ⇨ System tab ⇨ Backlight and uncheck the "Dim backlight if device is not used for. . ." checkbox. If this item is deactivated and the screen still dims, perform a soft reset on the device to restore it to its original brightness.

The screen has a green tint after installing the HP screen protector.

The screen protector has a removable protective film on both sides of the plastic. Be sure that you remove both protective sheets before installing the screen protector on your Jornada.

When I tap an icon or input data using the soft keyboard, the wrong buttons are pressed.

Your screen is out of alignment. Select Start ⇨ Settings ⇨ System tab ⇨ Align Screen and press the Align Screen button. Tap the target using your stylus at each point that the screen stops moving. Save the changes and test the new settings. Repeat if necessary.

Suddenly, Character Recognizer no longer recognizes the letters I am writing.

Chances are, you toggled the program from lowercase mode to uppercase mode, or vice versa.

To return the application to its previous setting, complete the following steps:

1. Select Start ⇨ Settings ⇨ Input ⇨ Options button.

2. Change the mode to the opposite of whatever mode is currently active.

3. Return to the application you were using and resume writing with Character Recognizer.

Someone borrowed my Pocket PC and now Transcriber does not recognize my writing accurately.

Hopefully, the person you loaned your Pocket PC to was kind enough to activate Guest mode before using Transcriber. The following steps attempt to recover your personal Transcriber settings and then return your device to the original settings so that you can customize it again:

1. Select Start ⇨ Programs ⇨ Transcriber ⇨ Letter Shape Selector.

2. When the program loads, open the File menu and check to see if the Guest profile is active (indicated by a check next to the word Guest). If it is activated, you can return to your settings by selecting Master.

3. If the Master mode was still active, try loading your profile by selecting Load from the file menu and searching for a saved version of your handwriting preferences in the pop-up window.

4. If you do not have a saved profile, select File ⇨ Use Original Settings to reset Transcriber to its factory settings and then run the entire Letter Shape Selector application again, resetting the program to your writing style.

The sound on my device no longer works.

This could be caused by a number of different settings on the Pocket PC.

1. Check to see if the sound has been muted by selecting Start ⇨ Today and examining the speaker icon in the bottom right corner of the screen. If the icon is gray, the system has been muted. Tap the icon once to deactivate the mute feature and the icon will turn yellow.

2. If the sound still does not return, select Start ⇨ Settings ⇨ Sounds & Reminders. Move the volume slider to the right side (loud) and ensure that all of the "Enable sounds for:" checkboxes are activated. This allows the operating system and applications to use sound feedback.

3. While still in the Sounds & Reminders applet, tap the Sounds tab at the bottom of the screen. Visually inspect each event to ensure that a speaker icon precedes the event name. This means that a .wav file has been assigned to the event.

4. If the sound is still not restored, perform a soft reset.

5. If the problem persists, you may have a malfunctioning speaker or sound system. Contact your hardware manufacturer for service or a replacement.

The alarm does not sound when an appointment reminder appears.

Select Start ➪ Settings ➪ Sounds & Reminders ➪ Reminders Tab. Activate the "Play sound" checkbox and ensure that a .wav file is selected in the sound window. If desired, activate the repeat sound feature to ensure that you hear the audible reminder.

Warning

The repeat sound feature will set the Pocket PC to sound the alarm continuously until you have dismissed the reminder from your screen. This may drain the battery considerably if the device is left unattended.

I lost the ActiveSync CD-ROM that came with my Pocket PC.

Most of the applications that came on the ActiveSync CD are available in the "Downloads" section at www.pocketpc.com.

I lost the CD-ROM that was provided by my hardware manufacturer.

Because third-party applications are constantly updated, you should check the software drivers and updates section of your hardware manufacturer's Web site. Chances are, most applications will have updated versions that can be downloaded free of charge. Otherwise, contact technical support for your hardware manufacturer and request a replacement disc.

I cannot use my scrolling controls or hardware buttons to play a game on the HP Jornada Pocket PC.

Hewlett-Packard has designed a special HP Game Buttons application to assist you in assigning directional (up, down, left, and right) and specialized game action (fire and open) commands to the hardware buttons on your device. If you have already launched the game, select Start ➪ Today and tap the icon in the taskbar that resembles a game controller. This application will allow you to configure your Jornada hardware controls to perform all of the game functions.

Cross-Reference

If you are interested in more information on the HP Game Buttons application, or if the HP Game Buttons icon does not appear on the Today screen, refer to the "HP Exclusive Software Applications" section of Chapter 18 for complete information.

I installed a third-party application but I cannot find the program's icon.

1. Select Start ➪ Programs ➪ File Explorer to launch the Pocket PC File Explorer application.

2. Tap the My Documents drop-down in the upper-left and select My Device to switch to the root directory of the device.

3. In the file window, select the Program Files folder.

4. Search for a folder with a name matching the application you installed. If you locate the folder, tap it and search for a file with a unique icon. This should be the application. Tap it to launch the program.

5. If you cannot find the file in the Program Files folder, tap the drop-down in the upper-left corner and select My Device again. Open the Windows folder and then open Programs. Search for a subfolder or file with a name matching the application you installed.

6. Some applications automatically install themselves to launch every time you reset your Pocket PC. Tap the drop-down in the upper-left corner of File Explorer and select My Device again. Open the Windows folder and then open Startup. Search for a subfolder or file with a name matching the application you installed.

7. Check to see if the application is only available in the Today screen. Select Start ➪ Today and look for a new icon in the taskbar at the bottom of the screen.

8. An error may have occurred during the installation of the application. Select Start ➪ Settings ➪ System tab ➪ Remove Programs and uninstall the application. Reinstall it from your desktop and repeat the installation process.

Cross-Reference

Once you locate the application, refer to the "Customize your Start Menu and Startup Applications" section of Chapter 17 to learn how to add the program to your Start menu.

How do I upgrade the operating system or Pocket PC applications?

As a general rule, the Pocket PC is not upgradeable. When system bugs occur, the hardware manufacturer releases software patches (found in the support section of their Web site). Otherwise, systems cannot be upgraded.

Desktop synchronization issues

I am setting up my Pocket PC to dock with my desktop using USB and it will not recognize the connection.

First, make sure you download the latest version of ActiveSync from the Pocket PC Web site (www.pocketpc.com). Microsoft has made a number of enhancements to ActiveSync's USB support, but this upgrade did not ship on the CD ROM included with your Pocket PC. Next, restart the desktop computer after installing ActiveSync, but before attempting a connection. On some systems, the desktop must be rebooted after installing the ActiveSync application in order for it to check the USB ports for docking stations, but the software does not automatically prompt you to do so.

I cannot connect my Pocket PC with the desktop computer.

Two types of disconnects can occur between the Pocket PC and the desktop: software and hardware. If you are having a software problem, the ActiveSync application will begin to synchronize, but will cease before establishing a connection. If you have a hardware issue, the ActiveSync window will not pop up and the ActiveSync icon in the taskbar will remain gray. Use this information to decide which of the following troubleshooting courses is appropriate for your needs.

All connection problems:

1. Visit www.pocketpc.com to download and install the latest version of the ActiveSync software.

2. If you previously owned a Palm Pilot device, uninstall or deactivate the desktop synchronization software.

3. Make sure that the Pocket PC is fully charged, because communications features often fail under low power situations.

4. Reboot the desktop computer.

5. Remove any cards (especially network cards) from the accessory slot of the Pocket PC and leave them out during the entire troubleshooting process.

6. Perform a soft reset on your Pocket PC.

7. Attempt to reconnect immediately after performing these steps to see if your problem has been resolved.

Software connection troubleshooting:

1. Ensure that your Pocket PC is configured to connect to the computer using the correct connection method. Select Start ⇨ Settings ⇨ Connect tab ⇨ PC and make sure the "automatically synchronize. . ." item is checked. From the drop-down box choose USB if you are using a Universal Serial Bus cradle/cable, or choose 19200 default if you are using the serial (com) port. If you have previously set the drop-down box to a higher communications speed than 19200, this might be a faster speed than your computer can handle. Return it to 19200 default and attempt to connect.

2. Run the Connection Wizard to establish a connection by double-clicking the ActiveSync icon in the desktop computer's taskbar and then select File ⇨ Get Connected . . . .

3. Uninstall the ActiveSync software from the desktop computer and then reinstall the software using the downloaded update from www.pocketpc.com. (Do not use the ActiveSync CD that came with your Pocket PC.)

Hardware connection troubleshooting:

1. Ensure that your desktop computer is configured to connect to the Pocket PC through the appropriate port by right-clicking on the ActiveSync icon in the desktop taskbar and selecting "Connection settings. . ." to display the available options for connecting your Pocket PC. Turn on the appropriate checkbox for the communications method that matches your Pocket PC's synchronization cable. If the connection method you are attempting to connect with is grayed out (so that you can not activate the checkbox), this means that the computer does not have the actual hardware port or that Windows is not correctly configured to access that port. If this is the case, ascertain whether your PC is equipped with a USB or com port, and then consult your desktop operating system manual to learn how to add the port drivers to the Windows system.

2. If the Pocket PC does not display the "Status: Connecting to Host" pop-up window when you dock your Pocket PC, check the cable connecting the PC to make sure that it is securely in place.

I have successfully made an ActiveSync connection in the past, but now I cannot connect to my desktop.

Perform a soft reset on your Pocket PC and reboot your desktop computer. This resolves 99 percent of all intermittent synchronization problems. If you still cannot connect, follow the instructions in the preceding tip.

The Pocket PC makes the successful-connect sound and my desktop activates ActiveSync, but after just a few seconds the Pocket PC makes the disconnect sound and a synchronization is never accomplished.

When this happens, soft-reset your Pocket PC and reboot your computer. This problem occurs most often when the device is inserted in the cradle with the power off. To prevent this from occurring, turn the Pocket PC on before connecting to the desktop computer.

I can connect to my desktop computer but items do not appear to be synchronizing in ActiveSync.

Open the ActiveSync window on your desktop by double-clicking the ActiveSync icon in the taskbar. If the category of items (i.e. Contacts) that you are trying to synchronize does not appear in the ActiveSync window, you need to activate synchronization for that group of items by selecting Tools ➪ Options and turning on the checkbox for that item.

After synchronization, I receive a message that says "x items not synchronized" or "attention required."

If this message is only received for Pocket Money items, skip ahead to the next tip. Otherwise, perform the following steps until the message disappears:

1. If available, select the "resolve items. . ." hyperlink on the top of the ActiveSync window. If it does not appear, press the Sync button.

2. Remove the Pocket PC from the cradle or disconnect the sync cable, and then reconnect to the desktop.

3. Select Tools ➪ Options from the ActiveSync window and deactivate the checkbox for the group of items that do not properly sync. Press Ok to save your changes and press the Sync button. Then open the Options window again and reactivate the checkbox. Press Ok to save your changes and resynchronize.

Warning

The following suggestions may delete items or cause duplicates in your personal information manager (PIM) applications. Perform them only as a last resort.

4. Delete the partnership to your Pocket PC by disconnecting the device from your desktop and selecting File ➪ Delete Partnership. Reconnect your device and create a new partnership.

5. Uninstall the ActiveSync software from your desktop computer and then reinstall it.

The Pocket Money item in ActiveSync continuously displays "x items not synchronized."

Occasionally, ActiveSync is not able to successfully synchronize information with the Pocket Money application. This may happen regardless of the number of times that you resynchronize your device. To solve this problem, perform the following steps:

1. While the device is docked with the desktop, press the Sync button on the desktop ActiveSync application numerous times in rapid succession. On occasion, this forces the Pocket Money items to synchronize one-at-a-time.

2. Should that fail, disconnect your Pocket PC from the computer and launch Microsoft Money on your desktop.

3. Select File ⇨ New ⇨ New File from the application's menu and create a new file called moneyfix.mny in a file folder you can quickly access, and then close the Microsoft Money application.

4. Open Microsoft ActiveSync by double-clicking the icon in the taskbar. Right-click on the Microsoft Money data option in the list and then select settings to open the Set Up applet for Pocket Money sync. In the "Select a Money file to synchronize" option make a note of the name and directory path of the current Money file being used. Next, click the browse button and locate the moneyfix.mny file you made in the last step. Press Ok to select that file and then press Ok on the Set Up applet to save your changes.

5. Synchronize your Pocket PC. ActiveSync will inform you that you are synchronizing a new set of data and suggest that you replace all of the items on your Pocket PC with the desktop information. Do so.

6. Remove your Pocket PC and repeat the preceding two steps, but return the "Select a Money file to synchronize" to the original file that was in the window before you modified it. When you dock your Pocket PC again, you should not have any non-synchronized items.

ActiveSync reports that I can not synchronize my e-mail because the device has a partnership with another device.

1. Remove your Pocket PC from the cradle.

2. On the PC with which you wish to establish e-mail synchronization, open the ActiveSync window. Select File ⇨ Mobile Device ⇨ [Name of your Pocket PC] to select the partnership for the Pocket PC with which you want to synchronize e-mail.

3. Select File ⇨ Delete Partnership to remove the old settings.

4. Synchronize your Pocket PC.

Following these steps creates a new partnership between your desktop computer and your Pocket PC that can successfully synchronize e-mail.

I cannot establish an infrared connection with a desktop or another Pocket PC.

Infrared connections should be established at a distance of no closer together than two inches, and no further apart than eight inches. In addition, some indoor lighting disrupts the infrared waves. Try this trick: put a piece a paper in the infrared path between the two units and reattempt communications.

When trying to connect with a Pocket PC, ensure that one device is set to send (by tapping and holding an item, and then selecting "Send via Infrared"), and one device is set to receive (Start ➪ Programs ➪ Infrared Receive). Both the send and receive modes attempt to connect for 30 seconds and then stop infrared communication if the attempt is not successful.

When I attempt to install a third-party application from my desktop computer by clicking on the .exe file, it pops up an error and reports that the program "can not be run because it is in an invalid format."

It is most likely that this application does not come with an install program. In this case, try copying the .exe file to the My Documents folder on the Pocket PC and launching it by loading File Explorer and double-tapping the copied file. If the application runs directly from the .exe that you copied over, review the "Menus Made to Order" section of Chapter 17 to learn how to add this program to your Start menu.

I turned on the device and it asked me to set up my Pocket PC screen alignment and location.

The data in your Pocket PC has been lost. Restore your data from a backup or connect to the desktop to download all of your Outlook data. All third-party applications must be reinstalled on your Pocket PC. You can quickly install them by selecting Tools ➪ Add/Remove Programs from the ActiveSync menu after you have established a partnership with the device. Activate each application's checkbox and then press Ok to begin the installation of all checked items.

Pocket PC Application Troubleshooting

This section pertains to the programs that ship with the Pocket PC. For assistance with third-party applications, contact the creator of the software application.

Files on my memory card do not appear in my file list when I load a Pocket PC application.

The Pocket PC applications (Pocket Word, Pocket Excel, and Media Player) only display files which are inside a My Documents folder. Create one on your storage card by completing the following steps:

1. Launch File Explorer by choosing Start ⇨ Programs ⇨ File Explorer.

2. Navigate to your storage card by tapping the My Documents drop-down in the upper-left corner, selecting My Device, and then opening the Storage Card folder in the file window.

3. Select Edit ⇨ New Folder.

4. File Explorer will prompt you to name the folder. Type **My Documents** and press enter.

5. Find all of your documents on the storage card and copy them into the My Documents folder.

The Help command does not work when I select it from the Start menu.

1. Rerun the application you are trying to get help on from the Programs menu (Start ⇨ Programs) and then select the Help command immediately after the program launches.

2. With the Help application open, select View ⇨ All Installed Help for a list of all of the help files installed on your Pocket PC. If the help file does not appear on this list, you may need to reinstall the application, or it may not include a Help file.

America Online for Pocket PC

When I connect to America Online and open Pocket Internet Explorer, the browser does not work.

At the time when this book went to press, America Online (AOL) did not support TCP/IP in the AOL client for Pocket PC. This means that Pocket Internet Explorer, all instant messaging applications, and any third-party software that makes use of the Pocket PC's Internet connection will not function while connected to AOL. Interested users should check for updates at keyword: "Anywhere on the America Online service."

A name that I have listed in my Pocket PC Contacts application does not appear in my AOL phone book.

Because the AOL phone book is only used for addressing e-mail, it does not display contacts without an e-mail address entry. To resolve this, open the Contacts application and add an e-mail address for the person to whom you are trying to direct the e-mail.

AvantGo

How do I begin receiving AvantGo content?

Complete these three steps to begin receiving AvantGo channels:

1. Establish synchronization: With your Pocket PC connected to the desktop, open the ActiveSync window and select Tools ⇨ Options. Activate the AvantGo (also called Mobile Link) checkbox and press Ok, and then click the Sync button to transfer the information to your Pocket PC. Make sure your desktop computer is connected to the Internet via modem or corporate network during this synchronization process. Once you have enabled synchronization you will have automatically downloaded AvantGo channels for Amazon, MSN Mobile, New York Times, and Sony.

2. Sign up for an account: If you are not already an AvantGo member, run Pocket Internet Explorer and open the AvantGo Channels menu by tapping the Favorites icon and selecting AvantGo Channels. Select "personalize this account" and enter your e-mail address. The next time you synchronize, you will receive account information for logging into AvantGo.

   If you are already a member of AvantGo, surf to their Web site from your desktop computer, log in on the homepage, and select My Account. Select Software Setup from the Web site navigation menu and click on the Configure Mobile Link option on the resulting page. When the pop-up dialog box appears, change the option to "Open this file from its current location" and then press Ok. After whisking you through a number of steps, the system will be configured to use your previous account.

3. Personalize your channels: To sign up for personalized content, point your desktop browser to www.avantgo.com/channels/. The Web site contains thousands of channels that you can subscribe to with the click of a mouse button.

Although it worked before, AvantGo does not properly connect to the Internet during synchronization.

First, ensure that your computer is connected to the Internet while you are synchronizing your AvantGo channels. Next, on your desktop computer, visit www.avantgo.com/channels/ and log in using your AvantGo account information. Within the Web site, select My Account ⇨ Software Setup ⇨ Configure Mobile Link. When the pop-up dialog box appears, change the option to "Open this file from its current location" and press Ok. Proceed through the steps and be sure to have the Mobile Link software test the Internet connection.

If after performing the preceding steps, you still cannot connect to the AvantGo server, you must uninstall the AvantGo and ActiveSync software from your desktop. Reinstall the ActiveSync software, download the AvantGo upgrade from `www.pocketpc.avantgo.com/`, and then install it on your desktop computer.

Warning

While uninstalling the AvantGo application from your desktop will not cause any data loss (because your channel preferences are stored on the AvantGo server), when you uninstall ActiveSync, it may delete items or cause duplicates in your PIM applications.

I am having trouble connecting to password-protected channel content.

Download the AvantGo upgrade for Pocket PC, which includes support for viewing of https pages and secure transactions. The upgrade is available at `www.pocketpc.avantgo.com`.

Pocket Excel

When I format a cell as currency, it displays the wrong currency symbol. For instance, the cell could be showing a UK monetary symbol and you are writing about American dollars.

These steps will enable you to format your cells so that the American dollar sign always pops up.

1. Select Start ⇨ Settings ⇨ System tab ⇨ Regional Settings.

2. Make sure that your location is correct in the Region drop-down.

3. Select the currency tab.

4. Pick the appropriate symbol for your local monetary system.

5. Press Ok to save the changes and close the window.

Pocket Internet Explorer

My mobile favorites are grayed out.

This occurs when the Web page data stored in your Pocket PC has been deleted or becomes outdated. To refresh the information, select Tools ⇨ Synchronize on your desktop version of Internet Explorer, and then select all of the checkboxes that reflect Mobile Favorites on your Pocket PC. Push the Synchronize button to update the desktop version of the Favorites content and, when the process is complete, dock your Pocket PC to copy the information to your device.

When I attempt to access a high-security Web site, such as online banking or online stock trading, the Web site denies me access or says I need 128-bit encryption.

An update is available from `www.pocketpc.com` to upgrade Pocket Internet Explorer to 128-bit encryption.

Pocket Outlook

Appointments synchronized from the desktop or received via e-mail as meeting requests do not appear in Calendar with the correct date or time.

Either your desktop or your Pocket PC has incorrect regional settings. On your desktop, double-click the clock in the taskbar and ensure the proper time zone is set for your current location. Then, on your Pocket PC, select Start ➪ Settings ➪ System tab ➪ Clock and check to make sure the clock time zone corresponds with the desktop.

When I send a meeting request, some recipients do not have the accept and decline controls.

If the e-mail travels between the Internet and a Microsoft Exchange server, (either on your end or the recipient's end) the *intelligent agent* controls will be stripped from the e-mail. The recipient is unable to press a single button to respond to your invitation and book the appointment in their calendar (as described in Chapter 6). They do, however, receive the complete meeting details in text format.

Pocket Reader

A book that I have installed on the Pocket PC does not show up in the Pocket Reader library.

Microsoft Reader books can be copied into the Pocket PC in two locations:

- Main memory: My Device ➪ My Documents ➪ [any subfolder]
- Memory card: My Device ➪ Storage Card ➪ My Documents ➪ [any subfolder]

If you have copied the books to a memory card, make sure that it is installed in the device when you launch Pocket Reader.

Pocket Streets

Does Pocket Streets support Global Positioning System devices?

Due to contractual agreements with the mapping vendors that Microsoft uses, they are unable to provide any kind of communications to Global Positioning System (GPS) devices that would pinpoint your location on the Pocket Streets map.

 Cross-Reference

For complete information on GPS software and hardware solutions, refer to the "Finding Your Way" section of Chapter 19.

When I try to load a Pocket Streets map on my Pocket PC, I receive a message that this map was made for another version of Pocket Streets.

If you download Pocket Streets from the www.pocketpc.com Web site, make sure that you download the maps from there as well. If you install Pocket Streets from your ActiveSync CD, install only the maps from the CD.

Why does Pocket Streets display a different road name than I see on my paper map or street sign?

Some roads have more than one name (for example, California's I-5 is also known as the Golden State Freeway) and Pocket Streets arbitrarily selects one of the two names to display on the device. Unfortunately there is no logic behind this decision and there is no way for the user to control it. Another common example of this discrepancy is a service road number showing up on the map rather than the actual street name.

Transcriber

Transcriber (the handwriting-recognition application) is not installed on the Pocket PC.

Transcriber is available for free on the ActiveSync CD-ROM that shipped with your Pocket PC, but it is not installed on the device automatically. To install it, insert the ActiveSync CD-ROM and run \Extras\TScribe\setup.exe.

The program recognizes my handwriting too slowly or too quickly.

Transcriber is set to a mid-level factory default delay for recognizing your handwriting. To adjust this delay, select Start ➪ Settings ➪ Input ➪ Options button ➪ Recognizer tab and adjust the recognition-delay slider to your liking.

Resetting Your Device

Soft reset

The soft reset is a cure-all for almost every problem relating to Pocket PC performance. It is the equivalent of rebooting your desktop computer to clear its memory and make it run smoother.

Warning

A soft reset will cause you to lose any information that has not been saved in your device. To ensure that you are not losing any information, select Start ⇨ Settings ⇨ System tab ⇨ Memory ⇨ Running Programs. Tap an item on the list and press the activate button. When the application appears, close any information windows that are open, return to the Running Programs dialog box (Start ⇨ Settings ⇨ System tab ⇨ Memory ⇨ Running Programs), and then repeat the manual shut-down process on the next application. Continue closing applications until you have checked every application for open data and then you may safely reset your device.

To perform a soft reset, locate the recessed reset button on your device. The approximate locations for the various models are as follows:

- **Casio E-1xx / Casio EM-500 / Compaq Aero 1550 / HP Jornada 540 Series**: on the back of the device

- **Compaq iPaq**: on the bottom of the device

Insert the Pocket PC stylus into the recessed hole and press with increasing pressure until the Pocket PC display clears and resets. You should see a loading screen and (if your sounds are activated) hear the system start sound. When the Pocket PC successfully restarts, it should display the Today screen after approximately five seconds.

Hard reset

When all else fails, a hard reset may be necessary to access your device. This is frequently called for when the device:

- Does not power up after trying all of the steps described earlier in this appendix

- Cannot be accessed because of a forgotten password

- Has a serious performance or synchronization problem that cannot be resolved

Warning

A hard reset deletes all of the information from your Pocket PC. Before performing a hard reset, ensure that you have synchronized your Pocket PC and have backup copies of all third-party software stored on your desktop computer's hard drive.

Each device has a unique hard reset process:

- **Casio E-1xx series:** While the power is on, press and hold your stylus on the reset button for a few seconds. A window pops up, warning you that you are about to initialize the device's memory. Press the Action button (straight down on the game pad) to perform the hard reset.

- **Compaq Aero 1550:** Remove the main and backup batteries for five minutes. Replace the main battery first and the backup battery second.

- **Compaq iPaq:** At the bottom of the device, use the stylus to open the sliding cover and slowly flip the white switch back and forth.

- **HP Jornada 540 Series:** While the power is off, press and hold your stylus on the reset button and press the power button.

Once you have performed a hard reset, the device requires that you align the screen and set the time zone for your location, and also demonstrates the Cut and Paste features of the Pocket PC. Once complete, you may restore your data from a backup or connect to the desktop to download all of your Outlook data. All third-party applications must be reinstalled on your Pocket PC. You can quickly install them by selecting Tools ⇨ Add/Remove Programs from the ActiveSync menu after you have established a partnership with the device. Activate each application's checkbox then press Ok to begin the installation of all checked items.

Hardware Vendor Technical Support Contact Information

If this appendix has not been able to solve your problem, or you have a critical need for customer support, or if you require hardware repair or replacement, you should contact the manufacturer of your Pocket PC. Following are the technical support phone numbers and Web site addresses.

Casio, Inc.

Technical Support: (888) 204-7765
Automated Support Line: (800) 962-2746
Web site: www.casio.com/support/

Compaq Computer Corporation

Technical Support: (800) 652-6672
Web site: www.compaq.com/support/

Hewlett-Packard Company

Technical Support: (970) 635-1000
Web site: www.hp.com/jornada/tech_support/

 **Windows CE Resources on the Internet**

This appendix provides Web site addresses for all major Pocket PC hardware manufacturers, software developers, and information resources. These sites are excellent starting points for getting to know the vast troop of Internet advocates for the Pocket PC platform.

Hardware Vendors

Casio, Inc.
www.casio.com

Casio has produced a wide line of Pocket PC products, including rugged, corporate, and stylish end-user devices.

Compaq Computer Corporation
www.compaq.com

Compaq offers a variety of Pocket PC devices, including the ultra-expandable iPAQ H3600 and the super-slim, black and white Aero 1550.

Hewlett-Packard Company
www.hp.com/jornada

HP has an entire line of Jornada series Pocket PCs for consumers and professional users. HP also has the widest array of Windows Powered devices with their popular Jornada Handheld PC product line.

Software Vendors

BSQUARE Corporation
www.BSQUARE.com

The long-standing Windows CE software developer BSQUARE has honed a number of top-quality programs, including bFax Pro, which brings send and receive fax capabilities to your Pocket PC, and the bUseful Utilities Pack, which contains their popular data protection and system maintenance applications.

Conduits Technologies Inc.
www.conduits.com

Developers of the innovative Peacemaker software, Conduits offers many software solutions for the Pocket PC, including a Macromedia Flash player and a Palm Pilot emulator.

Developer One, Inc.
www.developerone.com

In addition to the Today screen utilities Developer One has created, the company has a number of original applications for time and task management. Also, be sure to visit their "Pocket PC tips" page for information on how to customize your Today screen.

Ilium Software
www.iliumsoft.com

Ilium Software developed the innovative information storage application, eWallet, featured in Chapter 18. On their Web site, they also offer a number of equally indispensable applications available for 30-day trial, and a few freeware applications. One freeware gem is "Tipster," a program that quickly calculates the tip for a restaurant bill and then divides the total by the number of people in your party.

Stellarmetrics
www.stellarmetrics.com

This company produces fun and informational software for the Pocket PC, including Pocket Universe 2000, a full-featured astronomy program.

ZIO Interactive, Inc.
www.ziosoft.com

ZIO Interactive is of the most ambitious game developers for the Pocket PC. ZIOgolf, the golf simulation game introduced in Chapter 18, is their flagship product, followed by a handful of action and strategy games.

Pocket PC Accessory Manufacturers

Concept Kitchen
www.conceptkitchen.com

One of the originators of the screen protector, this company has a line of screen-maintenance accessories, including the popular Brain Wash and Karma Cloths. Exclusively designed for the maintenance of the Pocket PC's delicate touch screen, Brain Wash is a two-step process that gently cleans the screen. The Karma Cloth serves as a quick method to remove dirt and residue from the screen between cleanings.

E & B Company
www.ebcases.com

Custom case designer and manufacturer E & B Co. has developed a unique "slipper" case that protects the Pocket PC even during use.

Pretec Electronics Corporation
www.pretec.com

Pretec Electronics manufactures many innovative CompactFlash solutions for the Pocket PC, including CompactFM, an FM radio accessory, and CompactGPS, a one-body solution Global Positioning System accessory.

Socket Communications, Inc.
www.socketcom.com

In addition to the wireless connection kit mentioned in Chapter 16 of this handbook, Socket Communications offers an entire line of serial, USB, network, and vertical market accessories for the Pocket PC.

Targus Inc.
www.targus.com

Purveyor of fine leather cases, Targus markets an entire line of organizer cases that hold credit cards, cash, and checkbooks, in addition to your Pocket PC. Targus also recently released an accessory stowaway keyboard for the HP Jornada Pocket PC.

AvantGo Channels

AvantGo, Inc.
www.avantgo.com

The creators of AvantGo provide a rich online resource to help you extract the most from their application. Their online directory boasts over 1,000 channels and enables you to create your own AvantGo channels for personal or professional use.

E-book Resources

Audible, Inc.
www.audible.com

Audible has tens of thousands of hours of spoken audio text available for downloading from their Web site. When installed on the Pocket PC, the audio files can be played in the Reader application and are accessed via the Reader's library index.

BarnesAndNoble.com LLC
www.bn.com

In a partnership with Microsoft, Barnes & Noble has created one of the world's largest e-book libraries, with a collection that spans every literary genre and is available for downloading 24 hours a day.

DotLit Press
www.dotlit.com

A well-managed collection of free and low-cost fiction titles.

Elegant Solutions Software and Publishing Company
esspc-ebooks.com

The self-proclaimed provider of "eBooks for People Who Think", ESSPC offers a quaint collection of e-books for the Pocket PC Reader application.

Fictionwise, Inc.
www.fictionwise.com

A Web site that claims to provide the Internet's most comprehensive collection of fiction in e-book format. Short fiction (which they claim is optimal for reading as an e-book) is their specialty.

OverDrive, Inc.
www.readerworks.com

In cooperation with Microsoft, OverDrive has developed the ReaderWorks suite of products for publishing e-books that can be viewed on the Pocket PC Reader application.

peanut press.com, Inc.
www.peanutpress.com

The company's Web site contains a vast number of e-books available for download and viewing with their proprietary Peanut Reader application.

PocketPCpress
www.pocketpcpress.com

This Web site is dedicated to providing low-cost e-books exclusively for the Pocket PC.

University of Virgina's E-book Library
etext.virginia.edu/ebooks/

This public e-book center contains well over a thousand texts, including classic British and American fiction, major authors, children's literature, the Bible, Shakespeare, and American History categories.

News and Information Resources

Brighthand Consulting, Inc.

www.brighthand.com

Founded and managed by Steven Bush, Brighthand is one of the most popular news and information sites for Pocket PC users. The site includes reviews on devices, accessories, and software for the Pocket PC.

CEWire

cewire.com

The aptly named CEWire Web site features an up-to-the-minute news wire of all Windows CE broadcasts. And, since they cover hardware, software, books, training, and Web site announcements, I consider this one stop shopping for all of your Pocket PC news and information needs.

Microsoft Corporation

www.PocketPC.com

This is, unarguably, the largest single Pocket PC resource on the Internet. Microsoft has poured its vast resources into developing a massive digest of how-tos, help, downloads, and discussion group communities available free to Pocket PC users.

Microsoft's Mobile Devices site

www.microsoft.com/mobile/

Microsoft's site for the entire range of Windows Powered devices. Includes solution stories for vertical market applications of the Pocket PC, and news and information about the entire product line.

Pen Computing Magazine

www.pencomputing.com

As a bimonthly print magazine, *Pen Computing Magazine* offers in-depth reviews, software assessments, and feature articles on industry-specific PDA applications. Dan Hanttula was the staff Windows Powered editor for four and a half years.

Pocket PC Magazine

www.pocketpcmag.com

A monthly magazine dedicated to the Pocket PC platform. Their Web site includes an archive of past issues and up-to-date news, links, and downloads for the Pocket PC.

SemperAptus.com
www.semperaptus.com

SemperAptus is Latin for "always connected." The Web site, founded by this book's author, provides news, reviews and editorial commentary on Internet-connected devices, including the Pocket PC and smart phones.

Software Resources

Handango
www.handango.com

With a focus on handhelds and an entire section dedicated to the Pocket PC, this site should be your first stop for freeware, shareware, and commercial applications.

PocketGamer.org
www.pocketgamer.org

A news and information Web site that covers gaming and entertainment on the Windows Powered device platform.

PocketGear.com
www.pocketgear.com

This sleekly designed Web site pairs the latest in software with selected articles from top news sources on the Internet.

TUCOWS Inc. PDA
pda.tucows.com

Tucows is one of the Internet's most popular shareware directories. With massive vaults for each category of application, you can spend hours browsing through their archives for all kinds of useful software.

ZDNet CE Downloads
www.zdnet.com/downloads/ce/

Although the file descriptions are often more marketing fluff than informative portrayals of the programs, ZDNet offers a complete listing of Windows Powered device software with "Hot File of the Day," the most popular applications and reviewer's picks.

Pocket PC Advocate Web Sites

Craig Peacock's Windows CE Pages

www.craigtech.co.uk

This Web site is quite possibly the oldest and largest single resource of Windows CE information on the Internet. Craig is a Microsoft Windows CE MVP and has also launched a sub-site, www.pocketpchelp.com, to assist users who experience problems with their Pocket PC.

Dale Coffing's Pocket PC Passion

www.pocketpcpassion.com

One of the most ardent supporters of the Pocket PC platform, Dale has created his own Internet paradise of news, reviews, and information on the entire Pocket PC platform.

PocketProjects

www.pocketprojects.com

A Web site dedicated to helping third-party Windows Powered device software developers.

Zippy's Pocket PC Software List

www.ziplink.net/~zippy/pocketpc/

A thorough and frequently updated compendium.

Pocket PC Shopping Web Sites

CEShopper.com

www.ceshopper.com

An online shareware store for all Windows Powered devices.

MobilePlanet, Inc.

www.mplanet.com

One of the oldest and largest online retailers for Windows Powered devices and accessories.

Hardware and Software Specifications

This appendix is a technical information reference for the Jornada line of Pocket PCs. Chapter references indicate where detailed information on the topic can be found.

Hardware Specifications

Processor: 133 MHz 32-bit Hitachi processor

Memory (RAM): 16MB (HP Jornada 540/545) or 32MB (HP Jornada 547/548)

Memory (ROM): 16MB

Display: 240×320 pixels LCD rich color display

Input method: Pen-and-touch interface (stylus included)

Hardware input/output: Four user-configurable quick-launch screen icons and two quick keys (Record and Scroll/Action); notification LED

Battery: Built-in lithium ion rechargeable battery

Backup Battery: A reserved portion of the lithium ion battery

Communications: IrDA infrared port; RS232 serial port (Cable included with the Jornada 540, 545, and 548); USB (cradle included with Jornada 545 and 548)

Accessory Slot: CompactFlash (Type I) card slot

Power: AC input jack

Audio: Audio speaker, microphone, and stereo earphone jack

Size: 5.2"×3.1"×0.6"

Weight: 9.1 oz (including battery)

Operating temperature: 32 to 104°F (0 to 40°C)

Storage temperature: 32 to 131°F (0 to 55°C)

Humidity endurance: 90 percent relative humidity at 104°F (40°C)

Software Specifications

Pocket PC Software in ROM:

Microsoft Windows for Pocket PC (version 3.0.9348, build 9357)

Microsoft Pocket Outlook (Chapters 6 through 10)

Microsoft Pocket Internet Explorer (Chapter 16)

Microsoft Pocket Word (Chapter 11)

Microsoft Pocket Excel (Chapter 11)

Microsoft Pocket Money (Chapter 11)

Microsoft Reader (Chapter 12)

Microsoft Windows Media Player (Chapter 12)

Third-party developer software in ROM:

conduits technologies, inc. PeaceMaker 1.0 (Chapter 22)

LandWare OmniSolve

Socket Communications' drivers for Low-Power Ethernet (LPE) cards and digital phone cards (Chapter 16)

HP Exclusive Software in ROM:

HP Backup (Chapter 18)

HP Home Menu (Chapter 18)

Game Buttons (Chapter 18)

HP Security (Chapter 18)

HP Settings (Chapter 18)

Software included on the Microsoft ActiveSync CD-ROM:

Microsoft ActiveSync 3.1 (Chapter 15)

Microsoft Transcriber (Chapter 3)

Windows Media Manager (Chapter 12)

Microsoft Pocket Money synchronization setup application (Chapter 11)

Microsoft Pocket Streets and maps of major metropolitan areas (Chapter 13)

Microsoft Reader books (Chapter 12)

An introduction to AvantGo

Full retail versions of the Microsoft Outlook 2000 and Internet Explorer version 5 desktop applications

Software included on the HP Jornada CD-ROM:

AudiblePlayer 2.0 for Windows for Pocket PC and AudibleManager 2.5 (Chapter 12)

AOL Mail (Chapter 16)

EMusic.com (free sample digital music tracks for Media Player)

HPC Notes Lite full version and HPC Notes Professional trial version (to create and organize notes on the Pocket PC)

HP JetSend for Windows for Pocket PC 2.0 (Chapter 16)

MusicMatch Jukebox 4.4 (record, organize, and play digital music)

Sierra Imaging, Inc. Image Expert CE (Chapter 18)

Yahoo! Messenger (Chapter 18)

ZIOGolf five-hole demo (Chapter 18)

Software available for free download from the HP Jornada Web site (www.hp.com/jornada/**):**

ChaiVM for Pocket PC (a complete runtime environment for Java applications)

EzWAP (a Wireless Appication Protocol Internet browser application for viewing content designed for cellular phones)

PVPlayer (a video player that uses the MPEG-4 format)

WinPhone Pocket beta (manages cellular phone (SMS) Short Message Service messages, phonebook, and fax communications from your Pocket PC)

 # Hewlett-Packard Handheld Computing Milestones

Hewlett-Packard (HP) has been involved in Windows Powered devices since the inception of the platform. Furthermore, although the company is famous for their handheld calculators, HP had also developed their own line of handheld computing products in the early 1990s. Starting with the HP-95LX introduced in 1991, Hewlett-Packard created a line of DOS-based handheld computers with .5 MB and 1 MB of memory. The HP100LX included a larger screen and doubled the amount of built-in memory, but the HP200LX was the most popular of the line. The 200LX launched in 1994, equipped with Pocket Quicken and Lotus 1-2-3 (a spreadsheet application), but Hewlett-Packard discontinued the 200LX product line in 1999 in order to focus on the Windows Powered device platform.

The Windows Powered platform (formerly known as Windows CE) has created a number of important milestones for Hewlett-Packard and the company's innovative hardware and software development teams have played a critical role in greatly expanding the public awareness of the Windows Powered platform. Together, Microsoft and Hewlett-Packard have created some of the most exciting moments in handheld history. Here is a record of their achievements to date:

February 1997

Hewlett-Packard played an active role in helping Microsoft launch the Windows CE Handheld PC computing platform. As a result, HP garnered significant industry attention and acclaim for its Windows CE-based palmtop PCs, the HP 300LX, and the HP 320LX.

The HP 320LX was the first of the Handheld PC series to feature a full-width VGA screen. The 640 pixel wide (and 240 pixel high) screen enabled users to use applications without having to scroll left or right. In addition, the 320LX featured a whopping 4MB of random access memory (RAM), a 44-megahertz processor, and a backlit screen. Because it was the first version of the Windows CE operating system, the HP 320LX is said to run version 1.0 of Windows CE.

December 1997

Just before Christmas in 1997, Hewlett-Packard shipped the HP 620LX, the first Windows CE-based PDA with a color screen. The system nearly doubled the computing power of its predecessor with a 75-megahertz processor and included 16 MB of RAM. This model included the voice recorder feature that became a popular staple of all Windows Powered devices and the ability to add an extended battery, which doubled the battery life of the device to a reported 6-10 hours. The 360LX, an upgraded version of the 320LX, included the new version of Windows CE software, a 60 megahertz processor, and 8MB of RAM. With a slightly enhanced user interface, support for color displays, and the addition of Pocket PowerPoint, the next generation of Windows CE units was upgraded to version 2.0 of Windows CE.

May 1998

Hewlett-Packard quickly became recognized as the hardware manufacturer that revised its handheld computers to perfection. The first sign of their dedication to perfection was the HP 660LX (considered by many to be HP's performance model Handheld PC), the first color palmtop PC to ship with a bundled 56.6Kbps modem and 32MB of RAM. The processor was also upgraded for a slightly faster response time of 75MHz. The HP 660LX retained the Windows CE v2.0 operating system.

October 1998

Later that same year, with a new moniker for their Windows CE product line, Hewlett-Packard launched the HP Jornada 820 Handheld PC Professional featuring Pocket Access, a companion to the popular desktop database software application. The device was different from previous Windows CE models (and earned the Handheld PC *Professional* title) because of the new Pocket Access software and the nearly laptop-size form factor.

With a full VGA (640x480) screen and a laptop size keyboard, the HP Jornada 820 belonged to a group of "Jupiter" Windows CE devices because of the large form factor. However, the device surpassed laptop computers because the HP Jornada 820 featured a 190-megahertz processor (which performs much faster than the equivalent laptop processor)and a 10-hour battery life. Furthermore, the unit — when in full production — was available for under $800. HP Jornada 820 included v2.11 of the Windows CE operating system.

February 1999

Although Hewlett-Packard did not produce a black and white Palm-size PC, they were the first to introduce a color Windows CE Palm-size PC with the HP Jornada 420. The Palm-size PC was a precursor to the Pocket PC; it had a slightly less stylus-centric interface and lacked Pocket Word, Pocket Excel, and Pocket Money. But with a 100-megahertz processor and 8 MB of RAM packed into the stylish purple package, the HP Jornada 420 turned heads as a powerful and capable handheld device. Despite the fact that it did not feature the same applications as the larger Handheld PC line of products, the HP Jornada 420 Palm-size PC used v2.11 of the Windows CE operating system.

March 1999

Again upgrading their Handheld PC line of products, Hewlett-Packard launched the HP Jornada 680, a slimmer, 16 MB device with a 133MHz 32-bit processor. The HP Jornada 680 was the first clamshell Handheld PC to include both CompactFlash and PCMCIA slots. The HP Jornada 680 also added a built-in 56.6 Kbps modem. Finally, the keyboard on the device was changed from the old "chiclet-style" to keys that match the tactile feedback of the desktop keyboard.

June 1999

Hewlett-Packard launched the HP Jornada 690 Handheld PC as a minor upgrade. This device was identical to the 680, except that it included twice the memory, giving the 690 a total 32 MB of RAM.

November 1999

The HP Jornada 430se Palm-size PC was introduced with great fanfare. In mid-November the HP Jornada Palm-size PC appeared in the James Bond movie, "The World Is Not Enough," to aid Christmas Jones (portrayed by Denise Richards) in deactivating a nuclear bomb. As a result, the HP Jornada was seen on the Tonight Show, The Today Show, MTV.com, USA Today, The New York Times, and Elle Magazine. But public relations events aside, the device was a pocketable powerhouse featuring a powerful 133-megahertz processor and a formidable 16 MB of RAM in the same space as the HP Jornada 420 (released just 8 months prior). Like its recent ancestor, the HP Jornada 430se was based on Windows CE v2.11.

April 2000

At the launch party for the Pocket PC, Hewlett-Packard announced that the HP Jornada 545 was available in stores. As the first manufacturer with a newly designed Pocket PC, the media and consumer demand quickly sold out complete shipments of the HP Jornada Pocket PC at Best Buy, CompUSA, and Fry's within the first week of production. Clearly the 133MHz devices with 16-32 MB of RAM were the popular choice for the technologically advanced. The company released the HP Jornada 540, a business model with 16 MB of RAM, a serial connection cable, and INSO viewer to display files in proprietary formats. The HP Jornada 545 is a consumer version that replaces INSO with ZIOgolf and includes a USB synchronization cradle. The HP Jornada 548 includes everything that the 545 ships with, but is packed with 32 MB of RAM. This marks the change of the device category from "Windows CE Palm-size PCs" to "Windows Powered Pocket PC" systems. The Jornada 540 series operates on v3.0 of Microsoft Windows for Pocket PC.

September 2000

Still dedicated to providing the most extensive array of Windows Powered devices, Hewlett-Packard announced the HP Jornada 720, which is an upgraded version of the 600 series Handheld PC that includes a 206 MHz StrongARM processor and a Smart Card reader. The software applications installed on the device include the new Windows Media Player and an upgraded version of Pocket Internet Explorer, which includes all the features of of Microsoft Internet Explorer v4.0 on the desktop. The HP Jornada 720 runs version 3.0 of Microsoft Windows for the Handheld PC 2000.

Quick Reference: Character Recognizer

Writing letters

Letters are written in the first two panes of the Character Recognizer soft input panel. Capital letters are drawn in the first pane and Lowercase letters are written in the first pane and Capital letters are drawn in the second pane.

	Lowercase mode	*Uppercase mode*
A	a a	A A
B	b	B B
C	c	C
D	d d	D D
E	e	E
F	f	F F F
G	g g	G G
H	h h	h H
I	i i	I
J	J	J
K	k k	k k
L	L	L
M	m	m m
N	n	N N

	Lowercase mode	*Uppercase mode*
O	o o	o o
P		p	P P
Q	q q	Q Q
R	r	R R
S	s	S
T	t t 7	T T 7
U	u u	U U
V	v	V V V
W	w	w
X	x x	X X
Y	y y	y y
Z	z	z
Space	—	—
Backspace (right to left)	—	—
Period	·	·
Return (Enter key)	(On number pad for Lowercase mode)	/

Writing numbers and symbols

Numbers and symbols are written in the third pane of the Character Recognizer soft input panel.

1	
2	
3	
4	
5	
6	
7	
8	
9	
0	
Ampersand	
Apostrophe	
Asterisk	
At sign	
Backslash	
Backspace (draw from right to left)	
Cent sign (not available in Uppercase mode)	

Circumflex

Colon (not available in Uppercase mode)

Comma

Dollar sign (not available in Uppercase mode)

Quotes

Equals sign

Exclamation point

Forward slash

Greater than sign (not available in Uppercase mode)

Less than sign (not available in Uppercase mode)

Minus sign

Parentheses (open and closed)

Percentage sign (shown, respectively, in Lowercase and Uppercase modes)

Period

Plus (+) sign

Question mark

Return (Lowercase mode)

Semicolon

Glossary

A
AC adapter

The cable or power-supply device that provides the correct DC operating voltage for operating and recharging your Pocket PC from a standard household power outlet. AC adapters are frequently available in standard models, which connect to your Pocket PC or the docking station, and travel models, which are more compact and only connect to your Pocket PC.

Action button

The hardware button that has special directional (up and down) functionality, which enables you to navigate through menus, in addition to depressing the button. Depressing the Action button opens the item that is currently selected.

ActiveSync

This software application, shipped with every Pocket PC, enables you to synchronize data from your desktop computer with the information on your Pocket PC. This software is developed by Microsoft Corporation and upgrades are available for download, free of charge, from www.pocketpc.com. The ActiveSync software resides on your desktop computer, not your Pocket PC.

applet

A pop-up window that provides configurable information on a specific section of the device. Start ⇨ Settings contains a number of applets that enable you to configure many areas of the Pocket PC.

Application buttons

Also known as hardware buttons, these provide quick access to preprogrammed applications, which are indicated by the icons displayed on the buttons.

AutoPC

A Windows Powered device that replaces a car stereo with a voice-recognizing entertainment and information system.

AvantGo

A third-party product that enables you to download Web pages to your Pocket PC while synchronizing this information with your desktop. These pages can be reviewed later on either platform.

B

backup

The duplication of an item, portion, or entire set of data from the Pocket PC to a memory card or desktop computer in order to save the information in the event that the Pocket PC is lost or broken.

backlight

The illumination feature of the Pocket PC screen that increases brightness and enhances visibility in low-light conditions.

battery

This is the local source of power contained inside the Pocket PC. It's the battery that enables you to operate the device when it is not connected to any external power source.

Bluetooth

Bluetooth technology that enables products to network together using radio waves. Simply bringing Bluetooth devices close to each other establishes a connection to synchronize, print, exchange files, and share Internet connections.

C

channel

Also known as an AvantGo channel, this term describes a collection of contents designed specifically for handheld devices. Web site authors create channels using smaller graphics and text so that these items load quickly and use less memory.

ClearType

This Microsoft technology enhances the appearance of text in the Pocket Reader application.

communications (COM) ports

Also known as serial ports, these connectors, located on desktop computers, enable you to connect external devices (namely the Pocket PC) to the desktop.

CompactFlash

Available in Type I and Type II forms, this is a specific form factor of accessory cards that fit into a respective CompactFlash (CF) slot. Example CF cards include modems, network cards, and Global Positioning Systems.

CoolTown

Hewlett-Packard's research program and fictional future world, where everyday appliances can communicate with each other to perform higher level tasks.

conflict

A conflict is an issue that arises when the same item has been modified on both the desktop computer and the Pocket PC. ActiveSync will list conflicts and enable you to resolve them by selecting whether to overwrite the item on the desktop or the Pocket PC.

cradle

A Pocket PC docking station that usually provides both battery recharging and synchronization services. Although most Pocket PCs come with a cradle, some only offer it as an optional accessory.

CSTN

An abbreviation of color super-twist nematic, the screen technology used in the HP Jornada and developed by Sharp Electronics Corporation.

D

DC adapter

The cable or power supply device that provides the correct DC operating voltage from another battery source. A common example of a DC adapter is an automobile power adapter that plugs into the cigarette lighter in your car to power and recharge your Pocket PC.

dial-up connection

A link to the Internet or a corporate intranet server established via a phone line and requiring the use of a modem.

direct connection

A link to the Internet or a corporate server established directly, via a network card.

dots per inch (dpi)

The number of pixels (dots) which fit within a square inch of real estate on a computer screen. This term is frequently used to define how clearly a display can present small text and images — the more dots per inch, the finer the resolution.

E

e-book

An electronic book which stores the text and pictures of a book in one file. eBooks are available in many different formats, but the Pocket PC Reader application uses the LIT e-book format.

embedded system

A chip-driven control system or computer system inside an electronic device. Embedded systems exist in Coke vending machines, blenders and many other ordinary appliances.

E-Squirt

A software program that enables you to transfer a package of data or information via infrared light between devices in Hewlett-Packard's CoolTown.

F

filter

A method of displaying items that meet certain criteria in the Contacts and Tasks applications.

form factor

The shape or organization of a computer component. The CompactFlash form factor, for example, is a card that is approximately the size of a matchbook and includes a set of female connectors at one end.

G

Global Positioning System (GPS) unit

A hardware product that is able to ascertain its current location on the globe by locating various satellites orbiting the Earth. GPS units connect to the Pocket PC as an optional accessory.

guest connection

An ActiveSync partnership with the desktop computer that does not enable synchronization. Guest connections are usually established for copying files to and from the Pocket PC and software installations.

H

handheld computer

This term is used for a broad category of portable computers. A handheld computer is classified as any device (running any operating system) that is small enough to hold and use in the palm of your hand.

Handheld PC (HPC)

The first generation of Windows Powered devices. Generally identified by the ability to fold in half like a clamshell and hosting a very small keyboard.

Handheld PC Professional (HPC Pro)

A third generation of Windows Powered devices that are difficult to discern from laptop computers. Less expensive than laptops, most HPC Pro devices have a full-size keyboard and large touch screen, but still contain the Pocket

Office line of applications.

hardware buttons

Also known as "application buttons," these buttons provide quick access to preprogrammed applications, as indicated by the icons printed on them.

I

Internet Message Access Protocol 4 (IMAP4)

This newest version of the popular e-mail access protocol enables you to manage entire folders of e-mail on a remote server. Popular with bigger corporations, IMAP4 mail servers have more options on the Pocket PC than POP3, which is the other supported e-mail transfer method.

indicator light

The light on the Pocket PC that indicates charging status and visually notifies you of calendar alarms.

infrared port

The black glass outlet, usually at the top of the device, that enables data transfer using Infrared Data Association (IrDA) methods.

Internet

The global computer network, composed of thousands of wide area networks (WANs) and local area networks (LANs), which uses TCP/IP to provide world-wide communications to homes, schools, businesses, and governments.

Internet appliance

A device with a main purpose of connecting to the Internet for Web surfing and e-mail.

Intranet

A local (within a specific organization or corporation) computer network based on TCP/IP protocols.

IrDA

Short for *Infrared Data Association*, this communications standard uses infrared light (similar to a TV remote control) to exchange information between the desktop computer and Pocket PCs at 115kbps.

Internet service provider (ISP)

Providing access to the Internet, these companies make money from a monthly fee or by presenting advertising while you surf the Web. Services provided by ISPs include e-mail, Web browsing, FTP file transfer, and Web site hosting.

K
Kbps

An abbreviation for kilobytes per second, defining the amount of data that can be transferred via a modem or wireless connection. Higher numbers indicate a faster transmission speed.

kilobyte (KB)

A unit of measurement for memory or file size. One kilobyte equals 1,024 bytes.

L
lithium ion (Li-Ion) battery

A rechargeable battery that does not have a memory.

local area network (LAN)

A group of computers united by wired or wireless technology and confined to an immediate area. Corporate LANs, for example, usually only include one building or location. If a corporate network connects two different locations, it is called a *wide area network* (WAN).

M
memory card

An accessory that provides additional storage memory for your Pocket PC.

MIPS processor

Short for *millions of instructions per second*, this device is a chip that is used predominately in Windows Powered devices and developed by MIPS Technologies Incorporated.

modem

Hardware that provides telecommunications services for your Pocket PC. Modems can use telephone lines or wireless networks to connect to the Internet or corporate networks.

Mpeg

Short for *Moving Picture Experts Group*, this format of streaming media (video or audio) compresses the data before transferring it from the server to the playback device. Mpeg is an ideal file format for portable devices because of a faster download time and smaller file sizes, which reduces the amount of memory required to store the file.

MP3

An electronic form of music that is recorded into computer memory instead of onto an audio tape. MP3 files can be created from your music collection or downloaded from the Internet and played on a number of devices.

N

network

Multiple computers linked together to share data storage, printers, or information.

O

operating system (OS)

The software application responsible for controlling the memory, the interaction (input and output) with other devices, and all of the other programs on the Pocket PC. The Pocket PC operating system is installed in ROM, so even if the device is completely reset, the OS does not need to be reinstalled.

P
Palm

A competing personal digital assistant (PDA) developed and manufactured by Palm Incorporated.

palm-size PC

The previous generation of pocket-sized Windows Powered PDAs. The Palm-size PC did not have Pocket Internet Explorer, Pocket Word, Pocket Excel, Pocket Money, or any of the refinements in user interface that the Pocket PC contains.

partnership

An association made between the ActiveSync desktop software, which controls what specific sets of data to synchronize with the device, and the device itself, enabling the user to configure synched data.

PCMCIA card

A credit card sized accessory that (as with the CompactFlash card) comes in Type I, Type II, and Type III formats to provide additional functions. Examples of these cards include modems and network cards. The acronym PCMCIA stands for Personal Computer Memory Card International Association, which is the organization that developed the card's physical requirements and interface standard.

personal area network (PAN)

A new term for computer connections created in a relatively small space, to be used by a person or group of people. Bluetooth networks, for example, create personal area networks because they connect devices within a 30-foot range.

personal digital assistant (PDA)

An all-encompassing term for any handheld computing device that retains personalized information. The Pocket PC, Palm Pilot, and Apple Newton are all examples of PDAs.

personal information manager (PIM)

PIM software is specifically designed to deal with calendar, contact, and task information. This data is popular on PDAs because it is important information that can be easily synchronized with desktop PIM applications such as Microsoft Outlook.

Pocket Office

This suite of applications on Windows Powered devices mimics its desktop counterparts. Pocket Word, Excel, and the entire Outlook suite (Contacts, Calendar, In-box, Notes, and Tasks) are commonly referred to as Pocket Office.

Pocket PC

Any handheld device running the Windows Powered operating system with the Start menu in the upper left hand corner. Devices without a keyboard are usually Pocket PCs, except for the previous generation of handhelds that were referred to as the Palm-size PC.

POP3

This acronym stands for Post Office Protocol 3. POP3 is an Internet standard for e-mail transfer used by Internet Service Providers and many corporate organizations.

Point-to-Point Protocol (PPP)

A type of connection often used with TCP/IP to connect your Pocket PC to the Internet. PPP is a common protocol used by desktop computers and many Internet-connected PDAs. Compared to Serial Line Internet Protocol, PPP has additional advantages, including error correction and the ability to handle multiple processes at one time.

processor

The engine on which the Windows Powered operating system runs.

program memory

The portion of RAM memory (usually about half) dedicated to providing space for calculations and currently running programs. Program memory is likely to become filled with temporary information that can slow or stop the Pocket PC, and requires a soft reset to clear up.

R

random access memory (RAM)

One of two different types of memory, RAM is the erasable portion of memory that stores all of your personal settings and preferences, PIM data, and files. Installed third-party software is also held in RAM. RAM is divided into storage and program memory. When Pocket PC packaging declares that a device contains 32 megabytes of memory, it is referring to the amount of RAM it contains for your use. Information in RAM will be erased if the Pocket PC suffers complete power loss, or if you perform a hard reset.

Rapier

This was Microsoft's code-name for the Pocket PC during the early stages of development. Some smaller third-party developers may have separate downloads available for Rapier devices. These are applications specifically designed for the Pocket PC.

reset (hard or soft)

Performing a soft reset of the Pocket PC is equivalent to rebooting your desktop computer to clear the applications and information currently in program memory. A hard reset completely removes all of the information, personalization, and third-party applications installed on the Pocket PC.

read-only memory (ROM)

A portion of the memory dedicated to the Windows Powered operating system and applications that come preinstalled on the Pocket PC. A hard reset or complete power loss will not delete the items in ROM.

RISC chip

An acronym standing for *reduced instruction set computing*, this term describes processors that are specifically designed with a limited set of capabilities, so that the chip can perform those capabilities at faster speeds. Almost all Windows Powered devices use RISC chips.

S

scrolling controls

These hardware buttons feature directional (up and down and sometimes left/right) controls and can be used to navigate menus and lists.

serial connection

A link that uses the serial port of the desktop computer to unite the Pocket PC and the desktop.

Serial Line Internet Protocol (SLIP)

A specific type of TCP/IP connection that connects your Pocket PC to the Internet. SLIP offers fewer communications features and error-checking features than Point to Point Protocol, an alternate protocol used in TCP/IP connections.

SH3 processor

The 32-bit RISC chip inside the HP Jornada, designed by Hitachi Semiconductor.

Simple Mail Transfer Protocol (SMTP)

The language commonly used for sending messages to an Internet Service Provider'smail server.

soft input panel (SIP)

The pop-up window that appears at the bottom of the Pocket PC screen for entering text. Available SIPs include the keyboard and the Character Recognizer window. Transcriber does not have a SIP because you write across the entire screen.

stinger

This is the code name for a Windows Powered cellular phone that offers many of the capabilities of the Pocket PC in a cellular phone device.

storage memory

The portion of RAM memory (usually about half) reserved for installing applications and storing PIM data and individual files.

StrongARM

An extremely high-performance, advanced processor that conserves battery power, developed by Advanced RISC Machines Limited and Digital Equipment Corporation.

stylus

The pen used for navigation and data entry on the Pocket PC.

squirt

A term used when one PDA communicates to another using infrared ports.

synchronization

The act of comparing information on two different computers and copying the most up-to-date versions of the data to both devices.

T

Transmission Control Protocol/Internet Protocol (TCP/IP)

The communications standard that systems on the Internet or an intranet use to connect to one another. Using TCP, information is sent over the network in small packages; the IP portion of the standard creates a unique address for your device, so that it can be identified for receiving information.

U

universal serial bus (USB)

The high-speed port that connects your Pocket PC to the desktop computer. Unlike serial connections, the USB port of a computer provides plug-and-play functions and the ability to daisy chain (or connect multiple devices to a single port).

W

Wave (.WAV) files

The file format for sound recordings made on the Pocket PC. Audio files in Wave format can also be downloaded from the Internet or copied from the desktop computer to create customized sound schemes on the device.

wide area network (WAN)

Computers that are interconnected, but are located in more than one region.

Windows CE

The earlier name for the Windows Powered operating system.

Windows Powered

The title for all devices (including Pocket PCs) that contain the Windows Powered operating system. In addition to the handheld computing platform, Windows Powered devices are designed for automobiles, set-top boxes, and even home appliances. The Windows Powered operating system uses many of the most successful features from the desktop version of Microsoft Windows, but has been designed from the ground up for maximum handheld usability and minimum memory footprint.

Wireless Application Protocol (WAP)

A set of communications protocols developed by Ericsson, Motorola, Nokia, Phone.com, and others to provide a standard method of communications for wireless devices connecting to the Internet.

Wireless Markup Language (WML)

A language used to format Web page Internet content for viewing specifically on wireless phones and devices. WML is a portion of the Wireless Application Protocol (WAP).

802.11

A set of networking products named after the committee that developed the standard.

Index

X

Y

Z

my2cents.idgbooks.com